MUSIC WHILE YOU WORK

Music While You Work organiser Wynford Reynolds visiting a factory to canvass workers' opinions on the programme

MUSIC WHILE YOU WORK

An Era in Broadcasting

Brian Reynolds

Book Guild Publishing
Sussex, England

First published in Great Britain in 2006 by
The Book Guild Ltd
25 High Street
Lewes, East Sussex
BN7 2LU

Graphic design by
Alan Reading

Typesetting in Times by
Acorn Bookwork Ltd, Salisbury, Wiltshire

Printed in Great Britain by
CPI Bath

A catalogue record for this book is available from
The British Library.

ISBN 1 84624 004 2

DEDICATION

I dedicate this book to the many musicians who played in *Music While You Work* and whose performances have given me a lifetime of pleasure.

Contents

Foreword

It was a casual conversation with one of the musicians at the Palace Theatre Westcliff-on-Sea during a production of *Me And My Girl* which, by a circuitous route, led to the publication of this book. At the time I was appearing in the show, I was also presenting a weekly nostalgia music programme for BBC Radio Kent and mentioned to this colleague that I was keen to feature more light orchestral music in the programme. He said, 'You should get in touch with Brian Reynolds!' I did, and discovered that Brian had not only lovingly collected several hundred copies of *Music While You Work* transmissions, but also had a wealth of written material about the show and its contributors and an encyclopaedic knowledge of the subject. I made some hasty enquiries about the possibility of using some of Brian's material in a special radio programme and was given permission to start work. What followed was a series of twice yearly programmes featuring original recordings culled from Brian's collection worked into a documentary style discussion of the story of *Music While You Work* and its personalities, along with many of Brian's own personal recollections and anecdotes. These trips down memory lane proved popular with our audience and we continued to make a couple of programmes a year until I moved to BBC Radio Lincolnshire. There I introduced my new editor to the idea, and he approved. This gave Brian the opportunity not only to do some more *Music While You Work* specials, but also general light music programmes featuring BBC staff orchestras, such as the BBC Midland Light Orchestra. These programmes rekindled memories among 'listeners of a certain generation' of rushing off to get the accumulator charged in order to tune in to the next edition. It was whilst compèring a live military band broadcast that I suddenly found myself announcing a piece by Brian Reynolds. Apparently, since 1968, Brian had enjoyed some success on radio as a composer of light music with frequent studio performances of his compositions coupled with a number of commercial recordings.

It was whilst discussing one of the books I was to review for my programme with a colleague in publishing that I mentioned Brian, his collection and our broadcasts. His immediate response was, 'I don't suppose there's ever been a book about it, do you think he'd write one?' That was all the prompting Brian needed to set about a two year project to thoroughly research and write this volume. I have been privileged to have a small hand in helping with the construction of the book and have thoroughly enjoyed what has turned out to be a voyage of discovery. Whether you are a musicologist seeking a reference book on the subject or, like me, simply a lover of good music, then I am sure you will find this history an enjoyable one. I am too young to remember the original broadcasts and am extremely grateful that a small group of dedicated fans took sufficient interest in *Music While You Work* to preserve recordings of these wonderful performances for future generations. Through these recordings and my association with Brian Reynolds I have come to appreciate the sounds that inspired wartime workers and the generation that followed. *Music While You Work* was rightfully a British Radio institution, this is its remarkable story.

HOWARD LEADER

Introduction

Some people might be surprised that anybody would want to write a book about a radio music programme that has been off the air for many years, the names of many of its contributors being just a distant memory to all but their ardent followers. Well, that's precisely why I have written it. *Music While You Work* gave a lot of pleasure to people in their younger days and is remembered by many with great affection. Furthermore, the musicians who were associated with it, many of whom are poorly documented, deserve to be immortalized in some way. They were skilled artists, many with hundreds of broadcasts to their credit, spanning twenty or thirty years, and whose careers in broadcasting were abruptly cut short by the BBC's decision to remove from the airwaves styles of music which it deemed to be outmoded. The advent of Radios One and Two in 1967 saw the end of a number of long-established music programmes, and many popular orchestras and bands ceased to broadcast. In their place was a very different sort of popular music, mostly on record, aimed at the young and, to my ears, a lot less musical than that to which I was accustomed. It is a sad fact that few people of under forty years of age can have any conception of popular radio as anything other than 'wall to wall' pop records and personality presenters. If, from what I have written, you get the impression that contemporary 'pop' is not music to my ears then you would be right! I was fortunate to have been born early enough to experience the 'Golden Days of Radio' when the BBC unashamedly catered for all tastes, and orchestras and bands of every style and description were heard in their own shows every day.

I became 'hooked' on *Music While You Work* at about the age of twelve. I grew to love the individual sounds of its participating orchestras, bands and groups, the leaders of which became my heroes. Although at that time I had not met any of them, I felt that every time I switched on the radio I was inviting personal friends into my home. When, in later years, I was lucky enough to meet many of them, I found that, without exception, they were every bit as agreeable as their music. I suppose it would have been very disillusioning if they had been otherwise!

Music While You Work, as you will read, started as a morale boosting programme for factory workers during the war, but soon had the feet of the nation as a whole tapping to its tuneful, cheery sounds. Apart from the first couple of years, the programme contained no vocals – just an orchestra, band or ensemble playing good tunes without interruption for thirty or forty-five minutes – and usually sounding as if they were enjoying it as much as I was. I know many people who still share my affection for the programme. It really was high time somebody wrote a book about it!

There are a number of people whose assistance in the preparation of this book I would like to acknowledge. First of all, journalist and broadcaster, Howard Leader, with whom I've worked on a number of occasions and who suggested the idea of this book in the first place. In addition to writing the Foreword, for which I am most grateful, he has spent much of his valuable time in the capacity of Editor of my original draft, correcting grammatical errors, at the same time as ensuring that I was not too rude about the BBC's latterday music policy. (After all, he still has to work for them!).

My thanks also to Graphic Designer, Alan Reading for his excellent cover design and for the many hours working with me, advising on the layout of the book. My appreciation also goes to June Upton who kindly provided photographs from the late Stuart Upton's Vintage Light Music Society archive – notably the front cover picture of Anton and his orchestra, broadcasting from the Camden Theatre, London.

Thanks also to Sheila Tracy for graciously giving me permission to reproduce a number of photographs from her book *Who's Who on Radio*. To the BBC Written Archives for research facilities over the years and for allowing me to reproduce BBC internal memos from their files. Finally, my thanks to musicians Fred Alexander, Gerald Crossman and Jack Dorsey for kindly providing photographs as well as information about their careers. If I have left anybody out, I will put this to rights in subsequent editions.

Finally, if after reading this book, you feel a burning desire to hear actual *Music While You Work* broadcasts, well you can! O.R.C.A (Old-time Radio Collector's Association) have dozens of programmes which can be hired by members for just the cost of postage and packing. Full membership details from O.R.C.A. P.O. Box 1922, Dronfield, Sheffield S18 BRA.

Brian Reynolds

Chapter 1

How It All Began

There wasn't a lot to be cheerful about in 1940. With the nation at war, even the BBC was uncertain about precisely what should or should not be broadcast.

The outbreak of war in 1939 had a dramatic impact on BBC broadcasting, forcing the decision to confine output to the 'National' service for a very limited number of hours. For some months the BBC relied mostly upon its own musical resources, but by 1940, things had begun to improve. The 'National' became the 'Home Service' and the new 'Forces Programme' was introduced, consisting of continuous light entertainment, punctuated with news summaries in various languages – including English! Although aimed at the Armed Forces, it was, of course, available to the general public and became the 'Light Programme' at the end of the war.

Inevitably, there were differing opinions as to the type of programmes that should be broadcast in wartime, some feeling that, until peace returned, there should be no light entertainment whatsoever. Others suggested that religious programmes should predominate.

On the basis that 'you can't please all of the people all of the time', the BBC chose to adopt the majority view that radio should be cheerful and morale-boosting. At the same time broadcasts were arranged in such a way that last minute changes could easily be made in the event of an announcement of particularly grave news pertaining to the war.

Suggestions to the BBC from factories that certain musical programmes should be aimed at their workers were reinforced in 1940 when the War Department put it to the BBC that regular daily programmes of uninterrupted music would not only have a morale-boosting effect on workers, but were likely to increase production in industry, particularly in the munitions factories.

So, in the *Radio Times* for the week commencing 23rd June 1940, in an article debating whether wartime radio should be 'grave or gay', the following statement appeared: 'This coming week there will be, twice every day, half an hour's music meant specially for factory workers to

Jimmy Leach appeared on the first and last day of *Music While You Work*.

listen to as they work, you will find it in the programme pages for each
day under the title *Music While You Work*'. From this inauspicious
announcement was born a programme that was destined to become a
national institution in broadcasting, running without a break for the
next 27 years.

The first edition of *Music While You Work* was played on Sunday
23rd June 1940 at 10.30 a.m. by Dudley Beaven at the theatre organ,
with a further edition at 3.00 p.m. by a group called 'The Organolists'
– a trio comprising electric organ, drums and piano; the latter being
played by Jimmy Leach, who later took over the group.

As Jimmy Leach and his Organolian Quartet, they became regulars
on the show and, in fact, played the final edition in 1967. Jimmy Leach
was serving in the Royal Air Force during the war and had to cadge
lifts in Blenheim bombers in order to get to London in time for the
broadcasts!

The BBC's first task was to find the right formula for the show, and
in the early weeks it experimented with a wide range of styles from
light classical to the popular music of the day. It soon became
apparent, however, that what factories wanted was tuneful,
unpretentious and predominantly familiar music that workers could
sing along with or whistle to as they worked.

One thing that was missing in the early months was a signature tune, although some bands played their own themes which they used in other programmes. Hence, Harry Davidson signed on with *Sons of the Sea* and Henry Hall signed off with *Here's to the Next Time* – although in Henry's case there wasn't a next time as he was only used once in the series! It wasn't until October 1940, three months into the series, that Eric Coates's newly composed march *Calling All Workers* was adopted as the signature tune for *Music While You Work*, a piece destined to become Coates's most played composition. It was dedicated 'to all who work' and, even today, evokes memories of the programme whenever it is played in concert. Some say that the rapid semi-quaver figures in the 'trio section' (the point at which orchestras always began the programme) was representative of the sound of sewing machines in action. I suspect this was wishful thinking, as the composer hadn't even found a title prior to its completion, although he was known to have been inspired by the sight of people going off to work each day. It wasn't until he went to the cinema and watched a gangster film in which the phrase 'Calling All Cars' was repeatedly used, that he decided to adapt this to *Calling All Workers*.

Eric Coates, sometimes described as the 'father of light music', could have retired on the royalties earned from that piece alone but, quite apart from his other works, he was also responsible for the signature tunes of *In Town Tonight* and *Desert Island Discs*. It is all very well having a signature tune, providing that it is always played. There was an embarrassing occasion in 1941 when the Band of the Coldstream Guards failed to play it at either end of the programme – apparently their Director of Music was unaware of its existence!

Inevitably, there were early teething troubles, and if a particular programme did not go down well in the factories the BBC certainly got to hear of it. In those days broadcasts did not always come from studios. Theatres, restaurants, dance halls and even seaside piers were

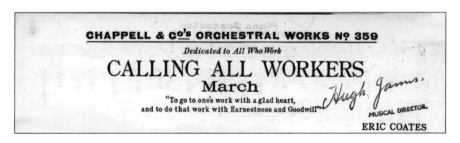

The famous signature tune of *Music While You Work*

3

**'MUSIC WHILE
YOU WORK'**

will be played to you
today at 10.30 by Harold
Smart on the theatre
organ, and at 3.0 with
records of dance music

utilised, if that was where a particular combination was based. In the first week of the series Geiger and his Orchestra broadcast from Claridge's Hotel in London, but the message that *MWYW* was to be a programme of continuous music had not got through to them and there were complaints that the musicians stopped to retune their instruments between pieces! Geiger and his Orchestra were soon dropped from the series, but Joseph Geiger's brother, Isy Geiger, later became a regular on the show.

Music While You Work soon settled down as a twice-daily, seven days a week series, employing a mixture of light orchestras, dance bands, brass and military bands and cinema organs – much in vogue in the forties and fifties, but sadly now gone the way of so much traditional entertainment. The cinema or theatre organ, although economical as far as the BBC was concerned, never really secured approval in the factories as it did not have a sufficiently abrasive sound to be clearly audible when played over the factory Tannoys. Consequently, organs were dropped in 1942 and, although given a further trial towards the end of the war, they were finally deemed unsuitable for the series.

During the early years of *MWYW*, certain editions consisted of gramophone records – about three shows per week at first, reducing to one, before disappearing for good in 1943.

Within quite a short period, *MWYW* had become indispensable to the factories, thousands of which had speaker systems installed to receive the programme; workers almost rioted if the factory management forgot to switch on! Although it started as an experiment, the BBC soon realised that it would be an on-going project (at least for the duration of the war) and decided, therefore, that it would be

4

desirable to have somebody specifically assigned who could devote all his time to the programme, its contributors and its content, and ensure that those at whom it was aimed were entirely happy with it.

So, in 1941, orchestra leader Wynford Reynolds was appointed to the position of *Music While You Work* Organiser, a post which, among other things, involved visiting factories around the country and ascertaining from the works managers which bands were the most effective and entertaining. In addition, he would listen to programmes in the prevailing conditions, thus gaining personal insight into the factory requirements. Not surprisingly, during his tenure in office, he was not allowed to allocate his own orchestra to the show, as this might have weakened his case when dealing with other contributors.

He drew up a number of ground rules for the programme: bright, tuneful and predominantly familiar music was the order of the day, nothing lethargic. In fact, all modern slow waltzes were banned because of their soporific qualities – they couldn't have workers 'nodding off' on the job! Also banned were pieces with distracting characteristics such as over-elaborate orchestration, the subtleties of which would be lost in factory conditions anyway. It was considered of paramount importance that the melody should always be audible above the factory noises; therefore there should not be much variation in volume – very soft sounds would not penetrate and *double forte* could be distressingly loud, possibly causing distortion when relayed over the Tannoys. There was a curious rule, never quite explained in the BBC files, which banned the playing of rumbas! Did the BBC expect workers to 'trip the light fantastic' on the shop floor, I wonder? This rule must have been relaxed at some point, as I often heard rumbas on the show.

Another requirement was that there were to be no noticeable gaps between pieces; the penalty for not playing *segue*, the musical term for this, was exclusion from the series. Certainly at least one Brigade of Guards Director of Music fell foul of the BBC on this point. On the subject of military bands, the BBC had, for some years been utilising its own BBC Military Band in its broadcasts, and this was duly conscripted to play regularly on *MWYW*. Unfortunately, being a virtuoso ensemble, the band had made quite a name for itself playing serious works and they did not take kindly to performing the lighter fare required for *MWYW*. In 1941 the band complained that they were being used too often, and not only did they find the programme 'arduous', but they also considered the repertoire to be 'beneath them'.

The BBC's response was swift and positive: 'If they feel like that about the programme, then we won't use them!' Happily the views expressed by the BBC Military Band were not shared by everybody as *MWYW* can boast editions conducted by Sir Adrian Boult, Sir Charles Groves and Sir Charles Mackerras.

During the war, factories did not just work on a nine-to-five basis; many (such as munitions factories) were in production throughout the night. With this in mind, in 1942, the BBC introduced a late-night edition of *Music While You Work* at 10.30 p.m., thus bringing the total number of editions per week to 21. If this wasn't enough, some of the programmes were repeated at breakfast time under the title *Music in the Morning*.

The factory broadcasting systems were also used for what might be termed 'propaganda records' issued on behalf of the Government, many of which implored workers to invest their wages in National Savings Certificates to help pay for the war.

Although most able-bodied musicians of military age were conscripted into the Services, resulting in the disbandment of many orchestras, it is amazing how many combinations were still available for broadcasting. One must assume, however, that most of these comprised musicians ineligible for the Services. There is an ironic story, told by pianist and organist Louis Mordish, concerning the orchestra of Alfred Van Dam, for whom Mordish had been the pianist. Van Dam suggested to the Royal Air Force the idea of forming a 25-piece orchestra to provide a variety of music for RAF personnel. The RAF thought this a marvellous idea and the Van Dam Orchestra joined the RAF 'en bloc'. The whole thing fell through, however, when Van Dam, whose eyesight was not very good, failed his medical examination. This left the musicians without the special posting for which they had volunteered, but in the RAF for the duration of the war! Poor Van Dam was left without an orchestra, and had to form one from musicians ineligible for service, and it was this orchestra with which he appeared on *MWYW* for many years.

Although a full list of contributors is given elsewhere in this book, it is worth mentioning that amongst the most frequently used performers on *MWYW* during the war were Victor Silvester and his Ballroom Orchestra, Debroy Somers and his Band, Primo Scala and his Accordion Band and the light orchestras of Harry Fryer, Harold Collins and Richard Crean.

Debroy Somers   Richard Crean   Harry Fryer

In wartime, the BBC was sensitive about being seen to employ Italians, so musicians working under Italian stage-names, such as Louis Voss (Luigi Voselli) and Harry Bidgood (Primo Scala), had to revert to their real names. Indeed, Harry Bidgood (son of march composer Thomas Bidgood) had a special billing in the *Radio Times* stating that he had 'taken over the Primo Scala Band before the war' – all the more ludicrous when you think that there was no such person as Primo Scala! It was just one of several aliases used by this British musician. Victor Silvester's wartime leader, the world famous Alfredo Campoli, had to become Alfred Campbell. Most amusing of all was Mantovani, a regular on *MWYW* during the forties. He was allowed to retain his own name, but had a special billing in the *Radio Times* stating that he was 'British despite his Italian surname'. This was true as Annunzio Paulo Mantovani, whilst originally hailing from Venice, had become a British citizen, swearing allegiance to the Crown in 1935.

Several directives were issued in respect of *MWYW* during the war and one even went as far as to suggest that the same tempo should be used throughout the programme (even though this would be considered bad programming as far as the domestic listener was concerned), going on to say that all attempts at subtlety should be avoided! I doubt if many bands observed this directive – indeed, if all the wartime directives had been observed to the letter, the results would have been so unmusical that it is unlikely that the programme would have survived the war, let alone continue into

<u>MUSIC WHILE YOU WORK</u>

<u>INSTRUCTIONS FOR ALL BROADCASTERS IN THIS SERIES</u>

It is essential that the following four headings are observed and strictly adhered to in the building and presentation of all programmes;

1. FAMILIARITY

Workers definately prefer tunes that they know and the most popular programme is one which enables them to 'join in' by humming or whistling. There must, therefore, be a minimum of twenty minutes of familiar music in every programme.

2. MELODY.

This heading is closely related to the above. Numbers that have no melody, or that are so orchestrated or played that the melody is lost are not satisfactory. The melody must always be clearly defined and never submerged by the 'inner parts'. If a scoring is too thick or the balance wrong the only effect in a factory is a meaningless blurred musical sound mingled with the machinery noise. Music of the 'hot' variety must never be included as this type of music does not answer to the need for familiarity and melody.

3. CONSTANT TONE LEVEL

Variation in Tone Level is one of the main grounds of complaint from factories generally, and it must be emphasised that for these programmes the dynamic range must be limited. Please note, therefore, that the dynamic range should lie between mezzo-piano and forte, and that the extremes of piano and double-forte must be avoided.

4. RHYTHM

    (A) Dance bands, Theatre Organs

The most suitable rhythm is obtained from a jig or quickstep tempo and programmes should be built around that ideal. As in Tone Level, extremes of tempo must be avoided. Slow tunes are unsuitable and too many very fast tunes create an atmosphere of unrest and irritation. Rhythm must not be too strongly accented and 'hot' rhythms must always be excluded. Programmes must not include any modern slow waltzes, and rhumbas are unsatisfactory.

    (B) Light orchestras, Military Bands, Brass Bands.

The rhythmic ideal as applied to dance bands cannot be applied here, but this loss can be made up in other directions. Programmes must have a cheerful, bright and lilting spirit running through them. Slow or too many very fast numbers must be avoided. Special attention must be paid to 'Familiarity' and 'Melody'. Popular selections from Musical Comedy and Light Opera are suitable, providing cuts are made to exclude any unfamiliar or too slow melodies. The changes of tempi in selections need cause no concern as these variations are well compensated for by the happy results obtained from 'Familiarity'. Waltzes with Viennese rhythm are suitable provided that they are familiar. Pay special attention to the first three headings.

Whenever possible, links must be played between items, or the programme so arranged that it can be played without breaks.

Wartime directive for *Music While You Work*

<u>MUSIC WHILE YOU WORK</u>

<u>Instructions for Dance Bands, Light Orchestras, Military and Brass Bands</u>

5th April 1943

In order to assist all those concerned in the building of "Music While You Work" programmes, I shall be glad if you will circulate the following general instructions. I may explain that dance music has been divided into four categories, i.e.:

1.   Banned completely (numbers with predominant rhythm, insufficient melody or other unsuitable characteristics).
2.   Banned completely (numbers that are too lethargic and unsuited to any speeding up of tempi).
3.   Banned completely (all modern slow waltzes owing to their soporific tendencies).
4.   Banned temporarily (as arranged with Dance Music Supervisor these numbers will only be released for this series when they are sufficiently familiar. The release dates will be issued periodically.)

In cooperation with Dance Music Supervisor I will advise you from time to time of the release dates of new numbers and of additions to the banned lists. Any new publications not appearing on the lists should be referred to Dance Music Supervisor or myself before inclusion in "Music While You Work" programmes.

Details of items, under the four categories, are attached.

Wynford Reynolds

George Scott-Wood

peacetime. Lists of pieces of music deemed suitable for *Music While You Work* were drawn up, together with even longer lists of pieces that were banned for one reason or another. Some of these pieces were only banned temporarily until they had become sufficiently well-known for inclusion in the series. Under the heading 'Banned Completely – numbers with predominant rhythm, insufficient melody or other unsuitable characteristics' were tunes such as the *Mexican Hat Dance, One O'clock Jump, Running Wild, Toy Trumpet* and *South Rampart Street Parade*. Most of these were regularly used in the series in later years. Also banned under this category was *Deep in the Heart of Texas*. It has a clapping motif which, it was feared, might encourage workers to 'down tools' and clap, or worse still, bang their tools on the machinery – sounds painful!

Although *Music While You Work* was primarily an instrumental programme, dance bands were allowed to include 'vocals' in the early days. George Scott-Wood, whose Accordion Band was a popular feature of the series, would occasionally sing one of the songs. There is an amusing memo in the BBC files from a producer reporting that he had told George Scott-Wood to stick to playing as he did not have a desirable voice. The producer adds, 'unfortunately he did not like this very much, as he thinks he is good!' Vocals were phased out entirely in 1943 as they were deemed to be a distraction.

In 1942 Wynford Reynolds had arranged for a survey to be done in a number of factories around the country to establish whether *Music While You Work* was succeeding, and if not, why not? Each Wednesday afternoon for 28 weeks a different band or orchestra would play, and 21 firms, incorporating 74,000 workers, would return questionnaires completed by both employers and workers' representatives. Industrial users were asked to grade the various

9

sessions in respect of 'audibility in noisy shops', 'audibility in quiet shops', 'general suitability of programme items', 'style of playing' and 'effect on workers'. The gradings A, B, C and D ranged from 'Excellent' to 'Unsatisfactory'. A points system giving a maximum of 300 points in each grading was also operated.

The overall 'winner' at the end of the six-month period was Debroy Somers and his Orchestra (232 points), with Felix Mendelssohn and his Hawaiian Serenaders coming last (107 points) Reports on the performance of this combination, which was very successful in other shows, indicated that it was thought 'too dreamy and lacking in clarity and crispness'. As a result of the survey, Mendelssohn was dropped from the series, as were several other bands.

For most of its existence *MWYW* was broadcast live, and it is probably not surprising that only a handful of the wartime shows are known to have been preserved for posterity.

From perusal of the programme listings at the BBC Written Archives, one can observe a strong patriotic feel about the wartime shows, with a much greater emphasis on medleys of community songs than there was in peacetime. One thing is certain, *Music While You Work* was a major success for the BBC, both in the home, and in its main role in the factories. With reports from industry noting a substantial increase in productivity whenever it was broadcast, the BBC was quite convinced that it made a significant contribution to winning the war.

SOME ACTUAL '*MUSIC WHILE YOU WORK*' PROGRAMMES BROADCAST DURING THE WAR

10.30 a.m.
10.7.40   **Sam Rogers and his Orchestra**
                 (From the Palace Theatre, Manchester)

Selection: *Bouquet of Memories*	arr. Bayford
Chase the Ace	Engleman
Foxtrot Medley	arr. Rogers
Melody in F	Rubinstein
Don't Ever Pass Me By	Watson/Denby
Selection: *The Count of Luxembourg*	Lehar

10.30 a.m.

18.8.40   **The Lewisham Hippodrome Orchestra**
              Conductor: Harold Collins (From the Lewisham
              Hippodrome)

Sons of the Old Contemptibles	Lynton
Selection: *Deanna Durbin Songs*	arr. Dexter
In the Mood	Razaf/Garland
I Hear Bluebirds (Concert Arrangement)	Woods & Tobias
	(arr. Bowden)
Toy Town Parade	Ferraris
Begin the Beguine	Porter
Classics of Rhythm	arr. Bowden

10.30 a.m

21.9.41   **The St. Annes Pier Orchestra**
              Conductor: William Rees (From the Floral Hall,
              St. Annes on Sea)

Calling All Workers (Sig)	Coates
Entry of the Toreadors (March)	arr. Zalva
Overture to The Arcadians	Monckton/Talbot
Rain in the Trees	Yorke
Bank Holiday (From *The Cockney Suite*)	Ketelbey
Tarantella (from *A Day In Naples*)	Byng
Two Irish Dances	Ansell
Lionel Monckton Melodies	arr. Robinson
Calling All Workers (Sig)	Coates

10.30 a.m.   **Torquay Pavilion Light Orchestra**
9.6.42   **Conductor: Ernest W. Goss (From The Pavilion, Torquay)**

Calling All Workers (Sig)	Coates
The Thin Red Line	Alford
The Girl Friend (Selection)	Rodgers
Estudiantina	Waldteufel
No, No, Nanette (Selection)	Youmans
Post Horn Galop	Koenig
El Capitan	Sousa
Teddy Bears' Picnic	Bratton
Calling All Workers (Sig)	Coates

11

10.30 a.m
26.9.43   **Richard Crean and his Orchestra**

Calling All Workers (Sig)	Coates
Parade of the Tin Soldiers	Jessel
Dream of Autumn	Joyce
Roundabouts	Wood
Wood Nymphs	Coates
The Valley of Poppies	Ancliffe
Happy Go Lucky	Crooke
Our Miss Gibbs (sel)	Caryll/Monckton
Calling All Workers (Sig)	Coates

10.30 a.m.
3.10.43   **John Blore and his Orchestra**

Calling All Workers (Sig)	Coates
Mazurka from *Coppelia*	Delibes
The Chocolate Soldier	Straus
In the Shadows	Finck
Slavonic Dance	Dvorak
Mountain Lovers	Squire
Merrymakers' Dance (from *Nell Gwynn*)	German
The Gypsy Princess	Kalman
Pas de Quatre	Lutz
Jeannie with the Light Brown Hair	Foster arr. Blore
Dance of the Mirlitons	Tchaikovsky
Musetta's Song (from *La Bohème*)	Puccini
Floradora	Stuart
Sleeping Beauty Waltz	Tchaikovsky
Faust Ballet Music	Gounod
Calling All Workers (Sig)	Coates

4.30 p.m   **Leeds Grand Theatre Orchestra**
24.4.45   **Conducted by Stanley C. Berkeley**

Calling All Workers (Sig)	Coates
Gipsy Blood (March)	Renner
Selection from *Hit The Deck*	Youmans
Lot 100	

Nothing Could be Sweeter
Sometimes I'm Happy
Join the Navy

Beautiful Spring (Waltz)	Linke
Selection from *The Geisha*	Jones
Nights of Gladness (Waltz)	Ancliffe
Selection from *The Lilac Domino*	Cuvillier
Spanish Gypsy Dance	Marquina
Selection from *Sally*	Kern

   Look for the Silver Lining
   Sally
   Wild Rose

Laughing Eyes	Finck
Three Little Maids From School	Sullivan
The Cachucha	Sullivan
Calling All Workers (Sig)	Coates

Chapter 2

The Post War Years

Music While You Work had been designed as a wartime measure and, as we have seen, had admirably succeeded in its main role in the factories. Nevertheless, the programme was available to the general public and had generated a considerable following among domestic listeners, in particular housewives, who found it an ideal accompaniment to the daily grind of dusting, polishing, washing and, believe it or not, hoovering! We are, of course, referring to an era when family roles were more clearly defined and a much smaller percentage of married women went out to work. As the years went on and radios appeared in cars, *MWYW* was deemed an ideal motorist's programme. Certainly its tuneful melodies and restrained dynamics were ideal listening, and very different from the ear-splitting boom-thud cacophony which is emitted from so many cars today.

So, in 1945, it was inevitable that *MWYW* would continue in its dual role. Although the weekend afternoon editions were no longer considered necessary, the late night programmes of uninterrupted music continued (albeit not under the title *Music While You Work*) until 1947, when the Sunday morning edition ended. In the Autumn of that year, however, the BBC instituted an early evening edition at 6.00 p.m. This continued, apart from a few months' break, until 1950, at which time the programme settled down to 11 shows per week, a format that was to remain unchanged for the next 14 years.

10.30 MUSIC WHILE YOU WORK Victor Silvester and his Ballroom Orchestra	3.45 MUSIC WHILE YOU WORK Jack Leon and his Orchestra	6.0 MUSIC WHILE YOU WORK Ralph Elman and his Bohemian Players

Throughout the run of *MWYW*, the morning edition was broadcast at 10.30 a.m., but the placing of the afternoon show altered considerably over the years. During the war, it had started at times varying between 3.00 p.m. and 4.30 p.m., the latter probably reflecting the Double Summer Time which was then in operation. It settled down

15

to 3.30 p.m. where it stayed until the end of the forties, when it was moved to 3.45 p.m.

By October 1957, the BBC had decided to increase the running time of the afternoon show to 45 minutes and initially placed it at 3.00 p.m., with a news summary at 3.30 p.m.. The factories, however, did not take kindly to the interruption of the programme and the BBC received many protests. So, in January 1958 it was moved back to its old time of 3.45 p.m. – continuing until 4.30 p.m. By the early sixties the programme had been brought forward to 3.31 p.m. at the request of the factories, many of which were now working a shorter day.

It was around this time that the BBC gave serious consideration to extending the morning shows to 45 minutes, or longer, but using exclusively BBC regional light orchestras (for example the BBC Midland Light Orchestra), but for some reason this idea never got off the ground. This was probably for the best, as such a plan would have meant many popular combinations being taken off the programme, particularly the small groups which were not considered suitable to service a programme of more than 30 minutes' duration. Wynford Reynolds relinquished his role as *Music While You Work Organiser* in 1944, returning to the programme in his capacity as orchestra leader. He directed several orchestras of different sizes on radio. For *MWYW* he used a small salon orchestra and a larger combination of about 20 players entitled the Raeburn Orchestra, so called because, as a composer, Reynolds used the pseudonym Hugh Raeburn.

Kenneth Baynes

His successors to the role of *MWYW* Organiser included organist Fredric Bayco and Kenneth Baynes, another one time orchestra leader whose father, Sydney Baynes, wrote the Destiny Waltz. It is somewhat ironic that Kenneth Baynes was instrumental in axing Wynford Reynolds' smaller orchestra from the programme in 1956, considering it 'too dated' and having outlived its usefulness. Personally, I thought that it was quite charming and some of the orchestra's records have been released on CD in recent times. Reynolds died in 1958 at the early age of 59.

Kenneth Baynes, who was also Head of Light Music and subsequently Head of the Popular Music Department, continued as *MWYW* supremo for many years. It is amusing to note from programme listings just how frequently his compositions would appear in orchestras' broadcasts – presumably because the musical directors thought that by regularly playing them, he would favour them with more broadcasts. Actually, Kenneth Baynes was not the sort of person to be so influenced and frequently removed his own pieces from pre-submitted programmes, substituting one of the alternative numbers that it was obligatory to provide.

The BBC was very strict when it came to the question of fair and unbiased treatment of composers, and instituted certain rules to ensure that favouritism was not apparent. A conductor could not play, in any one programme, more than one of his own compositions, or indeed more than one piece in which he had a financial interest – whether it be as an arranger (of non-copyright material) or as a publisher. For example, the well-known conductor Jack Coles ran his own publishing company.

Another problem related to reciprocal 'arrangements' between conductors who would play each other's works on the basis of 'if you'll play one of mine I'll play one of yours'. Although the BBC vetted the programmes for what it described as 'rackets', it was by no means easy to ascertain if the works of certain composers or bandleaders were being unfairly 'plugged' as most of them were written under pseudonyms. Indeed, I possess a recording of a broadcast by an orchestra (which for legal reasons I shall not name) whose conductor included three of his own compositions in the first 15 minutes – all written under different names, naturally!

The BBC was obliged, however, to take a hard line on song-plugging and, at one stage, required dance bands appearing on *Music While You Work* to play eight current tunes in each broadcast, believing that by making it an official requirement on the part of the BBC, the onus of responsibility would not fall upon individual bandleaders.

On one occasion, George Scott-Wood had his submitted programme returned to him because he had not included enough 'current pops'! When submitting his revised programme, he sarcastically commented that it now consisted entirely of pops, apart from one of his own compositions and a samba, adding that as this piece was also rubbish, the programme should be just what the BBC wanted! As this attitude was probably held by others, it might partly explain why, by the early sixties, the BBC had removed all obligations to play 'pop' tunes and, in fact, limited their inclusion to a maximum of five per programme.

Despite the BBC's efforts, song-plugging was difficult to control. Publishers' representatives would regularly turn up at the studios, armed with their latest numbers, hoping to persuade the musical directors to broadcast them. It became common practice for a publisher to provide a 'free' arrangement of a number, providing that the bandleader broadcast it an agreed number of times within the promotional period. Publishers employed their own staff arrangers whose task it was to arrange compositions accepted by conductors in the style of the orchestra in question. In the case of bandleaders who did their own arranging, publishers would 'reimburse' them with the arranging costs, subject, again, to the aforementioned performance criteria. So, it would be tough luck on a conductor who did not get sufficient broadcasts to satisfy these criteria within the promotional period.

Although the BBC was aware of this, it really was a *Catch-22*

WORKING MUSICIANS
Tommy Kinsman (left) and his Dance Orchestra at 10.30 and Jack Leon with the BBC Scottish Variety Orchestra at 3.45 play today's '*Music While You Work*'

18

situation as bandleaders were sometimes reprimanded for too frequent inclusion of certain items!

There was also a rule forbidding BBC executives to accept gifts, so when a well-known *MWYW* bandleader sent Kenneth Baynes a bottle of cognac, he was promptly told to come and collect it.

The allocation of dance bands and light orchestras on *MWYW* was in accordance with a set plan, that is to say that dance and light music were allocated fixed 'slots' each week. The Saturday morning edition, for example, was played by a light orchestra throughout most of the programme's run. The BBC's Variety Department (later to become the Light Entertainment Department) was responsible for providing the dance bands, with the Music Department providing the light orchestras, until a specific Light Music Department was set up in 1955. Light orchestras were permitted to play up to 10 minutes of dance music in a 30-minute programme, thus enabling them to include selections from musical shows such as *Annie Get Your Gun*, which contained mostly tunes that would be in the repertoire of the dance bands.

Every edition of *Music While You Work* would be preceded by a three-hour rehearsal and, like it or not, musicians performing in the morning session had to be in the studio in time to commence rehearsal at 7.30 a.m. The studio manager, who was often the only official present, had to be there much earlier in order to prepare the studio, set up microphones etc. in advance of the rehearsal. It was only when the musicians were actually playing, however, that he could 'balance' the orchestra, band or ensemble. Although a producer was allocated to every session, many of them, particularly on the light music side, didn't bother to turn up. In truth, they really did not have a major role to play in *MWYW* as most elements of the production of the show were the responsibility of the musical director, whose task it was to plan the programme (in accordance with the guide lines), arrange the music (or ensure that arrangements were done) and time each item. In effect, he was largely responsible for the end product.

As already mentioned, for most of its 27-year run, *Music While You Work* went out live and, inevitably, there were occasional mistakes. These were usually in the form of minor human errors, such as a split trumpet note, or a player coming in a bar early. Far from damaging the broadcasts, these minor glitches gave them a sense of 'reality'. Listeners got the feeling that these were real musicians actually performing at the time they were listening to them. There was a sense of spontaneity seldom experienced with modern compact discs, the technology of which permits all manner of 'faking'. In *MWYW*, the sound of sheet music being hastily changed between numbers added a certain charm and atmosphere to the broadcasts.

It was quite a rare event for anything to go seriously wrong; after all, these were professional musicians not 'end of the pier' buskers, but, with more than 16,700 broadcasts, it was inevitable that occasionally there would be a major hiccup.

One day in 1955, Frank Weir's orchestra was scheduled to provide the morning edition. As an unfamiliar studio had been allocated for the broadcast, most of the musicians, and even the producer, had difficulty in finding it and were very late arriving. Consequently, there was insufficient time to rehearse more than a few pieces before the call came to prepare to go on air, without a proper 'run-through'. Unfortunately, not all the band members had got their music in the correct order, and half way through the show all hell broke loose as the brass section played one tune whilst the saxes played another! The resulting cacophony meant that the band had to stop and reorganise before continuing. Such a situation was quite unacceptable to the BBC, and the Frank Weir Orchestra, despite being one of Britain's top dance bands, took no further part in the series.

Another embarrassing incident occurred one Friday morning in 1961 when Jack White and his Band were due on air at 10.31 a.m. On this occasion the band's pianist, who was also the librarian, was on holiday and had entrusted a publisher friend with the task of ensuring that the music arrived in the studio in good time for rehearsal. The publisher duly gave the manuscripts to a motor cycle messenger, with instructions to deliver them to the studio. Unfortunately, the messenger suffered a puncture and considered rectifying it to be of greater importance than the delivery of the music. It never occurred to him to hail a taxi! In consequence, the announcer, Frank Phillips, made the following statement at 10.31: '*Music While You Work* should be played this morning by Jack White and his Band – they are all in the studio, the only thing they haven't got is any music! In the meantime, I will play you a gramophone record'. The music soon arrived and the programme got under way at 10.40 a.m. Fortunately, the band was familiar with all the pieces, so the broadcast did not suffer from lack of rehearsal. Nevertheless, the BBC was none too pleased and gave Jack White an almighty rocket, informing him that the incident had caused them great embarrassment and, whilst acknowledging the difficult situation in which he had been placed, and the fact that nothing of this nature had occurred in many years of broadcasting, the BBC required his assurance that he would adopt a more reliable means of ensuring that music was available in time for rehearsal, or his further use in morning programmes would be viewed with reluctance.

In the mid-fifties Jack White's band, which had been established in the 1920s, was one of the most frequent and popular contributors to *MWYW*. Some of the producers, however, were critical of its style and submitted unfavourable reports. I think that the main problem was Jack's drummer, who had a distinctive but rather unconventional style. Unfortunately, he also happened to be Jack's brother, and a founder member of the band, who had been taught to play the drums by Jack himself. The BBC had to concede that the bad reports were inconsistent with the reality that they were Britain's most broadcast band, a fact that had not escaped the notice of a number of jealous bandleaders who felt that they could put on a better show. The BBC diplomatically wrote to Jack White informing him that there was criticism directed at his rhythm section. Jack pointedly replied that he

Jack White and his Band

21

felt his bass player was quite adequate! The truth is, however, that the band's down-to-earth style was attracting a number of appreciative letters and, happily for Jack, he had an ally in Kenneth Baynes, who wrote to him saying 'I don't care what they say – I think you've got a jolly good band'. Many would second that.

Indeed, a popular feature of *MWYW* was Jack White's Annual Christmas Special, which consisted predominantly of sing-along numbers such as *Maybe It's Because I'm a Londoner*, *I Do Like to be Beside the Sea Side*, *Knees Up Mother Brown* – topped and tailed with *Jolly Good Company* and *John Peel*, complete with barking and post horn effects. Although totally taboo at any other time, the band even got away with singing and cheering in some numbers. Okay, it was corny, but great fun.

Another incident which has gone down in *MWYW* folklore occurred during a broadcast by Ronnie Munro and his Orchestra; suddenly the pianist keeled over and fell off his stool. As it was nearing the end of the broadcast, nobody went to his aid – which was unfortunate as at the end of the programme he was found to be dead!

As stated earlier, each week of *Music While You Work* was divided fairly equally between light music and dance music, and the various combinations could best be summed up as follows:

LIGHT ORCHESTRAS

Bobby Howell

These would sometimes be theatre orchestras, that is to say orchestras of about 20 to 25 players, with an instrumentation similar to that found in the theatre pit, comprising strings, woodwind and brass. Many of these were indeed 'pit' orchestras, such as those of Harold Collins, Bobby Howell, Joseph Muscant and Hugh James.

There were also speciality orchestras – combinations which made a speciality of a particular style of music like Bernard Monshin and his Rio Tango Band, Harold C. Gee and his Maritza Players, and Ralph Elman and his Bohemian Players. These, and other ensembles, such as those directed

22

by Michael Freedman, Arthur Anton and Fredric Cooper, to name but a few, were rather smaller than the theatre orchestras and did not have a full brass section. An accordion was often used instead of brass.

Finally, there were the salon orchestras of about ten players, those led by Jack Salisbury, Marcel Gardner and Sidney Davey being typical examples in this category.

LIGHT MUSIC GROUPS

These were usually ensembles of four to eight players and, like most of the orchestras, had their own distinctive styles and instrumentation – the BBC liked all combinations to sound different. In this category were Ralph Wilson and his Septet, Louis Mordish and his Players, Maurice Arnold and his Sextet, as well as accordion ensembles (very popular in the fifties and sixties) such as George Scott-Wood and his Music, the Gerald Crossman Players and the Albert Delroy Sextet. Other virtuoso accordionists such as Henry Krein and Delmondi also appeared with their respective quartets.

Henry Krein   Delmondi   Ralph Wilson   Albert Delroy

DANCE ORCHESTRAS

These were carefully selected by the BBC for their ability to play 'straight'. Orchestras which favoured the 'big band' style were not considered suitable for factories, the ideal combinations being the 'strict-tempo' palais bands, such as those of Phil Tate, Lou Preager, Syd Dean and Harry Leader, or nightclub bands led by the likes of Jack Nathan, Ronnie Pleydell and Felix King. The orchestras of Bill

Savill and Tommy Kinsman (who played on the programme for nearly 20 years), did not have 'residences', but built their reputations on playing at high society functions and took engagements around the country, often performing for Royalty.

DANCE MUSIC GROUPS

As with light music, there were many small groups, some of which existed purely for broadcasting. Frank Baron and his Sextet, Cecil Norman and the Rhythm Players, Ken Beaumont and his Sextet, Eddie Strevens and his Quartet and the Jack Emblow Sextet are good examples. The famous dance band leader Lew Stone formed a sextet in 1959, specifically for broadcasting.

MILITARY BANDS

At least once a week service bands appeared on *Music While You Work*. Virtually all of the top bands took part. The various bands of the Brigade of Guards (as they were then known), together with the Royal Artillery and the Royal Air Force were regularly featured, as were most of the army 'corps' bands.

BRASS BANDS

Although they were not used to the same extent as military bands, and rarely after 1961, most of the leading brass bands of the day contributed to *MWYW*. Black Dyke, Brighouse and Rastrick, Grimethorpe Colliery, Fodens, Ransome and Marles were among the many bands used.

A full list of all the contributors to *MWYW* appears elsewhere in this book.

One of the reasons that the BBC did not favour the 'big-band sound' for *MWYW* was that 'hot solos' conflicted with the rule that the melody should be clearly defined at all times. Also, 'powerhouse' drumming could sound like gunfire over the factory Tannoys. By the sixties, however, fashions in music were changing, and even palais bands were becoming more 'up-tempo'. Jack Dorsey, whose ten-piece band was resident at the Astoria Dance Salon in London and had been

24

Jack Dorsey's Orchestra nearly got their marching orders for swinging the programme's signature tune!

playing regularly on *MWYW*, was suddenly given a 17-piece swing orchestra by the Rank Organisation, which managed the Astoria. Within months of its formation it was being heralded as the best band in the country, and duly replaced the ten piece band on *MWYW*.

25

Jack Dorsey had no intention of 'watering it down', indeed he was very proud of it. Predictably, he launched his powerhouse sound of quite exceptional musicianship upon a delighted *MWYW* audience, but much to the consternation of BBC officials. Jack, who did his own arrangements, even went as far as doing a 'hotted-up' version of the show's signature tune, *Calling All Workers* – a cardinal sin!

Consequently, he was summoned to a meeting of executives for a dressing-down, but the shrewd Jack Dorsey had checked the audience figures and knew that his band was near the top. When he informed the executives of this fact, they had to back down and let him continue. This seemed to set a precedent – after he had been seen to get away with it, other bandleaders started introducing more jazzy arrangements in their programmes.

It is reasonable to assume that the combinations which appeared most frequently on *MWYW* were also the most popular, although economics were undoubtedly an important consideration. Evidence of this is the formation of Lew Stone's Sextet after he had been informed that he could not expect to broadcast as frequently as he would have liked with a 14-piece band. Similarly, Ronnie Munro, who conducted a 17-piece light orchestra for some years, formed a sextet and, for a while, appeared with both combinations on *MWYW*, that is until some whiz-kid accountant at the BBC worked out that the sextet was cheaper. So the orchestra, a delightful combination of organ and strings, was axed. Although Ronnie Munro suggested that the sextet be used in early *Morning Music* programmes so that the orchestra was not completely lost from *MWYW*, his pleas were in vain.

The most used band was The Banjoliers, with 475 appearances in the series. Troise and his Banjoliers was formed in the early thirties and appeared regularly on *MWYW* until the death of Pasquale Troise in March 1957. The popularity of the band was such, however, that the BBC was anxious for it to survive, so, within days of Troise's death, the BBC was negotiating with his widow for Jack Mandel to take over the band. The Banjoliers, directed by Jack Mandel, continued to play an average of more than 20 editions per year for the rest of the series.

Some readers may recall Troise and his Mandoliers who toured the variety theatres in the thirties. They were exactly the same combination, merely swapping mandolins for banjos. During the first couple of years of *Music While You Work*, both Mandoliers and Banjoliers appeared on the programme but, after a few outings, it was established that the noisier factories found the more incisive-sounding

26

Jack Mandel conducting The Banjoliers in the 1960s

Banjoliers to be more satisfactory in terms of audibility. This determined the instrumentation subsequently used by Troise and Jack Mandel for *MWYW*. The Banjoliers were a unique and technically brilliant ensemble whose broadcasting spanned six decades – surely some sort of record! A particularly happy memory for me was attending the Banjoliers' final broadcast on 5th October 1982.

Cecil Norman at the piano

The next most used group was Cecil Norman and the Rhythm Players (466 shows). This was a quintet consisting of two pianos, bass, percussion and guitar. Cecil Norman, like so many musicians of that era, started in classical music and was, in fact, a child prodigy. Playing piano concertos at the age of eight, he was described as the finest pianist (of his age) in the country. However, neuritis in his right arm made it necessary for him to switch to less demanding music and his name subsequently became almost synonymous with the Light

27

Programme.

Although the rigid rules established for *Music While You Work* during the war were never officially relaxed (indeed, they were reiterated from time to time) there is no doubt that, during the fifties and sixties, more flexibility was applied and the programmes were all the better for it. The military bands and some dance bands maintained the non-stop performance directive but many light orchestras and some bands would pause for about three seconds between numbers. It was very important, when planning a programme, to keep a watch on the relative keys in which the pieces chosen were written. A piece in the key of C Major, for example, would sound very incongruous if it immediately followed one that ended in F Sharp Major; but if it followed one ending in F Major, it would sound fine.

It was, therefore, incumbent upon the musical directors to plan their programmes in such a way as to avoid jarring key changes. One way to do this was to use piano or guitar modulations between pieces. This also gave the musicians a little more time to change their music – except for the person playing the links, of course. It is not clear from the BBC files whether they condoned or condemned this practice, as conflicting instructions appear to have been given over the years. Wartime memoranda actually suggest the use of piano links, whereas a later instruction from Kenneth Baynes says that 'piano links are best avoided, it is much more satisfactory to play segue'. Yet, around this time, there is a letter from him to a bandleader, who was apparently guilty of untidy openings, actually suggesting that he give himself more time by using links! Whatever the official position, the use of links became more common as the years went by, and many light orchestras which rarely used them in the fifties introduced them in the sixties. Some used a few bars of their signature tunes. Accordionist Gerald Crossman used his own composition *A Night in Montmartre*, Falkman and his Apache Band appropriately used the *Apache Dance* by Offenbach, Bernard Monshin and his Rio Tango Band used their signature tune *Hear My Song, Violetta*, and Harold C. Gee and his Maritza Players used *Play Gypsy*.

Orchestra leader Sidney Davey played the piano for several of the light orchestras, and his distinctively styled modulations immediately identified him.

One rule which seemed to die a death concerned the use by MDs of top players from other bands to enhance their performances. The BBC adopted a 'one man, one band' approach, which meant that each band

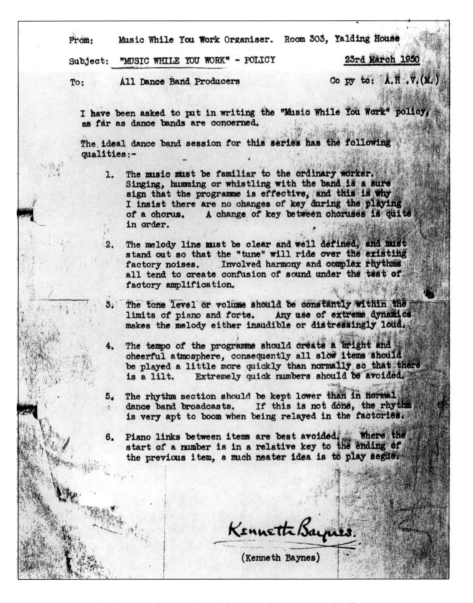

From: Music While You Work Organiser.   Room 303, Yalding House

Subject: "MUSIC WHILE YOU WORK" - POLICY   23rd March 1950

To: All Dance Band Producers   Copy to: A.H.V.(M.)

I have been asked to put in writing the "Music While You Work" policy, as far as dance bands are concerned.

The ideal dance band session for this series has the following qualities:-

1. The music must be familiar to the ordinary worker. Singing, humming or whistling with the band is a sure sign that the programme is effective, and this is why I insist there are no changes of key during the playing of a chorus. A change of key between choruses is quite in order.

2. The melody line must be clear and well defined, and must stand out so that the "tune" will ride over the existing factory noises.   Involved harmony and complex rhythms all tend to create confusion of sound under the test of factory amplification.

3. The tone level or volume should be constantly within the limits of piano and forte.   Any use of extreme dynamics makes the melody either inaudible or distressingly loud.

4. The tempo of the programme should create a bright and cheerful atmosphere, consequently all slow items should be played a little more quickly than normally so that there is a lilt.   Extremely quick numbers should be avoided.

5. The rhythm section should be kept lower than in normal dance band broadcasts.   If this is not done, the rhythm is very apt to boom when being relayed in the factories.

6. Piano links between items are best avoided.   Where the start of a number is in a relative key to the ending of the previous item, a much neater idea is to play segue.

Kenneth Baynes.

(Kenneth Baynes)

BBC memo from 1950 giving supplementary guidelines

or orchestra had to be 'fully constituted', that is to say that it should have regular personnel who did not play for other bands. This was rather a narrow view at the time when it was becoming common practice in the music business to borrow players from other bands to

29

Falkman and his Apache Band

cover absentees, or indeed to engage top session musicians as 'corner men' in a section of an orchestra. There were even instances of bands being taken off the air because they were deemed to be in breach of this rule. This smacked of hypocrisy, as the BBC was making more and more use of ensembles and orchestras which were brought together specifically for broadcasting and didn't exist outside the studio. These 'ad hoc' orchestras included those of Bernard Monshin, Louis Voss, Michael Freedman, Raymond Agoult and Sidney Davey. When these musical directors undertook non-broadcasting engagements, it was unlikely that it would be with the elite personnel which they used on broadcasts. The latter would be musicians whose expertise enabled them to play accurately, at sight, any music that was put before them.

Many musicians from symphony orchestras participated in *Music While You Work*. For example the well-known clarinet and saxophone player Jack Brymer (who also directed the London Saxophone Quartet and was one of the finest reed players in the country) took great delight in playing Latin-American music with Fredric Cooper and his Tipica Orchestra. Top instrumentalists from the world of light music, such as Reginald Leopold and Max Jaffa, would often be among the string players: indeed many an *MWYW* session would be a veritable who's who of light music.

The 'conscription' of players was usually organised by a 'fixer,' often a violinist, who would allocate himself a position in the orchestra which he had booked. It was by no means unusual for an orchestra to include within its ranks conductors of other *MWYW* orchestras. Hugh

James, whose light orchestra was one that also gave public concerts, often told me of his friendship with fellow conductor Arthur Anton (better known simply as Anton). This friendship went back to the days when they both played for the silent movies. He said, 'Anton would play in my broadcasting orchestra and I in his.'

It had become almost a standing joke at the BBC that on any day you could walk into a studio and see almost the same faces in each orchestra. Only the conductor was different, as was the repertoire and style of each orchestra. Gerald Crossman told me that, in addition to leading his own players, he would regularly play for Fredric Cooper, Ralph Elman, Anton, Sidney Davey, George Scott-Wood, Louis Voss, Bernard Monshin and many others.

Most of the orchestras, particularly in the fifties, played in programmes other than *MWYW* – early morning shows such as *Bright and Early* and *Morning Music*, for example. In these and other

Anton and his orchestra broadcasting from the Camden Theatre, London, in the fifties. This orchestra included no less than six *Music While You Work* bandleaders: front row left – Bernard Monshin; second from left – Ralph Elman; Harold C. Gee (to the right of Anton); accordionist Gerald Crossman and pianist Sidney Davey. In the second row left – Jack Mandel (conductor of The Banjoliers)

31

programmes, they often played pieces which, for one reason or another, they were not allowed to play on *MWYW*. Whereas an orchestra playing in *Morning Music* might include a rhapsody, an operatic selection, or movements from a suite, they would be unlikely to use them in *MWYW*. A more suitable repertoire would be a mixture of short, light pieces as typified by the works of Leroy Anderson, Robert Farnon, Sidney Torch, Ronald Binge, Clive Richardson and Ernest Tomlinson – all masters in the world of light music – with perhaps a show selection or popular ballad for contrast.

Sidney Bowman

Throughout its existence *Music While You Work* was dogged by musical snobbery. Certain top bandleaders didn't want to be associated with the concept of music played as a background to the sound of machinery, but in general the snobbery was not so much from the musicians as from some executives within the BBC who clearly regarded it as a low-brow programme. If it wasn't for the fact that the programme was wanted by industry, these executives would, in all probability, have advocated its removal many years before it actually ended. Whilst those directly responsible for *MWYW*, such as Kenneth Baynes, took the programme very seriously and demanded the highest standards, it is apparent from some programme reports in the BBC's files that others took a rather different attitude. A report on Sidney Bowman and the Promenade Players illustrates this:

'A refined orchestra consisting of rather superior personnel – Perhaps a little like putting the Derby winners drawing a milk cart to use them on MWYW.'

An audition report on what turned out to be a very successful dance band with hundreds of broadcasts to its credit and several commercial recordings reads:

'Dull by ordinary standards, but eminently suitable for MWYW.'

32

One of the most utilised light orchestras on the show (which shall remain nameless) was described in 1952 as:

'... *an orchestra of mediocre competency ... suitable for MWYW type of programme, but I doubt whether suitable for other light music periods.*'

This orchestra, which I considered to be of a very high standard, had several hundred broadcasts to its credit and appeared in a wide range of programmes. Its director frequently 'guest conducted' the various BBC Regional staff orchestras!

The snobbery which existed within the BBC, to some degree spilled over into the general public. Whereas today old recordings of the shows are much sought-after 'collectors' items' (many people recorded them – albeit illicitly!), in the fifties it was clearly regarded as 'non-U' to listen to the programme. I can well remember, as a child, being told, 'You don't want to listen to that – it's just for the factory workers!' Well, I did want to listen to it because it was so tuneful and enjoyable – it was only a programme title, after all. Clearly the factory connection inspired the notion in some people's minds that music intended for such conditions could not have much credibility. What its critics seemed to ignore was the fact that *MWYW* had become extremely popular in the home and, in 1955, was said to have a daily audience of four million, in addition to its 'captive' audience in the factories. To this figure must be added the burgeoning number of motorists for whom it was ideal entertainment. I can well recall that whilst still at primary school I used to dash home in order to catch the last 15 minutes of the afternoon edition. As a teenager I was really hooked, and began to regard *MWYW* orchestras in the same way as modern youth regard their favourite pop groups, and, like many of my contemporaries, I have never lost the taste for melodious music. Subsequent generations will never realise what they have missed.

For many years the morning edition of *MWYW* was transmitted simultaneously on the Home Service and the Light Programme, when it was the only broadcast entertainment available to the public from the BBC at 10.30 a.m. No wonder a whole generation grew up with the programme!

Music While You Work was by no means an easy programme for its participants. As we have seen, the morning sessions meant a very early start for the musicians. Cecil Norman regularly had to get up at 5.00

a.m. Of course, these days a lot of people get up at 5.00 a.m., but remember, many musicians will have been working late the night before, particularly those employed in the nightclubs and ballrooms. Ian Stewart, for example, who was the resident bandleader at London's Savoy Hotel for many years, got home at 3.00 a.m., so if he was on *MWYW* in the morning it was hardly worth going to bed!

As mentioned earlier, the conductor or bandleader was responsible for most elements of a *Music While You Work* broadcast: selecting and planning the programme, doing (or commissioning) the arrangements, ensuring that the necessary musicians knew when and where to turn up and, last but not least, timing the programme. The BBC liked at least 30 seconds of the closing signature tune, but did not like the orchestra to finish so early that *Calling All Workers* went on indefinitely. Getting the timing right was quite an art and just because it worked out perfectly at rehearsal did not necessarily mean that it would be the same on the broadcast. A conductor only had to take a couple of numbers slightly slower on transmission and he might not reach the signature tune before the red light went out.

Of course, it can work both ways. I well remember one programme in which the orchestra not only completed *Calling All Workers* but had to start it all over again! On another occasion an orchestra played the signature tune for a good three minutes before being 'faded out'. Could it be pure coincidence that the final item in the programme had been, appropriately, *Time On My Hands?*

Some musicians possessed a knack for precise timing. Cecil Norman had a reputation for being accurate to the second both at rehearsal and at the actual transmission. Isy Geiger, on the other hand, seemed to find the timing element very difficult and was regularly faded out before reaching *Calling All Workers*. He obviously established during rehearsals whether he was likely to be tight on time, and some of his broadcasts sounded rushed as a consequence. An amusing story concerning Isy Geiger was told by one of his musicians. On one occasion he was getting towards the end of his programme when he felt there was a danger of under-running (unusual for him), so he crept round the orchestra inserting an extra piece into the musicians' folders. As he reached the back of the orchestra, the red light went out. He had overrun!

The former BBC producer, the late Antony Askew, who for many years was the studio manager for the Saturday morning editions, spoke of an occasion when Fred Alexander and his Players discovered during rehearsal that they had insufficient music for the broadcast. There was only one solution: Fred had to telephone his wife to ask her to bring some more music to the studio. As a reward for doing this she was allowed to attend the live transmission.

The late Hugh James told me that in order to ensure the accurate timing of his broadcasts he would 'sing' the whole programme through in his own home. I'd love to have been a fly on the wall!

One would imagine that the military bands would have little trouble in timing their programmes, being in a position to rehearse at leisure in their own barracks. Nevertheless, on one occasion when the Band of the Irish Guards was broadcasting, their Director of Music, realising that they had not got time to complete their final march, decided to make an instant cut. This was a routine procedure which usually went without a hitch, so the conductor held up two fingers to instruct the band to go to the 'second time bar' (the second time bar is a musical shorthand to save the repeated section being written out in full – only the part at the end which is different the second time is written). Unfortunately, in this instance, half of the band had their music written out in full and, consequently, for them there was no second time bar. The ensuing cacophony was such that the Director of Music had no choice but to quickly stop the band and go straight to the signature tune. I have a recording of one of our most distinguished military bands getting lost in a piece called *The Dance of the Three Old Maids*. By the time the band got back together again – no easy task at the best of times – the Organising Director of Music must have been a nervous wreck. Ah, the joys of live radio!

Music While You Work conductors and bandleaders, like other entertainers, received their fair share of correspondence from listeners, either in the form of a fan letter, or simply to ask the title of a piece – *MWYW* was unannounced. From my own experience, I have found that musicians are very appreciative of listeners' interest in their work and will always provide a courteous reply. Just occasionally, however, the correspondence received can be of a rather different nature. Hugh James had included, in a 1952 Christmas broadcast, a medley of drinking songs and carols entitled *The Savoy Christmas Medley*, arranged by Debroy Somers, who had been a musical director at the Savoy Hotel in the 1920s. It was quite a famous number, having become a favourite with orchestras over the years, but following the transmission, Hugh James received quite a venomous letter from a listener accusing him of blasphemy on account of the fact that the

Hugh James and his orchestra in concert on London's South Bank in the fifties

carols in the medley had been played in a 'rhythmic' manner! The letter, which is now in my own collection, is frankly downright offensive. Hugh James took it very seriously and immediately sent it to Kenneth Baynes at the BBC, who promptly returned it, telling Hugh not to worry about it as this was a selection that had been played regularly by orchestras for decades. Nevertheless, Hugh James, being the gentleman that he was, wrote back to his correspondent apologising for his 'lapse of good taste' and assuring him that he would withdraw the item from his repertoire. He added:

'It is my desire to bring pleasure to people through my music – not to offend them'.

The complainant, who happened to be the editor of a well-known magazine, returned a very conciliatory letter apologising for being boorish and rude and asking for forgiveness. This seems to prove the old adage that says 'you can kill more flies with honey than with vinegar'.

During the fifties there was no great change in the style and content of *Music While You Work*. The mixture of old favourites and current tunes seemed to work well and, whilst no attempt was made to emulate particular fashions, the music was very much in line with that played in other programmes, although there was greater emphasis on bright, tuneful music with the minimum of affectation. The programme was a gift to the light music composers of the day, many of whom wrote with the programme in mind. Also, to a certain extent, *MWYW* reflected the output of record companies. In this area, however, things began to change in the late fifties with the advent of rock and pop music, aimed predominantly at the young. By the early sixties, pop groups were becoming the main money-earners for record companies, which largely abandoned light orchestral and dance music for that which was of greater financial benefit to them.

Although *MWYW* continued to use current numbers, bands were limited to those pieces which were tuneful enough to be adapted as 'instrumentals'. To attempt to use some of the material perpetrated by the rock groups would have completely altered the character of the show. At this point the BBC was beginning to wonder if *MWYW* was still wanted by industry, and Kenneth Baynes visited a considerable number of factories in 1962 with a view to establishing this. Having discussed the question with directors, personnel officers, managers, welfare officers and public relations managers as well as shop stewards and operatives, he was able to report a resounding YES! In his report he quoted the following phrases to substantiate this:

'A most useful aid to keeping staff happy ... an everyday necessity ... very glad to have it and when not available due to football etc. we replace it with our own records ... a National institution ... Most useful as a livener-up, especially during the afternoon ... uproar if not available ...' and so on.

There was competition however. Firms specialising in the provision of piped music such as MUZAC and REDITUNE were using high-pressure salesmanship to persuade factories to use their products, although some establishments which tried piped music found it monotonous by comparison with *Music While You Work*, and did not continue with it.

Nevertheless, the BBC's audience research figures seemed to indicate that the number of listeners to the morning editions outnumbered those listening to the afternoon show by three to one, and that it was apparent that up to 85% of the afternoon audience was in the home. The BBC's budget for *MWYW* was separate for the 30-minute

Gerald Crossman (left) discussing a final point with producer Edward Nash before going 'on air'

morning and longer afternoon editions, the latter having a greater allocation because small groups were rarely used in the 45-minute programmes. In view of this it would have seemed more logical to have had the longer shows in the morning – a premise that was certainly discussed.

In Chapter One, I explained that light orchestras and dance bands on *MWYW* were provided respectively by the BBC's Light Music Department and Light Entertainment Department. Although not known to the general listener, in 1963 it was decided that both elements of the programme would come under the control of the newly-formed Popular Music Department, into which the other departments had been integrated. With this change came the decision to pre-record the majority of *MWYW* sessions, with the exception of the Wednesday morning military band spot, which would continue to be live.

By recording some of the programmes in the evenings and on Sundays, the BBC hoped to increase the daytime availability of some of its studios for other programmes. The majority of *MWYW* sessions came from its Maida Vale studios, although some came from the Aeolian Hall, some from the Playhouse Theatre near Charing Cross, as well as from other studios dotted around London. The Concert Hall at Broadcasting House was also used for the occasional programme. There was concern amongst musicians, and even BBC officials, that the pre-recording of *MWYW* might cause it to lose some of its sense of immediacy. So, with a view to avoiding this, strict instructions were given that the show must be recorded 'as if live'. This directive precluded breaks or retakes in the event of mistakes. Well, that was the official line, anyway! I am inclined to think that the musicians, who undoubtedly took pride in their work, would not have tolerated a serious error going out on air if it could possibly be avoided. If they had stopped playing and demanded a retake, I doubt if there was much the studio manager could do about it! Orchestra leader Cyril Watters, who joined the show in 1965, told me that he recorded his shows in two halves, the ensemble taking a 20-minute break half way through the recording. This became standard practice in later years. By

Bernard Monshin and his Rio Tango Band. This orchestra also included a number of well-known musicians. Henry Elman (second from left); Louis Voss (partially obscured); guitarist Billy Bell behind Bernard Monshin (centre); Alec Firman (fourth from right); Edward Rubach (third from right) and Gerald Crossman (extreme right)

the mid-sixties, there was audible evidence of breaks or even editing in some broadcasts, with opening notes being clipped off, or reverberation (electronic echo) being suddenly turned on or off.

It was noticeable, after *MWYW* ceased to be live, that broadcasters overran more frequently. This was not necessarily the fault of the musicians. If there was an important story in the news, the one minute news summary that preceded the programme sometimes lasted for two minutes. A gale warning would sometimes be enough to delay the programme to the extent that it had to be faded out before the closing signature tune. When *MWYW* had been live, bandleaders had been able to adjust their tempos or make cuts during the broadcast in order to complete their programme of music – although, unbeknown to listeners, completion was often only achieved by the studio manager leaving his cubicle and holding up a placard saying something like 'cut the repeat' or 'go straight to the coda'.

After *MWYW* had been under the auspices of the Popular Music Department for some while, it became noticeable that some of the light music combinations became lighter and 'more commercial', both in choice of music and style. It was as if they had a premonition that if they did not update, they might not continue broadcasting. They may well have been right as some of the more traditional-style ensembles were being used less frequently in the programme. I well remember Jack Mandel, conductor of the Banjoliers, saying that he quite deliberately modernised the style of the band at this time. I am not sure that 'modernise' was quite the right word, but their programmes certainly became more up-tempo and many of the genuine light music numbers were replaced by dance tunes such as *Limehouse Blues* and *Alexander's Ragtime Band*. Entertaining though these arrangements were, some listeners were not entirely happy with this change, as it was not quite the sort of music with which the Banjoliers had long been associated; there were, after all, other banjo bands which played the popular repertoire.

In 1964 came the first sign that *Music While You Work* might not be immortal. Whereas the programme was heard simultaneously on the Home Service and the Light Programme on weekdays, the Saturday morning edition had, for several years, been broadcast only on the Home Service, and then not in the Western Region. The BBC now decided that with music (albeit of a different type) being available on the Light Programme, it was desirable to replace *MWYW* with further education programmes. This came as something of a blow to those people who, because of their occupation, could only hear the Saturday edition. Since 1961, the morning slots for light music had been on Monday, Wednesday and Saturday, the Wednesday show always being played by a military band. So, with the removal of the Saturday show, there remained only one morning session per week for light music ensembles, some of which were not stylistically suitable for the 45 minute shows and, consequently, now had fewer opportunities to play in the series.

Although not apparent at the time, the decision to discontinue the Saturday morning show was just the thin end of the wedge. Techniques for broadcasting music were forever evolving; whereas in the fifties just a few microphones (sometimes only two) would suffice to broadcast an orchestra, by the early sixties every musician was 'miked-up'. No doubt every sound engineer would consider this to be an improvement, but was it? Whilst the sound produced was crisper and cleaner, it was, to my ears anyway, a flatter, more one-dimensional sound. Remember, this was before stereo had become commonplace. In the fifties it was possible to conjure up a mental picture of an orchestra playing in the studio, purely from the sound which came over the air. Somehow the percussion actually sounded as if it was at the back of the orchestra, its traditional position. With the advent of updated technology, it became less easy to create this mental picture as the musicians often sounded on top of one another. (If the broadcast was coming from Maida Vale Studio 5 – they probably were!)

Another disadvantage of the multi-microphone technique was that the overall balance of an orchestra was no longer in the hands of the conductor; it was now completely at the mercy of the studio manager, all adjustments to volume and internal balance being made in the control box. This was fine when the broadcast was being managed by an experienced technician (who also needed to be a musician, by the way). Problems occurred if the 'man in the box' was inexperienced or unsympathetic to the style of music being broadcast. Such a situation sometimes adversely affected the sound that came over the air. It didn't do a lot for the reputations of some musicians either, as the layman would, in all probability, put it down to a bad performance. Understandably, bandleaders often took an interest in the internal balance that was being created in the box, however, those who wanted their broadcasting careers to continue were wise to remember that nobody, whether he is a sound engineer or musician, likes to be told how to do his job by the unqualified. A one-time *MWYW* studio manager, who later became a respected producer, once revealed that when bandleaders came into the box to hear the sound that was being recorded, he would turn up the volume – 'everything sounded good then!' he said.

I do not pretend to have technical knowledge concerning broadcasting equipment, but I do know that by the sixties, increasing use was being made of reverberation, otherwise known as 'electronic echo'. In the right hands, this technique can enhance a performance by 'lifting' the sound of a band or orchestra, creating a 'presence' – a simulated natural acoustic that could not be attained in certain BBC studios which are intentionally acoustically dead. These, however, were pioneering days and some broadcasts were certainly not in the right hands and were often marred by a distant, tinny and altogether unnatural sound, the clarity of individual instruments often being lost. I have a recording of a 1966 broadcast in which the echo was turned up to the extent that single notes were repeating several times, causing a completely jumbled sound. I am sure that such a situation would never occur today.

The next major change to affect *Music While You Work* was the decision to end the afternoon editions in the summer of 1966. The listening figures, which, as previously mentioned, had for some time indicated a smaller audience in the afternoon, must have had a bearing on this decision.

Iain Sutherland, who was the conductor of the BBC Scottish Radio Orchestra

This was a major blow to the larger orchestras which provided the afternoon broadcasts. Whilst, in theory, these could have been transferred to the 30-minute morning editions, the smaller budget allocation would only permit the occasional use of an orchestra. The programme was now down to five editions per week, one of which – the military band spot – took up a large part of their budget. Perhaps it would have been logical to have placed these bands on a fortnightly basis at this stage, in order to accommodate the orchestras. The fact that this didn't happen might have had something to do with agreements with the Music Department, whose weekly military band spot was its sole contribution to *MWYW*. The blunt fact was, however, that the BBC felt no obligation to the outside orchestras, which, in the opinion of some, had outlived their usefulness, particularly at a time when the broadcasting of light orchestral music had reduced to the extent that such programmes still remaining could be serviced by the BBC's own staff orchestras. Indeed, with a view to maintaining the orchestral element of *MWYW*, the BBC Scottish Radio Orchestra was given a weekly slot in 1967. As BBC orchestras were on an annual salary, regardless of which programmes they provided, this would also have been deemed cost-effective.

Another cost-effective measure was the decision, in the autumn of 1966, to repeat most of the programmes a few weeks later, thus further reducing the number of actual performances.

By early 1967, plans were well advanced for a major overhaul of BBC broadcasting. The BBC no longer had a monopoly on listeners; threatened initially by 'pirate radio' – offshore broadcasting and then legalised commercial radio stations churning out pop music, the BBC felt an obligation to compete. Radios One, Two, Three and Four were to replace the existing networks, the Light Programme being separated into Radios One and Two. The pop-orientated Radio One would have long record-dominated programmes fronted, not by announcers, but by what were termed 'personality presenters', whose task it was to create a cheery aural wallpaper that could be heard rather than listened to. One wonders what Lord Reith, the BBC's first Director General, would have thought of these changes, but change the BBC did and the new format was a success, surviving almost unaltered to the present day – its contemporary audience never having heard anything different.

Whilst the pseudo jolliness and apparent inanity of some of the presenters irritated those used to more traditional presentation, it has to be admitted that others were intelligent and professional in their approach. Jimmy Young, for example, was to be allotted a daily programme consisting of a mixture of music and interviews, and one hour of this programme was to be 'shared' with Radio Two between 10 a.m. and 11 a.m., replacing the programmes broadcast at this time. So, whilst Jimmy Young's programme survived into the 21st century, the new schedules meant the end for *Music While You Work* after 27 years. Thus, on 29th September, the last day of the Light Programme, Jimmy Leach and his Organolians played the final show, ending with *Say It With Music* and the familiar signature tune *Calling All Workers*, which, instead of being faded out as usual, was brought to a conclusion with a decisive chord.

The BBC's stated reason for ending *Music While You Work* was that, as there was so much music coming over the airwaves, there no longer seemed to be a need for a programme that was designed in very different circumstances. Furthermore, the BBC felt that it could no longer accommodate such a programme because of the *Jimmy Young Show*. However, had they not decided to broadcast part of this programme simultaneously on Radios One and Two, this situation might not have arisen. Let's face it, some of the BBC management had long grown weary of *MWYW*, which they clearly felt belonged to another age. Indeed, rumour has it that there was one quite well-known musical sophisticate at the BBC, with a penchant for 'avant-garde' music, who could not wait to see the back of the small outside orchestras that had been part of the BBC's output for decades.

The BBC quite expected a backlash from industry over the decision, which indeed it received, but executives felt that the advancement of piped music in factories from commercial organisations such as

David Curry conducting the BBC Northern Ireland Light Orchestra in the fifties

MUZAC justified their action. They did not expect much reaction from the general public, and it is a sad fact that just two letters in the *Radio Times* marked the passing of *MWYW*, one referring to the pleasure that various artists had given over the years. At no time did this magazine mention that the show was ending, indeed, I can't recall having seen any press coverage on the subject at all.

Whatever the listening public may have thought about it, the loss of *MWYW* was a greater blow to the musicians who played on it. With the noticeable reduction in the broadcasting of light music over the preceding years, the use of outside orchestras and groups had diminished to the point that, apart from the breakfast-time programmes, which themselves were becoming increasingly record dominated, there was little broadcasting opportunity for them. As stated previously, the BBC had its own regional orchestras under contract: the Midland Light Orchestra, the Northern Ireland Light Orchestra and the Scottish Radio Orchestra amongst others, all of which needed to be used several times per week to justify their salaries. Nevertheless, the clock was ticking even for them, as they all disappeared in the early eighties.

With the demise of *MWYW*, many long-standing orchestras, bands and ensembles never broadcast again. Reginald Pursglove, whose Albany Strings had been a regular feature of the Light Programme for many years, asked the BBC why it was that his orchestra had received 23 broadcasts in 1966 but only one in 1967, despite the fact that the orchestra was as good as ever. The BBC had to concede that it was unfair to a broadcaster of 30 years' standing but it was difficult to find a slot for him as *MWYW*, and several other suitable series, were no longer being broadcast. Eventually, he was given three weeks deputising for the BBC's London Studio Players as 'holiday relief', but nothing else was forthcoming. With no future hope of broadcasting, many musical directors left the music profession, some emigrating. Others found alternative employment; Michael Freedman, one of the *MWYW* stalwarts, became a London taxi driver. The late Hugh James once said that '*Music While You Work* was a labour of love – we gave so much pleasure to people yet we were cast out like old clothes!'

Over the years, I have had the good fortune to meet many of the artists associated with *Music While You Work* and have, without exception, found them to be the most agreeable of people, happy to talk nostalgically about their careers and their music; I think that those who are left are pleased that there are still people around who care, and that young people are discovering, even now, the joy of light music through the few surviving recordings of their work.

So, what legacy remains of *MWYW*? Certainly none of the 16,781* broadcasts had been retained in the BBC Sound Archives, although this has, to some extent, been remedied from private sources.

Between 1943 and 1947 the Decca Record Company produced a series of *Music While You Work* records for use in factories. They instituted a special black and white label, and some 420 records were made by a variety of bands and orchestras, most of which appeared in the series. Although the project was totally independent of the BBC, the recordings were supervised by the first *MWYW* Organiser, Wynford Reynolds, and Edgar Jackson. To this day, these records still turn up in vintage record bazaars and are sought-after collectors' items. Many have now been re-released on CD.

In 1963, the one and only long-playing record of *Music While You*

---

*Note: The figure of 16,781 can only be regarded as approximate as *MWYW* was sometimes cancelled at short notice, particularly during the war.

45

Work was issued; it was an authentic recreation of a typical programme by Stan Reynolds and his Octet, with sleeve notes by Kenneth Baynes, who, as I have recounted, had a long association with the programme, finishing up as Head of the BBC's Popular Music Department.

At the end of the final edition of *MWYW* in 1967, to the accompaniment of *Calling All Workers*, the continuity announcer said 'Well, ladies and gentlemen, that's the last time you'll ever hear THAT tune and it has been played for many years ...' Actually, he was wrong – as we shall see in the next chapter!

SOME ACTUAL '*MUSIC WHILE YOU WORK*' PROGRAMMES BROADCAST IN PEACE-TIME

**10.30 a.m.   Harry Fryer and his Orchestra
7.7.45**

Calling All Workers (Sig)	Coates
Wings Over the Navy	Warren
Community Songs:	
I've Made Up My Mind to Sail Away	Scott
Are We Going to Part Like This?	Collins
Waiting at the Church	Pethers
Masquerade of the Waltz	Hildebrandt
Medley of popular songs:	
Don't Fence Me In	Porter
Can't Help Singing	Kern
Waiting	Lawrence/Milton

46

I'm Ridin' White Horses	Halifax
Selection: *Finckiana*	arr. Finck
Community Songs:	
Ta-Ra-Ra-Boom-De-Ay	Asher
In the Good Old Summer Time	Evans
My Gal is a High Born Lady	Morton
Gaily Through the World	Macbeth
Calling All Workers (Sig)	Coates

10.30 a.m.   Terence Casey at the Organ
3.7.45   of the Trocadero, Elephant & Castle

Calling All Workers (Sig)	Coates
Marche Lorraine	Ganne
Pierrette Cherie	Ives
Cockney Capers	Crantock
Let the Rest of the World Go By	Ball
We'll Gather Lilacs	Novello
Wedding of the Rose	Jessel
Sweet Dreams	Jerome
Medley:	
Touch of Texas	McHugh
I'm Thinking Tonight of My Blue Eyes	Carter
Whistler's Ma-in-Law	Stevens
Kiss Me Again	Velazquez
Amour Amour	Ruiz
Echo of a Serenade	Brever
You Are My Sunshine	Davis
Calling All Workers (Sig)	Coates

10.30 a.m.   BBC Midland Light Orchestra
29.9.46   Conductor: Gilbert Vinter

Calling All Workers (Sig)	Coates
The Galloping Major	arr. Jacob
As Time Goes By	Hopfield
Jealousy	Gade
Phil The Fluter's Ball	French arr. Hartley
Cacucha (from *In Malaga*)	Curzon
Septembre (Waltz)	Godin

47

Firefly	Friml
Calling All Workers (Sig)	Coates

**10.30 a.m.   Harry Davidson and his Orchestra
19.10.46**

Calling All Workers (Sig)	Coates
Twostep: *The Jungle Jubilee*	Bratton
Waltz: *A Toi*	Waldteufel
Stepping Stones	Reeves
Wedding in the Highlands	Ewing
Selection: *Sweethearts*	Herbert
Fragrance	Ancliffe
The Pig and Whistle	Elliott Smith
Calling All Workers (Sig)	Coates

**10.30 a.m.   The London Coliseum Orchestra
3.12.46   Conductor: Reginald Burston**

Calling All Workers (Sig)	Coates
Here Goes	Baynes
Double or Nothing	Johnston
Fascination	Marchetti
Medley:	
All Through the Day	Kern
Blue Skies	Berlin
I Don't Know Enough About You	Lee
Five Minutes More	Cahn/Styne
In a Country Lane (From *Summer Days*)	Coates
Moontime	Collins
Selection: *The Country Girl*	Monckton
Calling All Workers (Sig)	Coates

**3.30 p.m.
3.12.46   Jack Leon and his Orchestra**

Calling All Workers (Sig)	Coates
Selection: The Passing Show	Finck
Phantom Melodie	Ketelbey
Spring In Vienna	Stoltz

48

Medley:

Mister Moon You've Got a Million Sweethearts	Chester/Morris
Anytime At All	Gold/Emmerson
One Night in Old Seville	Foley
Do You Love Me?	Ruby
The Cactus Polka	Plumb
My Best to You	Jones
Selection: *Song of Norway*	Greig
Baby's Sweetheart	Corri
Lupita	May
Calling All Workers (Sig)	Coates

10.30 a.m. Dudley Hippodrome Orchestra
7.2.49   Conductor: William Hand

Calling All Workers (Sig)	Coates
March: *Spirit of Youth*	Gilbert
Selection: *The Merry Widow*	Lehar arr. Godfrey
Intermezzo: *The Boulevardier*	Curzon
Fantasy: *The Wearing O' the Green*	arr. Hanmer
Rhythm of the Clock	Hunt/Kane
Selection: *Communityland*	arr. Stodden
Calling All Workers (Sig)	Coates

6.00 p.m. Percival Mackey and his Orchestra
17.7.50

Calling All Workers (Sig)	Coates
Samovar	Lowry/Richardson
Selection: *King's Rhapsody*	Novello
High Heels	Duncan
Blue Dreams	O'Hagan
I Remember the Cornfields	Ralton
Delibes Ballet Memories	arr. Geiger
Festival Scene	Buder
Five Minutes with Waldteufel	arr. Hartley
Galopade	King Palmer
Calling All Workers (Sig)	Coates

10.30 a.m.   **Birmingham Hippodrome Orchestra**
7.8.52   **Conductor: Frank Hagley**

Calling All Workers (Sig)	Coates
Ascot Parade	Strachey
Flanagan's Mare	Stanton
Fireside Fusiliers	Mayerl
Belle of the Ball	Anderson
Carriage and Pair	Frankel
Pampanella	Michelo
On a Spring Note	Torch
Galloping Major	Leigh/Hastow arr. Jacob
Selection: *Blue for a Boy*	Parr Davies
Calling All Workers (Sig)	Coates

10.30 a.m.   **The Albert Cazabon Orchestra**
15.12.55

Calling All Workers (Sig)	Coates
The Dam Busters	Coates
Peacock Patrol	Barrington
Gaytime	Crossman
The Last Tango	Monshin
The Stein Sing	Fenstad
Lady of Spain	Evans
Sleigh Ride	Anderson
Scotch and Chaser	Croudson
The Waltzing Bugle Boy	Martin
Selection: *The Water Gipsies*	Ellis
Calling All Workers (Sig)	Coates

10.30 a.m.   **The Jack Emblow Sextet**
16.3.56

Calling All Workers (Sig)	Coates
Medley:	
I've Got a Pocketful of Dreams	Monaco
Sing a Song of Sunbeans	Monaco
An Apple for the Teacher	Monaco
When You Lose The One You Love	Pelosi

A Room With A View	Coward
Moments To Remember	Allen
Nicolo Nicolo Nicolino	Winkler
Medley:	
There's Always a First Time	Tibsen
Everywhere	Evans
Fascination	Marchetti
Pickin' a Chicken	Bernfield
Penny Serenade	Wecsma
Robin Hood	Sigman
Close to Me	Carr
Life Could Not Better Be	Fine
Medley:	
Shine	Dobny
I Can't Give Anything But Love	McHugh
That's My Weakness Now	Green
Pasadena	Warren
Calling All Workers (Sig)	Coates

**10.30 a.m.   The Bobby Howell Orchestra
14.1.57**

Calling All Workers (Sig)	Coates
Mexican Hat Dance	arr. Hanmer
A Woman in Love	Loesser
Yodelling Mountaineer	Rogez
Fascination	Marchetti arr. Jupp
Brahms' *Hungarian Dances*	arr. Charrosin
Butterflies in the Rain	Myers
Cachucha (from *In Malaga*)	Curzon
More	Alstone
Paso-Bolero	Hanmer
Selection: *Salute To Jolson*	arr. Hanmer
Calling All Workers (Sig)	Coates

**10.30 a.m.   The Coventry Theatre Orchestra
30.5.57   Conductor: William Pethers**

Calling All Workers (Sig)	Coates
The Merrymakers' Dance	German

Georgian Rumba	Slaney
Piccaninny Puppets	Rogez
Bouquet De Paris (2nd. Selection)	arr. Hanmer
Bella Musica	
Clopin Clopant	
Valse Grise	
Le Petit Cordonier	
The Westminster Waltz	Farnon
Mexican Serenade	Coles
Breath of Spring	Hart
Heart	Adler/Ross
Baby Ballerina	Strachey
Selection: *Oklahoma*	Rodgers
Calling All Workers (Sig)	Coates

3.45 p.m.   Van Dam and his Orchestra
14.6.57

Calling All Workers (Sig)	Coates
Entry of the Gladiators	Fucik
Carousel Waltz	Rodgers
Marigold	Mayerl
Fiesta	Coles
Two Guitars	arr. Martin
The March Hare	Green
Theme from the Threepenny Opera	Weill
Shooting Star	Torch
Selection: *Maid of the Mountains*	Fraser-Simpson
Calling All Workers (Sig)	Coates

10.30 a.m.   Frank Baron and his Sextet
23.8.57

Calling All Workers (Sig)	Coates
I Love My Baby	Warren
I'm Gonna Sit Right Down	Ahlert
We Will Make Love	Hulme
The Military Polka	Thomas
Wonderful, Wonderful	Edwards
Island in the Sun	Belafonte

Rotten Row	Baron
With All My Heart	Marcucci
Cold Cold Shower	Waller
Guardian Angel	Roberts
Parakeet	Lobsa
When Somebody Thinks You're Wonderful	Elliott
The Very Thought of You	Noble
Why Do I Love You?	Kern
Who's Sorry Now?	Snyder
Don't Dilly Dally	Leigh
Calling All Workers (Sig)	Coates

3.00 p.m.   **BBC Northern Ireland Light Orchestra**
25.10.57   **Conductor: David Curry**

Calling All Workers (Sig)	Coates
Theatreland	Strachey
Valse Bluette	Drigo
Beguine: *This Time is for All Time*	Rivers
Selection: *The King and I*	Rodgers
Tango: *Jealousy*	Gade
Peanut Polka	Farnon
Mr Wonderful	Bock
Five Minutes with Gung'l	arr. Hartley
Reel: *Kate Kelly's Fancy*	*trad.* arr. Curry
We Saw the Sea	Berlin
Strings on Parade	Martin
Love Letters in the Sand	Coots
Tyrolean Revels	Cardew
Jig: *Maguire's Jig*	Curry
Calling All Workers (Sig)	Coates

3.00 p.m.   **BBC Scottish Variety Orchestra**
11.12.57   **Conductor: Jack Leon**

Calling All Workers (Sig)	Coates
The Dam Busters March	Coates
Amoureuse	Berger
Messenger Boy	Goodwin
Selection: *The Student Prince*	Romberg arr. Fones

Rio Chambira	Muller
Five Minutes With Gung'l's Waltzes	arr. Hartley
Selection: *Sing, Everybody Sing*	arr. Caryll
Sing, Everybody Sing	
Bye Bye Blues	
I Never Knew	
Me and My Shadow	
Rolling Round the World	
Tango: *Dark Eyes*	trad. arr. Martin
Frankfurt Polka	Dexter
Dance of the Panpipes	Coles
Da Capo	Boulanger
Rise and Shine	Howlett
Selection: *Bells Are Ringing*	Styne
Calling All Workers (Sig)	Coates

3.45 p.m.   **The Regent Orchestra**
21.2.58   **Conductor: John Thorpe**

Calling All Workers (Sig)	Coates
Selection: *Free as Air*	Slade
Sarda	Alessandro
Tritsch Tratsch Polka	Strauss
The Doll Medley:	arr. Michaeloff
Dainty Doll	
Lonesome Little Doll	
Rag Doll	
Little Dutch Doll	
The Doll Dance	
Wedding of the Painted Doll	
Portuguese Party	Vinter
Selection: *Hit The Deck*	Youmans
Vanity Fair	Collins
Slavonic Dances	Dvorak arr. Hanmer
Frankfurt Polka	Dexter
Dance of the Panpipes	Coles
Flat Foot	Whiteley
Selection: *A King in New York*	Chaplin
Calling All Workers (Sig)	Coates

10.31 a.m.   **Lionel Monte and his Orchestra**
1.3.58

Calling All Workers (Sig)	Coates
Spanish Dance No.5	Moszkowski
Shooting Star	Torch
Waves of the Danube	Ivanovici
Macnamara's Band	O'Connor
Napolitana	Troise
Poupee Valsante	Poldini
The March Hare	Green
Slavonic Dances	Dvorak arr. Hanmer
Selection: *The King and I*	Rodgers
Calling All Workers (Sig)	Coates

10.31 a.m.
22.4.58   **Victor Silvester and his Ballroom Orchestra**

Calling All Workers (Sig)	Coates
Ma, He's Making Eyes at Me	Conrad
Magic Moments	Bacharach
Cry My Heart	Trapani
Mandy	Rendine
The Breeze and I	Lecuona
Linke in the Ballroom	Linke
Chicago	Fisher
While We're Young	Wilder
Conchita	Silvester/Wilson
April Love	Fain
The Story of My Life	David
Calling All Workers (Sig)	Coates

10.31 a.m.   **Charles Mackerras conducting**
10.5.58   **his Light Orchestra**

Calling All Workers (Sig)	Coates
Knightsbridge March	Coates
The Skaters' Waltz	Waldteufel
Blue Tango	Anderson
Ragamuffin	Rixner

Selection: *Where's Charley*	Loesser
Blue Moonlight	Norman
Westminster Waltz	Farnon
Little Serenade	Tomlinson
Finale *(Pineapple Poll)*	Sullivan
	arr. Mackerras
Calling All Workers (Sig)	Coates

3.45 p.m.   Owen Walters and his Orchestra
16.5.58

Calling All Workers (Sig)	Coates
Great Day	Youmans
Robert Farnon Medley:	Farnon
Jumping Bean	
Westminster Waltz	
Peanut Polka	
I'm Getting Sentimental Over You	Bassman
The Gainsborough Waltz	Hellier
Medley:	
All the Way	Van Heusen
Once in Love with Amy	Loesser
My Darling, My Darling	Loesser
I May Never Pass This Way Again	Wizell
The Red Sombrero	Binge
Medley:	
La Ronde	Strauss
Two Hearts in Waltz Time	Stolz
The Whistling Waltz	Woods
Live, Laugh and Love	Heymann
The Poodle Polka	Walters
Medley:	
Mexican Serenade	Coles
Pepita	Versey
Fiesta	Coles
Toy Shop Ballet	Mantovani
Ballet Music from *Les Sylphides*	Chopin
Waltz in F	
Grande Valse Brilliante	
Spanish Dance No.5	Moszkowski

Tarantella From *A Day in Naples*   Byng
Calling All Workers (Sig)   Coates

3.45 p.m.
7.11.58   Joseph Muscant and his Orchestra

Calling All Workers (Sig)   Coates
March: *The Royal Blue*   Marsden
Waltz with Waldteufel   arr. Wilkinson
The March Hare   Green
Serenade No.1   Heykens
Cascade of Stars   Moderna
Un Carnet Du Bal   Jaubert
Cornflakes   S. Norman
The Wee Macgreegor   Amers
Mexican Serenade   Coles
Trudie   Henderson
Runaway Romance   Andrini/Zabach
Donkey Serenade   Friml
Dusky Aristocrat   Whiteley
Leroy Anderson Medley   arr. Tomlinson
   Sleigh Ride
   Syncopated Clock
   Plink, Plank, Plunk
   Blue Tango
   Serenata
   Belle of the Ball
Calling All Workers (Sig)   Coates

10.31 a.m.   Harold Geller and his Orchestra
19.12.58

Calling All Workers (Sig)   Coates
Sobbing Women   De Paul
Real Love   Harris
Farrago   Wright
S'Wonderful   Gershwin
All of You   Porter
Pick Yourself Up   Kern
Home   Clarkson

There Goes My Lover	Leonard
Ballet Shoes	Dempsey
Volare	Modugno
More Than Ever	Taccani
John and Julie	Green
Pico Carpentero	Amado
Tulips from Amsterdam	Arnie
Loudenboomer Bird	Manning
Nice to Know You Care	Baguley
Bye Bye Baby	Styne
Calling All Workers (Sig)	Coates

10.31 a.m.   Lew Stone and his Band
16.1.59

Calling All Workers (Sig)	Coates
Everybody Loves a Lover	Adler
Isle of Capri	Grosz
The Glory of Love	Hill
Red Sails in the Sunset	Grosz
Mandolines in the Moonlight	Weiss
Tom Dooley	Warner
Trudie	Henderson
Cha cha cha	Paverman
More Than Ever	Taccani
Medley:	Coward
Dance Little Lady	
Dear Little Cafe	
Room With a View	
The Green Cockatoo	Geller
Tea for Two	Youmans
Apple Blossom Time	Tilzer
Calling All Workers (Sig)	Coates

10.31 a.m.   Norman Whiteley and his Sextet
16.9.59

Calling All Workers (Sig)	Coates
Wait for Me	D'Anzi
Swedish Polka	Alfven

58

Cat on a Cool Tin Roof	Granville
Hayride	Goodwin
Swiss Dancing Doll	Ketelbey
I Know Why	Warren
Country Rig	Clifford/Payne
Trampolina	Love
Lock Up Your Daughters	Johnson
Jamaica Walk	Norman
Ragtime Medley:	arr. Whiteley
Tiptoe Through the Tulips	Burke
Rock-a-Bye Your Baby	Schwartz
Black-Eyed Susans Grow	Whiting
Oh You Beautiful Doll	Ayer
Dusky Aristocrat	Whiteley
The Trolley Song	Martin/Blane
Calling All Workers (Sig)	Coates

10.31 a.m.   Maurice Arnold and his Sextet
1.2.60

Calling All Workers (Sig)	Coates
Swedish Polka	Alfven
Under the Linden Tree	Felix
Spinning Wheel	Rawicz
Manhattan	Rodgers
Caracas	Monshin
Miss Melanie	Binge
Runaway Romance	Zabach
Baion de Santos	Jupp
Consuela	Logan
Wonderful Illusion	Mores
The Man Who Plays the Mandolino	Fancuilla
Plantation Medley:	arr. Arnold
Polly Wolly Doodle	
Camptown Races	
Oh Dem Golden Slippers	
Calling All Workers (Sig)	Coates

59

3.45 p.m. Sidney Bowman and the Promenade Players
23.2.60

Calling All Workers (Sig)	Coates
Here We Are, Here We Are, Here We Are Again	Knight/Lyle
The Whistler and His Dog	Pryor
Ad Infinitum	Baynes
That's a Plenty	Pollack
Juliette	Mirros
Singing in the Rain	Freed
Scots Reels: *The Kilt Is My Delight*	arr. Gourlay
Peter Pan Polka	Watters
When You Wore a Tulip	Wenrich
El Choclo	Villoldo
Kisses in the Dark	De Micheli
Ida, Sweet as Apple Cider	Munson
Canadian Capers	Cohen
Pink Lady	Caryll
Here's to Love	Mougeot
Calling All Workers (Sig)	Coates

3.45 p.m. Jack Salisbury and his Orchestra
24.3.61

Calling All Workers (Sig)	Coates
Lady of Madrid	Evans
Begin the Beguine	Porter
Galop: *Vienna Dash*	Strauss
Chiribiribin	Bucalossi
Spanish Main	Anales
Waltzes:	Baynes
Destiny	
Mystery	
Ecstasy	
Military Shuffle	Blackmore
Swiss Dancing Doll	Ketelbey
Live Love and Laugh	Heymann
Punch and Judy Polka	Munro
Selection: *The King and I*	Rodgers
Calling All Workers (Sig)	Coates

3.31 p.m. Fredric Cooper and his Tipica Orchestra
6.10.61

Calling All Workers (Sig)	Coates
El Relicario	Padilla
Whatever Will Be Will Be	Livingston
Romantica	Rascel
La Cannebiere	Agoult
Israeli Carnival	Phillips
Moonlight Over Tahiti	Bridgmont
Cha Cha Cha	Ramos
Hyde Park Polka	Chacksfield
Hear My Song, Violetta	Klose
Consider Yourself	Bart
Shy Serenade	Scott-Wood
La Petite Polka	Paramor
Portugese Party	Vinter
Around the World	Young
How Wonderful to Know	D'Esposito
Song of the Gaucho	Manilla
Tinkle Box Samba	Rubach
Selection: *Fifty Years of Song*	arr. Kennett
Calling All Workers (Sig)	Coates

10.31 a.m. Raymond Agoult and his Players
16.12.61

Calling All Workers (Sig)	Coates
Ad Infinitum	Baynes
Runaway Romance	Zabach
Piping Hot	Leach
The Laughing Seine	Scott-Wood
House of Bamboo	Crompton
Little Shepherd Boy	Hughes
Page Boy	Leonard
Boutade Basque	Ruis
Tulip Chimes	Norman
La Cannebiere	Agoult
Ca C'est Paris	Padilla
Honouring the Haggis	Agoult

Calling All Workers (Sig)   Coates

10.31 a.m.   Louis Mordish and his Players
25.8.62

Calling All Workers (Sig)   Coates
Medley:
   Portuguese Washerwoman   Popp
   Undecided   Shavers
   Music Music Music   Baum
Lazzarella   Modugno
Windmill Waltz   Madin
Tears   Maxwell
Rainbow Run   Mers
Windows of Paris   Osborne
Sunset   Woodman
Rooney   Green
Ginny Come Lately   Gold
Spectre on the Spree   Mordish
Medley:
   Mammy   Donaldson
   Anniversary Song   Jolson
   April Showers   Silvers
   The Spaniard That Blighted My Life   Merson
   California, Here I Come   Jolson
Calling All Workers (Sig)   Coates

10.31 a.m.   Central Band of the Royal Air Force
24.10.62   Conducted by Wing Commander J.L. Wallace OBE

Calling All Workers (Sig)   Coates
March: *Bravest of the Brave*   Gay
Selection: *Can-Can*   Porter
You Belong to My Heart   Lana
Folies Bergère from *Parisian Sketches*   Fletcher
Lady of Spain   Evans
Selection: *Bouquet de Paris*   arr. McInnes Smith
Waltz: *Nights of Gladness*   Ancliffe
Selection: *Top Hat*   Berlin
Tango Bolero   Llossas

62

March: *Anchor's Aweigh*   Zimmerman
Calling All Workers (Sig)   Coates

10.31 a.m.
23.2.63   **The Sidney Sax Strings**

Calling All Workers (Sig)   Coates
Never on Sunday   Hadjidakis
Globetrotter   Meek
Cochinelle   Hill Bowen
Cuban Boy   Chacksfield
How Wonderful to Know   D'Esposito
Tango de la Zarzuela   Rogers
The Lawrence Theme   Jarre
Tonight   Bernstein
Boulevard de Paris   Michael
Street of Linden Trees   Geller
Tango Bolero   Llossas
Calling All Workers (Sig)   Coates

10.31 a.m.   **Ralph Wilson and his Septet**
30.3.63

Calling All Workers (Sig)   Coates
Honouring the Haggis   Agoult
Medley:
    Every Little While   Tate
    Lily of Laguna   Stuart
    They Didn't Believe Me   Kern
Petite Waltz   Heyne
The Little Lobster   Rico
Whisky Galore   Hartley
Medley:
    Demoiselle Chic   Fletcher
    In the Shadows   Finck
    Glow Worm   Lincke
    Down South   Myddleton
Fireside Fusiliers   Mayerl
Mademoiselle de Paris   Durand
Pianissimo   Alstone

Luxembourg Polka	Reisdorff
Lady of Spain	Evans
Calling All Workers (Sig)	Coates

10.31 a.m.   Anton and his Orchestra
26.10.63

Calling All Workers (Sig)	Coates
Zaragoza	Baynes
Under the Bridges of Paris	Scotto
Romantic Gipsies	Raphael
Little Brazilian Soldier	Rossiter
Selection: *The Merry Widow*	Lehar
Carlo's Theme	Slaney
Playboy in Paris	Gledhill
El Pandero	Lanjean
Selection: *Boys of Syracuse*	Rodgers
Laughing Polka	Steurs
Can Can Dancers	Crossman
Calling All Workers (Sig)	Coates

10.31 a.m.   Harold C. Gee and his Maritza Players
18.1.64

Calling All Workers (Sig)	Coates
Bravo-Bravo	Monshin
Little Senorita	Watters
Song of the Gaucho	Manilla
Brise de Paris	Delroy
Song of the Sea	Trinidade
Tango of the Violins	Spivakowsky
Lady of Spain	Evans
Felicidades	Rosada
Fascination	Marchetti
Kiss of Fire	Hill
Bandarilla	Marland
Calling All Workers (Sig)	Coates

10.31 a.m. **The Albert Delroy Sextet**
19.9.64

Calling All Workers (Sig)	Coates
A la Francais	Martin
Merry Go Round	Van Parys
Ukelele Boy	Supran
Bar Americano	Richardson
Desafinado	Jobim
Playtime for Poodles	Strevens
Autumn Leaves	Kosma
Jangle Bells	Baynes
Brise De Paris	Delroy
September in the Rain	Warren
Nicola	Race
Medley:	
Bella Musica	Fontenoy
Clopin Clopant	Coquatrix
Valse Gris	Jaubert
Little Shoemaker	Revil
Calling All Workers (Sig)	Coates

10.31 a.m. **Band of the Coldstream Guards**
15.9.65   **Director of Music: Captain Trevor L. Sharpe MBE**

Calling All Workers (Sig)	Coates
Marching Around the Shows:	arr. Sharpe
Strike Up the Band	
Get Me to the Church	
June is Bustin' Out All Over	
With a Little Bit of Luck	
Some Girls We Have Known:	arr. Sharpe
Miss Annabelle Lee	
I Love You, Samantha	
Margie	
Lulu's Back in Town	
If You Knew Susie	
Sweet Georgia Brown	
French Festival:	arr. Osser
Pigalle	

Domino
Selection: *New Moon*   Romberg arr. Sharpe
Italian Holiday: arr. Sharpe
  Romantica
  Eterno Ritornello
  Scalinata
The Coldstream Play Some Blues: arr. Sharpe
  My Blue Heaven
  The Blue of the Night
  Blue Room
  Birth of the Blues
  Bye, Bye, Blues
  Blue Skies
Calling All Workers (Sig)   Coates

3.31 p.m.   Claude Cavalotti and his Orchestra
27.9.65

Calling All Workers (Sig)	Coates
From This Moment On	Porter
A Bedouin in Baghdad	Leach
Love Me with All Your Heart	Rigual
Everything's In Rhythm With My Heart	Hoffman
Spooky	Deane
Heartaches	Hoffman
Tangerine	Schwartzinger
Bacciar	Brandez
Look Through Any Window	Silverman
Spoonful of Sugar	Sherman
My Favourite Things	Rodgers
Tango '65	Ponticelli
University Rag	Michael
Zorba's Dance	Theodorakis
You've Done Something to My Heart	Gay
Vino Tinto	Coles
Unchained Melody	North
Brazil	Barroso
If Ever I Would Leave You	Loewe
Camelot	Loewe
Calling All Workers (Sig)	Coates

3.31 p.m.   **The Banjoliers**
12.5.66   **Directed by Jack Mandel**

Calling All Workers (Sig)	Coates
Colonel Bogey	Alford
Swinging Safari	Kaemfert
Riviera Nights	Alstone/
	Chacksfield
Medley:	
Ain't That a Grand and Glorious Feeling	Agar
I Can't Give You Anything But Love	McHugh
Shine	Dabney
Phantom Riders	Dabson
Felicidades	Rosada
This Little Piggy	Jupp
Nebraska	Revel/Sissle
The Petite Waltz	Heyne
Jangle Bells	Baynes
Can Can Polka	Mordish
Whistling Boy	Stewart
Bond Street Rag	Holland
Washington Square	Goldstein/Shire
Suntan	Douglas
Redwing	Mills
Medley:	
Four-Leaf Clover	Woods
Baby Face	Davis/Akst
Chinatown, My Chinatown	Jerome/Schwartz
Toot Toot Tootsie, Goodbye	Keyes/Erdman/
	Russo
Calling All Workers (Sig)	Coates

A typical schedule from 1964 showing dance bands and light orchestras

Wk com	Mon	Tues	Wed	Thurs	Fri	Sat
APRIL 26th	RONNIE MUNRO SEXTET / RONNIE PLEYDELL and his ORCHESTRA	KEN BEAUMONT SEXTET / SIDNEY DAVEY and his PLAYERS	ROYAL ARTILLERY MOUNTED BAND / BILL SAVILL and his ORCHESTRA	CHRIS ALLEN SEXTET / The BANJOLIERS directed by JACK MANDEL	FREDDIE BALLERINI Sextet / ANTON and his ORCHESTRA	The ALBANY STRINGS directed by REG PURSGLOVE
MAY 3rd	GERALD CROSSMAN Players / JACK NATHAN BAND	CECIL NORMAN RHYTHM PLAYERS / HAROLD COLLINS ORCHESTRA	Band of the ROYAL ARMY SERVICE CORPS / CLAUDE CAVALOTTI ORCHESTRA	IAIN KERR KEYBOARDS / The BANJOLIERS directed by JACK MANDEL	JIMMY LEACH ORGANOLIAN QUARTET / HUGH JAMES and his ORCHESTRA	ANTON and his ORCHESTRA
MAY 10th	GEORGE SCOTT-WOOD MUSIC / PHIL TATE and his ORCHESTRA	KEN BEAUMONT SEXTET / BERNARD MONSHIN and his RIO TANGO BAND	Band of the GRENADIER GUARDS / ERIC GALLOWAY and his ORCHESTRA	FREDDIE BALLERINI Sextet / HAROLD C GEE and his MARITZA PLAYERS	EDDIE STREVENS QUARTET / SIDNEY DAVEY PLAYERS	JACK SALISBURY and his ORCHESTRA
MAY 17th	WHIT MONDAY	CECIL NORMAN RHYTHM PLAYERS / The BANJOLIERS directed by JACK MANDEL	Band of the ROYAL ARTILLERY (Woolwich) / BILL SAVILL ORCHESTRA	JIMMY LEACH ORGANOLIAN QUARTET / MICHAEL FREEDMAN ORCHESTRA	HARRY GOLD and his BAND / GEORGE SCOTT-WOOD MUSIC	RAYMOND AGOULT PLAYERS
MAY 24th	HAROLD C GEE MARITZA PLAYERS / JACK WHITE BAND	STAN REYNOLDS OCTET / LOUIS VOSS KURSAAL ORCHESTRA	WELSH GUARDS / JACK DORSEY and his ORCHESTRA	KEN BEAUMONT SEXTET / BERNARD MONSHIN RIO TANGO BAND	SYD DEAN BAND / The BANJOLIERS directed by JACK MANDEL	ANTON and his ORCHESTRA
MAY 31st	FRED ALEXANDER PLAYERS / HAROLD GELLER ORCHESTRA	HARRY GOLD and his BAND / GERALD CROSSMAN Players	Band of the IRISH GUARDS ORCHESTRA / TOMMY KINSMAN DANCE ORCHESTRA	CLAUDE CAVALOTTI ORCHESTRA / The BANJOLIERS directed by JACK MANDEL	CECIL NORMAN RHYTHM PLAYERS / HUGH JAMES and his ORCHESTRA	ALBANY STRINGS directed by REG PURSGLOVE
JUNE 7th	FREDRIC COOPER TIPICA ORCHESTRA / RONNIE PLEYDELL and his ORCHESTRA	JIMMY LEACH ORGANOLIAN QUARTET / ALBERT DELROY Sextet	SCOTS GUARDS / NAT TEMPLE and his ORCHESTRA	ROBIN RICHMOND QUINTET / LES PERRY PLAYERS	KEN BEAUMONT SEXTET / ANTON and his ORCHESTRA	GEORGE SCOTT-WOOD MUSIC
JUNE 14th	MAURICE ARNOLD SEXTET / PHIL TATE and his ORCHESTRA	KEN BEAUMONT SEXTET / BERNARD MONSHIN RIO TANGO BAND	METROPOLITAN POLICE BAND / EDDIE STREVENS QUARTET	DANNY LEVAN QUINTET / DELMONDI QUARTET	LEW STONE SEXTET / RONNIE MUNRO SEXTET	MARCEL GARDNER ORCHESTRA
JUNE 21st	MICHAEL FREEDMAN ORCHESTRA / BILL SAVILL and his ORCHESTRA	CECIL NORMAN RHYTHM PLAYERS / BERNARD MONSHIN RIO TANGO BAND	RANSOME AND MARLES WORKS BAND / JACK DORSEY ORCHESTRA	JIMMY LEACH ORGANOLIAN QUARTET / RALPH ELMAN BOHEMIAN PLAYERS	EDDIE STREVENS QUARTET / HAROLD C GEE MARITZA PLAYERS	JACQUES VALLEZ and his PLAYERS
JUNE 28th	RALPH WILSON SEPTET / RONNIE PLEYDELL and his ORCHESTRA	JIMMY LEACH ORGANOLIAN QUARTET / ANTON and his ORCHESTRA	ROYAL ARTILLERY MOUNTED BAND / BOB POTTER and his ORCHESTRA	CECIL NORMAN RHYTHM PLAYERS / HAROLD C GEE MARITZA PLAYERS	GRAHAM DALLEY MUSIC / The BANJOLIERS directed by JACK MANDEL	ISY GEIGER and his VIENNESE MUSIC
JULY 5th	LOUIS MORDISH PLAYERS / BILL SAVILL ORCHESTRA	SYD DEAN BAND / MARCEL GARDNER ORCHESTRA	Band of the ROYAL ARMY SERVICE CORPS / JACK WHITE BAND	ROY HERBERT / RAYMOND AGOULT PLAYERS	CECIL NORMAN RHYTHM PLAYERS / HUGH JAMES and his ORCHESTRA	ALBANY STRINGS directed by REG PURSGLOVE
JULY 12th	RONNIE MUNRO SEXTET / JOHNNY KILDARE ORCHESTRA	STAN REYNOLDS OCTET / RALPH ELMAN BOHEMIAN PLAYERS	Band of the ROYAL ARMY MEDICAL CORPS / JACK DORSEY ORCHESTRA	JIMMY LEACH ORGANOLIAN QUARTET / The BANJOLIERS directed by JACK MANDEL	LEW STONE SEXTET / FREDRIC COOPER TIPICA ORCHESTRA	JACK SALISBURY ORCHESTRA

Note: Dance bands shaded

Chapter 3

The Revivals

The BBC likes to remember anniversaries and, as October 1982 was the 60th anniversary of its formation, the Corporation's Diamond Jubilee, it was decided to celebrate the occasion with a number of special programmes. This included a week-long revival of *Workers' Playtime* – the popular variety show which was broadcast from factories. To the amazement of many, David Hatch, the enlightened Controller of Radio Two at the time, also decided to revive *Music While You Work* for one week.

Brian Willey, a radio stalwart of many years' standing, was appointed as Producer for these shows and he decided to make the five revival programmes as much like the original series as possible, using original contributors, even if it meant reforming their bands for the occasion. It was no easy task as many of the regulars had died since 1967. Willey wanted to use the Jack Emblow Sextet, one of the most skilful and entertaining groups of the fifties and sixties, but Jack, whose group had not broadcast for some years, had apparently discarded his library. Brian Willey thought that the 'string element' of the series could be provided by the Harold Geller Orchestra, but once again he came up against a brick wall – Geller had emigrated to the States!

Eventually Willey settled for the dance orchestras of Nat Temple, Jack Dorsey and Phil Tate, plus The Banjoliers directed by Jack Mandel, along with the Latin-American sounds of Lou Whiteson and the Southern Serenade Orchestra. This orchestra was the 'odd one out' as it had never previously participated in *MWYW*, although it had been used regularly in other programmes since the forties. According to the *Radio Times* its inclusion was because neither authentic light orchestras of the period nor their libraries existed! Not quite true, I would venture to say, but Brian Willey did confide in me that he wanted this to be a happy week and had deliberately chosen musical directors with whom he could be sure of having a good working relationship and achieve the objective with the minimum of fuss. I suspect that one of the reasons why Lou Whiteson's orchestra had not

69

previously been used on *MWYW* was the fact that its repertoire was largely of authentic Spanish and South American music, some of which would not have been deemed familiar enough for the original series. Nonetheless, they used their typical repertoire for their 1982 programme and, whilst it was not quite in the classic *MWYW* vein, it was nevertheless most enjoyable and David Hatch thought it the highlight of the week.

At this stage *Music While You Work* had been off the airwaves for 15 years – apart from a half-hearted and short-lived attempt by Radio One, which, for a while, put on an unannounced programme of vocal records topped and tailed with an electronic version of *Calling All Workers!* Frankly, the least said about that, the better.

Over the years, I had often regretted the fact that I had never attended any of the shows. I probably didn't think that I would be permitted to 'sit in'. However, as soon as I heard that the programme was to be revived, albeit only for one week commencing 4th October 1982, I immediately contacted Brian Willey and explained my interest, and he kindly gave me the necessary permission to attend the shows, for which, incidentally, no music written after 1967 was to be included.

The programmes were broadcast live at 3.30 p.m., preceded by a three-hour rehearsal. I was permitted to sit in the studio with the musicians except during the actual transmission, when I went into the 'box'. Nat Temple and his orchestra played the first edition; they had been stalwarts of the programme since the forties and I'm not ashamed to say that as the band struck up *Calling All Workers*, I felt a tingle go down my spine. However, I wasn't the only one to be caught up in the emotion of the occasion as, by the time the broadcast was drawing to a conclusion, I could not help noticing that Nat Temple was in tears. At the end of the broadcast the telephone rang in the control room. It was the Radio Two Controller wishing to convey his congratulations to the bandleader.

The following day, The Banjoliers were due to broadcast for the first time in many years and their conductor, Jack Mandel, was able to get together most of the surviving players. I will never forget the sight of the musicians' faces lighting up as they played the signature tune once again; they were grinning broadly and were flushed with emotion. I had been tipped off that they were going to commence with *When the Saints Go Marching In*, so I took a small tape player and a recording of The Banjoliers playing the same piece in 1964. Although I had taken it to the studio purely because I thought it might be of interest, it

70

Jack Mandel directing The Banjoliers in their final broadcast on 5th October 1982, an amazing 50 years after their first broadcast

actually came in rather useful. At the first run-through of the programme, I thought that the band took *The Saints* rather slowly and, more importantly, the drummer was ignoring some drum breaks which were integral to the arrangement. So, rather undiplomatically, I told Jack Mandel how it should be played and invited him to listen to the 1964 performance. Jack called the drummer over so that he, in particular, could hear the correct interpretation. All agreed that it was wrong and that it needed to be played faster, Jack then re-rehearsed it with them. Apparently, although Jack Mandel had done the arrangement about 20 years earlier, he had mislaid his conductor's score and was conducting from a cello banjo part which, obviously, gave no indication of what the drummer should have been doing. It is, of course, hardly the done thing for a guest in the studio to tell a conductor that he is doing it wrong; however, in this case I got away with it as I was not only right but I could prove it! Frankly, had I not intervened and the band had broadcast it as first rehearsed, I would have regretted it to this day.

When I first heard that The Banjoliers were taking part in this

71

special week, I contacted Jack Mandel to suggest that he include in his programme a piece called *Red Wing* which his predecessor, Pasquale Troise, had recorded with the band during the forties. Jack was happy to oblige and they played it at both rehearsals, but ten minutes before the live transmission, Brian Willey came out of the box and said: 'You're running two minutes over – something will have to be cut.' Jack replied: 'Okay, we'll cut the Scottish medley.' This was greeted with howls of protest from the Scotsmen in the band, so Brian Willey said: 'No, we'll cut out Red Wing'. Jack replied 'I can't cut that out, Mr Reynolds has requested it!' This cut no ice with the Producer, who repeated his instruction and with only a few minutes to go before transmission, there was no time to argue. Brian Willey later told me that *Red Wing* was his least favourite item in the programme as he always associated it with 'some stupid words written to it in the fifties.' Oh well, you can't win 'em all!

After Lou Whiteson's Southern Serenade Orchestra the following day, Jack Dorsey recreated his big band sound with an orchestra that was virtually a who's who of the dance band world, including some of Britain's top session men, many of them bandleaders themselves. It was no wonder that, after the first rehearsal, Jack Dorsey said to the band, 'Okay, there were a few mistakes but you know what they were!' He obviously knew better than to talk down to musicians of that calibre.

The nostalgic week concluded in fine style with Phil Tate and his Orchestra, which was a 15-piece dance orchestra with nine woodwind players. There were three flutes, clarinet, five saxes, trumpet, two pianos and rhythm. The blend of flutes and saxes produced an attractive, spine-tingling sound which had always been very popular with *MWYW* listeners. At the end of the programme, I told Phil Tate that I considered him to be Britain's answer to Glenn Miller, to which he replied, 'I'm so glad you said that. This was my idea when I first formed the orchestra, but you are the first person to notice!' This final edition was, in the opinion of Brian Willey, the best programme of the week.

Amazing though it was that the BBC should revive *Music While You Work* in this way after 15 years, it was nothing like as amazing as the audience reaction to the shows. The BBC was bombarded with some 10,000 calls and letters of appreciation, together with requests for the resumption of the programme.

Just four weeks later, newspapers were carrying the front page news

Phil Tate rehearsing his orchestra for the live broadcast on 8th October 1982

headline: **MUSIC WHILE YOU WORK TO RETURN**. The decision had been taken to reinstate the programme on a daily basis, commencing 4th January 1983.

Charles Clark-Maxwell was appointed Producer of the series, with John Meloy as Executive Producer, and the programme was to be transmitted at 12.02 p.m. every weekday, sandwiched between the Jimmy Young and Gloria Hunniford shows. There were, however, to be a number of changes. Unlike the Diamond Jubilee week, the programmes were not to be nostalgia-based, the brief being that they should reflect the styles of the eighties. A substantial budget was allocated to the new show, thus enabling the use of much larger orchestras than before. One important change was that the series was no longer aimed at factories and was, simply, to be a programme of continuous instrumental music with the accent on melody. Most of the restrictions on what could be played no longer applied and conductors and bandleaders were given a free hand to build their programmes as they wished. All broadcasts were pre-recorded, usually in two halves – the intention being for them to be repeated after two or three months.

For the first time, jazz and big-band music were welcomed into the series, as were lush, string-dominated orchestras playing popular music, old and new. In all honesty, some editions were far removed from the *MWYW* that fans of the earlier series remembered.

As a framework for planning the programmes, a different style of music was allocated to each day of the week. Monday was what the production team called modern light music (perhaps more accurately described as glossy popular music), played by large and lush orchestras under the direction of musicians such as Frank Chacksfield, John Fox, Ray Davies, John Gregory, Roland Shaw and Stanley Black. All these were big names in the record world, but few of them were previously associated with *MWYW*. Tuesday was given a jazz feel with artists like Acker Bilk, Dave Shepherd, Allan Ganley and the Pete Allen Jazzband. Wednesday was for dance and swing bands, ranging from the palais style of Joe Loss, Tony Evans, Ray McVay and Andy Ross, to the Don Lusher Big Band and the Syd Lawrence Orchestra. Also included in this category was the old-time style of the Bryan Smith Orchestra.

It had become commonplace for ballroom bands to include vocalists who sang wordlessly along with the players, and this wordless singing was now permitted on *MWYW*. Apart from this, the programme remained as it had been since 1942, strictly instrumental. It would appear, though, that Syd Lawrence was unaware of this; he planned his first programme to incorporate several vocals and brought his two regular singers to the studio for this purpose. Presumably the Producer felt that it was too late to re-plan the programme; in any case he would have had to pay the singers whether they were used or not, so this became the first *MWYW* since the war to include vocals. It was also the last, as Syd's next appearance was strictly instrumental.

Friday was allocated to the traditional light orchestral sounds of musicians like Iain Sutherland, Geoffrey Brand and Reg Leopold, plus the occasional appearances by brass and military bands. Thursday was given over to styles which, in the Producer's opinion, did not fit into any other categories and included Geoff Love's Banjo Band, The Robert Docker Sextet, Jack Peberdy's Flutes 'n' Things and the virtuoso two-piano team of Christine and Sandy Blair who, amazingly, played the whole programme from memory.

As with the original series, not everything went to plan. I attended several sessions with Iain Sutherland's orchestra, one of which was scheduled to end with Eric Coates's *Dance in the Twilight*. Under the

Christine and Sandy Blair

impression that the programme was going to overrun, the Producer told the conductor to play only one minute, fourteen seconds of the piece. Somewhat nonplussed, Iain Sutherland duly complied and it wasn't until the musicians had gone home that it was discovered that it was the Producer whose timing was wrong, not the conductor's. To rectify the shortfall on the tape, the engineers had to make a copy of the one minute, fourteen seconds already laid down and splice it on the end. It sounded strange, to say the least!

Unlike Brian Willey, Charles Clark-Maxwell was strangely reluctant to use bands that had been regulars in the original series. One would have thought that their experience would have been an asset to the show, but Clark-Maxwell thought that they sounded too dated. To be fair, he did use a few of them, but there were certainly several previous contributors whose applications were rejected.

One aspect of *Music While You Work* which had completely disappeared by 1983 was the snobbery. Just about everybody who could get a band together wanted to play on the show. As it was no longer policy to audition bands, they were either engaged on the basis of their reputation or on the acceptance of tapes which they provided as an example of their work. This resulted in the use of several bands which were new to broadcasting, even though their musical directors were known in the music business. Some, such as John Brown's Bodies, were excellent, whereas a few bands were, frankly, tedious. The fact that the individual musicians may have been proficient on their respective instruments should not be confused with their ability to be entertaining. That is an altogether different skill. Charles Clark-Maxwell was quite convinced that the musicians broadcasting in 1983 were better than those of 20 years earlier. That may have been true in some instances – it is a widely held opinion that some of the most famous bandleaders of the past would have failed an audition into their own bands! Nevertheless, they possessed the 'know-how' to be entertaining for 30 minutes or more, whereas a few of their eighties equivalents became boring after about 10 minutes. Obviously, I am writing from my own perspective and my likes and dislikes may not necessarily accord with other people's, but the *MWYW* production team was quite willing to admit that certain programmes were less than satisfactory, and that some bandleaders had been warned to 'do better next time'. Others didn't even get a next time – a couple never even got the 'repeat airing' for which they had been paid. One of those was a technically brilliant big band which the Producer thought was excellent; unfortunately his Executive Producer considered its modern style to be 'over the top' even by the new standards that were being applied.

The 'no audition' policy led to what was perhaps the most unfortunate incident to befall the new series. An unknown band had sent in an audition tape which so impressed the production team that no time was wasted in contracting them for a broadcast. The standard of performance in the studio, however, in no way matched the audition tape and the Producer asked for an explanation. The bandleader then admitted that the tape submitted had been of another band and had he submitted a recording of his own band he wouldn't have got the broadcast. Needless to say, the programme was never transmitted and proved to be a costly mistake as far as the BBC was concerned.

There were some excellent editions of *Music While You Work* in 1983. Most of the 'old names' such as Phil Tate, Johnny Howard, Iain Sutherland, Nat Temple, Harry Leader, Sidney Sax and Jack Coles put on first-rate shows, as one would expect, but there were also some memorable performances from bands, orchestras and combinations which had not previously played on the programme, many of them stalwarts of other radio shows. These included Reg Leopold, Neville Hughes, Carlos Romanos, Grant Hossack, George French, Dave Shepherd, Andy Ross, Tony Evans, and 'Pianorama' featuring the two pianos of Harold Rich and Colin Campbell. There was also a delightful band called 'Bones and Fifes' which featured trombones and flutes. Other notable groups included the Robert Docker Sextet and Christine and Sandy Blair, the two-piano team mentioned earlier.

However, there were ensembles that seemed to have little idea of programme building, sometimes playing several consecutive slow pieces; and some small groups did not appear to have the right style or instrumentation to sustain a 30-minute programme. The increased budget for the 1983 series meant that orchestras of 40 or more players were regularly used; these were twice the size of the largest orchestras in the original series. Cyril Ornadel, whom many will remember as the

Neville Hughes

Sidney Sax

George French

Harold Rich

Johnny Howard

Musical Director of television's *Sunday Night at the London Palladium*, used no less than 52 players at a cost of more than £2,500. Naturally, small groups had to be used to offset such costs, but *MWYW* was proving to be quite an expensive series, although the Executive Producer told me at the time that if the budget was reduced to the point that only small groups could be used, he would consider this to be detrimental to the series and would, in such circumstances, not wish the show to continue.

I had the pleasure of attending a number of recordings, including sessions by the orchestras of Iain Sutherland, Reg Leopold and Nat Temple. Indeed, Reg Leopold made a last-minute change to his intended programme to include a piece which he knew to be a particular favourite of mine. Iain Sutherland kept a notebook in which he had listed items requested by listeners and used some in each programme. Bearing in mind that conductors were simply doing a job for which they were paid, it is to their credit that they gave such consideration to their listeners. I well remember a telephone conversation with Nat Temple in which he told me that the BBC wanted him to include more contemporary pieces in his programmes. I remarked that I thought it important that whatever he played should not seem out of character with the style of music with which he was associated, and suggested a piece called *We'll Meet Again*; not the Vera Lynn favourite, but the theme to a then current television drama series set during the Second World War, which was played in the Glenn Miller style. Nat was unfamiliar with it and asked me to sing it to him! Having listened, he proceeded to sing it to his wife, who immediately recognised it. When he came back to the phone he said: 'My wife says it's good, so we'll use it on our next broadcast' – and he did.

During one of my visits to Maida Vale Studios, I came across a draft of a forthcoming broadcast by Harry Leader and his Band, a famous outfit formed in 1934 which had an impressive broadcasting history. This was to be their first broadcast in about ten years and I felt that their programme, mostly pop tunes of the day, was more appropriate to a current band than a vintage combination which was being brought together again for the broadcast. I therefore wrote to Harry Leader and, without revealing my surreptitiously obtained advance information, suggested that he gave emphasis to arrangements which his fans would remember and associate with him, leaving current numbers to the many modern bands on the show. I even gave him examples of pieces that he might like to include. To my amazement he completely changed his programme and the resulting broadcast was very much in line with my suggestions! He told me that he would have to put in one or two modern arrangements just to prove that he could play them.

Harry seemed rather proud of a brand-new arrangement which he had penned of the old song *They Can't Take That Away From Me* but the musicians didn't like the rather unconventional modern harmonies which he had used – and they told him so. 'Ah!' he said, 'the trouble with you chaps is that you're not used to playing good arrangements!' This was not, perhaps, the most diplomatic remark to make to some of Britain's top session players, and their stony expressions said it all. Harry, however, decided that he wanted to hear the performance in the control box. As soon as he was out of earshot, the musicians had a hasty discussion: 'We can't play these harmonies – they're all wrong,' said one. 'No, you're right, we'll have to change them,' said another. So, during rehearsal and the subsequent broadcast, the band played the piece the way *they* thought it should go and it sounded much better than before. If Harry Leader realised what they had done (and he surely must have) he didn't say anything!

Actually, the Harry Leader broadcast nearly didn't happen. It was scheduled to be recorded one Thursday evening and, having obtained the date and time of the session, I duly went to the studio at Maida Vale. To my surprise, the only people in the studio were the Producer and the Studio Manager, both of whom were wondering what had happened to the band. After waiting for some time, the Producer telephoned Harry Leader's home and Harry answered! Apparently, he was under the impression that the recording was not due for a couple of weeks and was quite surprised to learn that he and the band were supposed to be in the studio in London. Clearly a misunderstanding had occurred and perhaps we shall never know who was to blame. What is certain is that the Producer was none too pleased, as the recording had to be rescheduled on a day when he was supposed to be on holiday.

The revival of *Music While You Work* had come about because the then Controller of Radio Two, David Hatch, believed in the programme. During the autumn of 1983 his tenure of office came to an end and his successor was Bryant Marriott, a former producer of *MWYW*. Any hopes that this fact would prove beneficial to the series, however, were shattered when it was announced that *MWYW* would end in January 1984. Unfortunately, Mr Marriott considered the programme dated in concept and belonging to another age. It is known that the Producer, Charles Clark-Maxwell, regretted the decision as he had hoped to be associated with the programme for many years to come.

One of the excuses given for ending the series was that some of the smaller groups were stylistically unsuited to sustaining a half-hour period. Well, that was true, but surely the answer would have been to use only those combinations that were suited to the show.

Another reason given was that up to half a million people were switching off their radios at 12.00 noon before the programme started, but as *MWYW* immediately followed the *Jimmy Young Show* – Radio Two's most popular programme – it was surely logical that any subsequent programme would have a smaller audience. Personally, I thought that it had been placed at the wrong time – a time when many would have been preparing to have lunch.

The die was cast. After just over a year, the final show was transmitted on 18th January 1984. It was played by Iain Sutherland

Iain Sutherland conducting *Music While You Work* for the last time in December 1983

and his Orchestra and was a repeat of a broadcast of 30th December, so its final item was appropriate on both dates – *Auld Lang Syne!*

This was, however, not quite the end. In June 1990, the BBC decided to celebrate the 50th anniversary of *Music While You Work* with a week of programmes at the traditional afternoon time of 3.30 p.m. They were played by Phil Tate and his Orchestra, the Band of the Royal Military School of Music (Kneller Hall), the Victor Silvester Orchestra, the George French Orchestra; and Ken Mackintosh and his Band. This group of programmes was repeated at the end of the year.

In 1991 *Music While You Work* appeared again – this time for six Saturday afternoon editions, commencing on 18th May with the Victor Silvester Orchestra, followed by the Band of the Irish Guards, the Robert Docker Sextet, the John Fox Orchestra, the Harry Stoneham Band and lastly the Don Lusher Big Band. This turned out to be the final series of *MWYW*. There was a one-off special in 1995, as part of a nostalgia weekend, in which Victor Silvester Jnr. directed the famous Victor Silvester Orchestra in what transpired to be their final broadcast. Curiously, their famous signature tune *You're Dancing On*

My Heart was added to the end of *Calling All Workers,* rather spoiling its authenticity.

So, that was the end, or so we must assume, of a legendary programme. I hope I am wrong, but I cannot really see it returning, certainly not for an extended series. It is questionable whether there are now sufficient orchestras and groups of a suitable nature to service such a programme; furthermore, studio broadcasting of the types of music covered by the programme has all but disappeared from Radio Two. Nevertheless, the belief that *MWYW* had become a part of our heritage is borne out by the fact that many amateur light orchestras around the country perform 'mock' *MWYW* shows to appreciative audiences.

In the next chapter I shall tell you about some of the musical directors, most of whom are no longer with us, whose music gave so much pleasure to so many.

Finally, here is a desperately sad, yet poignant story concerning a former *MWYW* contributor, whom I have been asked not to name. Towards the end of his life he was so ill that he could no longer communicate or indeed comprehend. In an attempt to communicate with him, a family member played him a tape of one of his old broadcasts, wondering if it would stir any visible emotion. The result was instantaneous; the tears ran down his face – a clear indication of the memories which the music brought back to him. *Music While You Work* meant a great deal to many people, not least to the musicians involved.

It was an unforgettable programme, truly an era in broadcasting.

SOME ACTUAL *MUSIC WHILE YOU WORK* PROGRAMMES BROADCAST IN 1983

(All performances 12.02 p.m. to 12.30 p.m.)

4.1.83   The Neville Hughes Orchestra

Calling All Workers (Sig)	Coates
One (from *Chorus Line*)	Hamlisch
I Will Wait for You	Legrand
Love is in the Air	Vanvy/Young
Moon River	Mancini
Stranger on the Shore	Bilk
Swinging Safari	Kaempfert
Moonlight in Vermont	Sues
Days of Wine and Roses	Mancini
You Stepped out of a Dream	Brown/Kahn
Here We Are Falling in Love Again	Sedaka/Cody
Autumn Leaves	Mercer/Kosma
Dancing in the Dark	Schwartz
I'll Be Seeing You	Fain
Calling All Workers (Sig)	Coates

21.1.83   Lou Whiteson and the Southern Serenade Orchestra

Calling All Workers (Sig)	Coates
Chiqui Chiqui Cha	Quintero
Componte Condunga	Perez
Alma Llanera	Guitarez
Come Closer to Me	Farres
Sucu Sucu	Rojas
Bomba	Gomez
African Dawn	Gardner
Grey Skies (Nube Gris)	Talledo
Mexican Mambo	Gomez
Maria Dolores	Garcia
Calling All Workers (Sig)	Coates

7.2.83   **Stanley Black and his Orchestra**

Calling All Workers (Sig)	Coates
The Hustle	McCoy
A Woman in Love	Loesser
How High the Moon	Lewis
Wave	Jobim
Vereda Tropicale	Gonzalo
Serenata	Anderson
Chariots of Fire	Vangelis
Frenesi	Dominguez
Canadian Sunset	Heywood
That Old Black Magic	Arlen
Calling All Workers (Sig)	Coates

17.2.83   **Bones and Fifes (Trombones, Flutes, Rhythm)**

Calling All Workers (Sig)	Coates
Thou Swell	Rodgers
It Might As Well Be Spring	Rodgers
Always True to You in My Fashion	Porter
Volare	Modugno
Jeepers, Creepers	Mercer/Warren
Zing Went the Strings of My Heart	Hanley
Only Sixteen	Cooke
Smile	Chaplin
On a Clear Day	Lane
My Heart Stood Still	Rodgers
La Raspa	Garcia
Calling All Workers (Sig)	Coates

18.2.83   **Iain Sutherland and his Orchestra**

Calling All Workers (Sig)	Coates
Covent Garden	Coates
Manhattan Playboy	Farnon
Sailing By	Binge
Edinburgh Castle	Sutherland
Rotten Row	Stott
March from the *Little Suite*	Duncan

Cumberland Square	Tomlinson
Waltz: *Murder on the Orient Express*	Bennett
Calling All Workers (Sig)	Coates

2.3.83   Johnny Howard and his Orchestra

Calling All Workers (Sig)	Coates
At Long Last Love	Porter
Call Me Irresponsible	Van Heuson/Cahn
When You're Smiling	Fisher/Goodwin
Give My Regards to Broadway	Cohan
Who's Sorry Now	Kalmar/Ruby/Snyder
Love is All	Tilzer
I've Told Every Little Star	Kern/Hammerstein
Blue Skies	Berlin
I'm Putting All My Eggs in One Basket	Berlin
You're Just in Love	Berlin
Dream	Mercer
The Importance of Your Love	Becaud/Newell
Games That Lovers Play	Last
What Now My Love	Becaud
I Get a Kick Out of You	Porter
Stranger on the Shore	Bilk/Mellin
Love For Sale	Porter
Calling All Workers (Sig)	Coates

26.5.83   The Christine and Sandy Blair Two-Piano Rhythm

Calling All Workers (Sig)	Coates
Casatschok	Runaschkin
Zambesi	Carstens/De Waal
Doll Dance	Brown
The Wedding of the Painted Doll	Brown
Maigret Theme	Grainer
One Note Samba	Jobim
Romanza de Amor	Trad. arr. Blair
Gilbert and Sullivan Medley:	Gilbert/Sullivan
Three Little Maids	
Dance a Cachucha	
Bluesette	Thielemans

Yellow Bird	Luboff
Zorba's Dance	Theodorakis
Calling All Workers (Sig)	Coates

6.6.83　　John Gregory and his Orchestra

Calling All Workers (Sig)	Coates
One (from *Chorus Line*)	Hamlisch
Aquarius	Macdermott/Rado
Mozart 40	Mozart
Arthur's Theme	Bacharach/Sager
Fame	Gore
Chariots of Fire	Vangelis
Raiders of the Lost Ark	Williams
Theme from E.T.	Williams
Superman Theme	Williams
Calling All Workers (Sig)	Coates

20.6.83　　The Sound of Strings Directed by David Francis

Calling All Workers (Sig)	Coates
Holiday in Rio	Richardson
Sunny	Hebb
Where There's Love	Armstrong
The Girl from Ipanema	Jobim
Double Scotch	Martin
Romeo and Juliet Theme	Tchaikovsky
High Heels	Duncan
Red Roses for a Blue Lady	Brodsky
Marching Strings	Ross
Manhattan Playboy	Farnon
Calling All Workers (Sig)	Coates

27.6.83　　John Fox and his Orchestra

Calling All Workers (Sig)	Coates
On The Street Where You Live	Loewe
Mr Sandman	Ballard
With You I'm Born Again	Shire
Ramblin' Rose	Sherman

The Rainbow Connection	Williams/Ascher
More	Ortolani/Newell
Smoke Gets in Your Eyes	Kern
Yours Sincerely	Fox
Manhattan	Rodgers/Hart
Don't Give Up On Us Baby	Macauley
Chattanooga Choo Choo	Warren
Calling All Workers (Sig)	Coates

31.8.83   Joe Loss and his Orchestra

Calling All Workers (Sig)	Coates
Spanish Gipsy Dance	Marquina
Crazy Rhythm	Caesar/Meyer/Kahn
Men of Harlech	Trad.
My Guy's Come Back	Powell/McKinley
Never on Sunday	Hadjidakis
Song of India	Rimsky-Korsakov
The Village Band	Fryberg
A Man and a Woman	Lai
Y Viva Espana	Caerts/Rozenstraten
How About You	Freed/Lane
Calling All Workers (Sig)	Coates

15.9.83   Carlos Romanos and his Orchestra

Calling All Workers (Sig)	Coates
I'll Be Around	Wilder
Summer Love in Napoli	Todd
Up Up and Away	Webb
Marina	Webb
Once I Loved	Jobim
Scalinatella	Bonagura/Cioffi
Manha de Carnival	Bonfa
Moonglow	Hudson/Mills
Yena Stranieva	Unknown
How Insensitive	Jobim
Calling All Workers (Sig)	Coates

6.10.83   The Bill Jackman Group

Calling All Workers (Sig)	Coates
18th Century Drawing Room	Scott
World on a String	Arlen
Toy Trumpet	Scott/Mitchell
By Strauss	Gershwin
A Handful of Songs	Bart/Steele/Pratt
Yes We Have No Bananas	Silver/Cohn/Carlton
Soft Shoe Shuffle	Burman
Cavaquinho	Nazareth
Windy	Friedman
Betty Dear	Agoult
Under the Double Eagle	Wagner/Agoult
Calling All Workers (Sig)	Coates

7.10.83   The GUS Band

Calling All Workers (Sig)	Coates
Presto (*Norwegian Rhapsody*)	Lalo
Rhythm and Blues	Sparke
Memory (from *Cats*)	Lloyd Webber
Bandology	Osterling
Trumpets Wild	Walters
My Ain Folk	Trad.
Trombola	Bryce
Lisbon Carnival	Vinter
Sons of the Brave	Bidgood
Calling All Workers (Sig)	Coates

27.10.83   Pianorama directed By Harold Rich
(Harold Rich and Colin Campbell at Two Pianos
with Orchestra)

Calling All Workers (Sig)	Coates
Medley:	
Camptown Races	Foster
Toot Toot Tootsie	Keys/Evdman/Russo
Waiting for the Robert E. Lee	Wolfe/Gilbert/Muir

Medley:
   All of Me   Simons/Marks
   I'm Confessin'   Neilberg/Dougherty
   Little Dolly Daydream   Stuart

Medley:
   Won't You Come Home Bill Bailey   Cannon
   Swanee   Gershwin
   I'm Just Wild About Harry   Sissle/Blake

Medley:
   That Old Feeling   Brown/Fain
   That Old Lucky Sun   Gillespie/Smith
   Over the Rainbow   Harburg/Arlen

Medley:
   Dark Town Strutters Ball   Brooks
   Oh You Beautiful Doll   Ayer
   Miss Annabelle Lee   Clare/Pollock

Medley:
   You Must Have Been a Beautiful Baby   Dubin/Warren
   Shanty in Old Shanty Town   Young/Siras/Little
   By the Light of the Silvery Moon   Madden/Edwards
   When Day is Done   De Sylva/Katscher

Medley:
   Thank Heaven for Little Girls   Lerner/Loewe
   Ma, He's Making Eyes at Me   Clare/Conrad

Medley:
   April Showers   De Sylva/Silvers
   Side By Side   Woods
   Carolina   Kahn/Donaldson
Calling All Workers (Sig)   Coates

28.10.83   Geoffrey Brand and his Orchestra

Calling All Workers (Sig)   Coates
Belle of the Ball   Anderson
Summertime   Gershwin
Prestbury Park   Lane
Come Follow the Band (from *Barnum*)   Stewart/Coleman
Selection: *West Side Story*   Bernstein
Don't Cry For Me Argentina   Lloyd-Webber
March of the Toys   Herbert

Calling All Workers (Sig)   Coates

17.11.83   The Robert Docker Sextet

Calling All Workers (Sig)   Coates
Astaire/Rodgers Medley:
   We Saw The Sea   Berlin
   Waltz In Swingtime   Kern
   Cheek To Cheek   Berlin
   I'm Putting All My Eggs in One Basket Berlin
   They Can't Take That Away From Me   Gershwin
   Let Yourself Go   Berlin
Buffoon   Confrey
Ray Noble Medley: Noble
   The Touch of Your Lips
   The Very Thought of You
   Goodnight Sweetheart
Pavanne   Gould
Girls Medley:
   Louise   Whiting
   Sally   Haines/Leon/Towers
   Stella By Starlight   Young
   Charmaine   Pollack/Rapee
   If You Knew Susie   De Sylva
Dizzy Fingers   Confrey
Music Hall Medley:
   Down The Road   Gilbert
   The Galloping Major   Bastow
   Little Dolly Daydream   Stuart
   After the Ball   Harris
   Waiting at the Church   Pethers
   Put On Your Ta Ta Little Girlie   Leigh
Calling All Workers (Sig)   Coates

5.12.83   Ray Davies and his Orchestra

Calling All Workers (Sig)   Coates
Country Style   Burke/Van Heuson
Goofus   King/Harold/Kahn
Someday I'll Find You   Coward

Linger Awhile	Rose
Balmoral Waltz	Jones/Davies
El Pato Loco	Davies
Autumn in New York	Duke
Imagine	Lennon
Plaisir d 'amour	Trad.
Sweet Georgia Brown	Bernie/Pinkard
Calling All Workers (Sig)	Coates

Chapter 4

The Men Behind the Music

In this chapter I'll tell you something of the careers of a selection of band and orchestra leaders who helped to make *Music While You Work* the success it undoubtedly was. A full list of contributors is given elsewhere and it would be impossible to profile all of them in a book of this size, even if the necessary information could be obtained. Although there were many regulars playing on the programme, some for the entire 27-year run of the original series, others had only a handful of broadcasts before disappearing into the obscurity from which they had come. A glance at the list of contributors will reveal many famous names, as well as others whose names will mean nothing to most readers. I would venture to say that only the most ardent of enthusiasts of the show will remember all the artists profiled in this chapter, even though all of them were prolific broadcasters in their day. Artists are featured in alphabetical order.

FRED ALEXANDER

Fred Alexander, a Londoner, studied violin at the Guildhall School of Music until the death of his father made it necessary for him to find a way to supplement the family income. He decided to use his musical talents by playing in the local cinema. Initially he was an apprentice for the princely sum of five shillings per week but, at the tender age of 16, he was quickly promoted to the post of Musical Director at a new Super cinema in London Fields. By the time he was 18 Fred was Musical Director at the Watford Super Cinema, but the talkies were arriving and it was not long before the only music required was for big stage shows. This was not the only time in the 20th century that progress was to oust art!

For several years, with the door shut on cinema work, Fred resumed his studies, this time with the well-known teacher Sasha Lasserson. He then started doing session work and around 1936 joined a broadcasting combination called The Karl Kaylus Players in the capacity of solo violin. When guitarist Karl Kaylus became disenchanted with the group and left, Fred Alexander, realising its potential, took over as Musical Director. Although initially retaining its original name, it was not long before the group became Fred Alexander and his Players. This combination's broadcasting was destined to span four decades.

During the Second World War, Fred served in the Royal Artillery, playing in their famous orchestra, but after being invalided out at the end of hostilities, he resumed free-lance work (as well as directing his players). Fred played in the Harry Fryer Orchestra, a frequent *MWYW* contributor, but in 1946 Fryer became terminally ill and it fell to Fred to conduct the orchestra's last broadcasts. With Fryer's death, the orchestra would have ceased to exist but, once again, Fred's preservation instinct came into play and he thought of a way to keep the orchestra going, at least for radio. After discussions with the BBC, he formed the Portland Light Orchestra, consisting largely of members of the Harry Fryer Orchestra. Over the next few years, this 32-piece orchestra played many times in programmes such as *Strike Up The Band* and *Morning Music*, not forgetting 33 editions of *Music While You Work*, for which the size of the orchestra had to be reduced in order to keep within the show's budget! After a few years, however, the orchestra's broadcasts fizzled out, though Fred Alexander's Players continued to receive regular airings. Their instrumentation consisted of violin, cello, accordion, piano, guitar, bass and percussion and included top instrumentalists such as Henry Krein, Edward Rubach, Billy Bell and Henry Elman (brother of orchestra leader Ralph Elman).

Fred tells me that in the early fifties he did theatrical work, leading the orchestra for the Cicely Courtneidge show *Gay's the Word*, and then working for Jack Hylton in *Paint Your Wagon* and *Pal Joey*. Unfortunately, Fred had to forsake theatre work because of the increasing demands of session work. In the BBC studios he regularly played for Anton, Michaeloff, Harold Collins, Bernard Monshin, Harold C. Gee, Sidney Bowman and Les Perry as well as accompanying top vocalists as diverse as Gigli, Frankie Vaughan and Petula Clark.

During the post-war years, Fred Alexander and his Players were

92

regularly broadcasting, often in daily shows such as *Bright and Early* and *Morning Music*. Between 1955 and 1965 the ensemble chalked up 90 editions of *MWYW*. Fred was also a composer and his paso doble *Sarda*, written under the pseudonym of Alessandro, became quite a favourite.

Most of the light music ensembles, including Fred's, were withdrawn from broadcasting in the mid-sixties, but Fred continued with session work into the seventies, becoming leader and orchestral manager of the Johnny Patrick Orchestra in television's *New Faces* talent show. At the time of writing this profile, Fred Alexander is living comfortably in retirement at his home in Worthing, aged 94.

(I am indebted to Fred Alexander for providing me with detailed information on his career.)

The following is an example of a *MWYW* programme by Fred Alexander and his Players, broadcast on 1st June 1964 at 10.31 a.m.

Calling All Workers (Sig)	Coates
Bravo, Bravo	Monshin
Oh Donna Clara	Peterburkski
This is My Prayer	Nisa
Baveno	Prince
Sidewalk Serenade	Fotine
E Fantastico	Di Ceglia
Parakeets of Paraguay	Dumont
Kisses in the Dark	Micheli
'Appy 'Arry	Jupp
Carlo's Theme	Slaney
Vilia	Lehar
Marbella	Kerry
Calling All Workers (Sig)	Coates

KEN BEAUMONT

Ken Beaumont was one of those radio 'names' who had many hundreds of broadcasts to his credit and yet is so poorly documented that I doubt if many of those who remember him even knew what instrument he played, let alone anything about his career! Indeed, his fame as a bandleader represented only the last 20-odd years of a very diverse career.

Ken Beaumont was born in Blackpool on 24th October 1913. His musical education was at the Royal Manchester School of Music, and even whilst still a student he gave recitals of *Lieder* and ballads. During his career he was a singer, disc jockey and actor, taking part in many North Region Revue programmes prior to moving to London in 1936. Whilst living in the North he had played and sung with Larry Brennan's Winter Garden Dance Band in Blackpool, with which he broadcast and recorded.

He was one of the first radio artists to become a disc jockey, and he presented a programme entitled *With Vocal Chorus* between 1937 and 1945. He also broadcast on television and radio from Hollywood, as well as performing on commercial radio. Ken was with several leading dance bands, including those of Henry Hall, Oscar Rabin and, notably, Billy Ternent and the BBC Dance Orchestra, being one of their featured vocalists for much of the war when he was with the BBC's Variety Department, which, at that time, was based in Bangor.

It was in 1946 that Ken Beaumont formed his sextet for broadcasting. Initially billed as Ken Beaumont's Music, this ensemble was clearly a favourite with radio listeners, becoming particularly associated with *Music While You Work* and playing no less than 289 editions. The sextet performed in other shows as well, and I have clear memories of setting my alarm clock for 6.30 a.m. in order to hear their regular *Bright and Early* broadcasts. By the early sixties they were also frequent contributors to *Morning Music*. Ken Beaumont's ensemble was essentially a dance band but often included light music novelties in its programme for contrast. Listeners may recall that they liked to commence and conclude their broadcasts with medleys of traditional folk tunes which Ken arranged for the group.

Ken Beaumont and his Sextet comprised the following instruments: violin, saxophone/clarinet, piano, bass, drums and two guitars, one of which was played by Ken himself. Curiously, he adopted a rather low profile within the group, playing the rhythm guitar rather than the lead. The band's violinist was Danny Levan, who also had his own sextet.

In the 1950s, in between 'bashing out *Music While You Works*', as Ken put it, it would appear that he was doing a stage act with Margaret Heath (soprano and violinist). Around this time he occasionally broadcast in variety shows and had his own series – *Tuneful Twenties*.

By the sixties, Ken was broadcasting exclusively as a bandleader and, around 1963, possibly with a view to updating his style, he dispensed with the violin, substituting an electronic keyboard (probably an electronic accordion). In my opinion this lost the band a lot of tone colour.

The BBC was very particular about bands being in the studio in time for the *MWYW* rehearsals at 7.30 a.m., and so was Ken Beaumont, who, on New Year's Eve 1962, insisted that the sextet sleep in the studio overnight as there was snow on the ground and he didn't want to risk a delay. The fact that the musicians might 'over-celebrate' the New Year might just have occurred to him as well!

Following the demise of *MWYW* in 1967, Ken Beaumont's broadcasts became infrequent, with just the occasional session for *Breakfast Special* in the late sixties. When *Music While You Work* was revived in the early eighties, Ken rang the Producer to advise that, as he had retired, he did not want to participate. Given the reluctance on the part of the production team to use 'old names' at that time, it is unlikely that he would have been invited anyway.

Ken Beaumont died on 11th March 1996, aged 82.

Music While You Work at 10.31 a.m. 24th October 1963
Played by Ken Beaumont and his Sextet

Calling All Workers (Sig)	Coates
Traditional Medley No.19	arr. Beaumont
My Love is Like a Red, Red Rose	
My Love is but a Lassie Yet	
Sospen Bach	
The Rakes of Mallow	
In Summer	Adams
I'm Telling You Now	Murray
It's My Party	Gold

Things are Swinging	Lee
Hey Neighbour	Parker
Bad to Me	Lennon
It's All in the Game	Dawes
Applejack	Vandyke
Frimley Green	Baynes
I'm Sitting on Top of the World	Young
Porta Rossa	Bennet
Charmaine	Rapee
This Can't Be Love	Rodgers
Bacciar	Brandez
Shindig	Welch
The Cruel Sea	arr. Maxfield
Traditional Medley Nos 43 And 44	arr. Beaumont
La Golondrina	
Shortnin' Bread	
Tom Dooley	
The Caviare Song	
The Girl I Left Behind Me	
Calling All Workers (Sig)	Coates

JACK COLES

Jack Coles was born in London on 28th April 1914. After studying the trumpet at the Royal Military School of Music, Kneller Hall, from 1933–34 and winning the Gold Cup for the best all-round pupil, he played with leading dance bands until the outbreak of war in 1939. After serving with the King's Royal Rifle Corps, he joined the British Band of the AEF as trumpeter and arranger for its conductor, George Melachrino.

Jack Coles started broadcasting in 1946 with a ten-piece dance band called the Music Masters. Subsequently, at the request of the BBC, he formed a 22-piece light orchestra consisting of strings and woodwind, piano, percussion and two French horns. Specialising in light music of the day, this was called Jack Coles and his Orchestre Moderne and, unlike the Music Masters, which only survived a few years, was destined to become a major contributor to the light music scene for over a decade.

Jack Coles and his Orchestre Moderne contributed to programmes such as *Melody Hour*, *Morning Music* and, of course, *Music While You Work*, for which the orchestra did 51 programmes. (The Music Masters did 16 in the late forties.) I well remember listening to a live *MWYW* by the orchestra on one blisteringly hot August afternoon in 1959 when the music suddenly stopped and the announcer explained that the very hot weather affected the tuning of the musical instruments, going on to say '...the orchestra crave your indulgence for a few moments whilst they retune their instruments in order that they may continue to play in concert pitch'. Their retuning was not heard on air and they soon resumed playing.

From the outset, Jack had always impressed the BBC with his musicianship, programme building and ability as a conductor. It was, therefore, no surprise when, in 1958, he was invited to take part in the annual BBC Festival of Light Music at the Royal Festival Hall in London. He was also invited to conduct the Continental Orchestra of Hilversum. His many talents included composing and arranging for radio, television, film and stage productions, his own musical tastes ranging from jazz to operatic and symphonic works. He was also one of the leading composers of light music in this country. His best known composition, *Tyrolean Tango*, written under the pen-name of Paul Stewart, was recorded by George Melachrino and in America by Duke Ellington, re-titled *The Echo Tango*. Jack also recorded it, together with some of his other compositions, on a 1966 Columbia LP entitled *The Music of Jack Coles*. His numerous compositions included *Mexican Serenade, Dude Ranch, Dance of the Pan-pipes, Fan Tan, The Girl From Cadiz, Parakeets and Peacocks, Positano, Prochida, Sparky, Cowbell Polka* and *Joy Ride*.

By the late 1950s, Jack Coles was regularly 'guest conducting' the various BBC Regional Light Orchestras, and a tour of Holland with the BBC Studio Choir so impressed the BBC that it was decided that his was a skill that needed to be exploited at a higher level. Since early in 1959, the BBC Midland Light Orchestra had been without a permanent conductor and Jack Coles, Gilbert Vinter and Leo Wurmser were holding the fort until a fixed appointment was made. In 1960 it was decided to make changes to the orchestra's instrumentation, reducing its size and making it more suited to a lighter, more modern style. Jack Coles, having already introduced a number of modern arrangements to the orchestra, was seen as the obvious man to develop this on a permanent basis and was duly appointed conductor in August 1960.

Jack lived in London and commuted to Birmingham, staying for three or four days each week. As he was not available full time, Gilbert Vinter, who had previously been the resident conductor, was drafted in for the days that Jack couldn't be there, playing the more traditional style of light music with which he was associated. This arrangement gave the orchestra an unusual versatility. Jack held the post of conductor of the MLO until 1972, when he retired to Italy – to Positano, the title of one of his compositions.

Returning to London in the early eighties, he recorded programmes for the revived series of *MWYW*. Jack Coles died on 24th April 1991, four days before his 77th birthday.

Music While You Work at 3.45 p.m. on 15th June 1956
Played by Jack Coles and his Orchestre Moderne

Calling All Workers (Sig)	Coates
Shooting Star	Torch
Songe d'Automne	Joyce
Without Your Love	Noel
Mexican Serenade	Coles
Shimmering Silk	King Palmer
In a Persian Market	Ketelbey
Napolitana	Troise
Bluebell Polka	Stanley
Lady Beautiful	Bayco
Petite Waltz	Heyne
The March Hare	Green
Calling All Workers (Sig)	Coates

HAROLD COLLINS

Many *Music While You Work* contributors had long associations with the theatre and, of these, Harold Collins and his Orchestra were one of the most popular. In common with so many musicians in the light music field, Harold Collins is poorly documented, therefore it is possible to say only that he was born in Birmingham on 4th June; the year remains a mystery but was probably around 1900. Harold started as a pianist in a concert party at the age of 18, subsequently spending some years with the Archie Pitt Organisation as a conductor in revue. (Archie Pitt was Gracie Fields' first husband.)

In the thirties, Harold was resident conductor at the Palace, Plymouth, from where he gave his first broadcast in 1936. Subsequently, he returned to London and formed a broadcasting orchestra at the Lewisham Hippodrome; this was regularly featured 'on air' and made an early appearance on *MWYW* in August 1940. In December of that year he played the first of 227 programmes in the series as Harold Collins and his Orchestra. His broadcasts were not confined to *MWYW*, however, as he was a regular for many years on *Morning Music,* also appearing on *Melody on the Move.* During the forties, Harold Collins made a considerable number of records for Decca on their special *Music While You Work* label.

Harold acted as musical director for a succession of stage shows, both in London and the provinces. He was at the London Coliseum in 1947, the London Casino 1951/2 with the show *Folies Bergere.* He also toured, during the fifties, with *The Student Prince.*

It was evident from listening to his broadcasts that Harold Collins was the ultimate professional who went to a lot of trouble to ensure a good performance. His programme building was very imaginative, never more so than on 5th November 1953 (Bonfire Night) when his programme included *Here Comes the Guy, Dancing Around the Bonfire,* and a selection from the show *Mister Cinders!* All items were orchestrally linked with a few bars of *I Don't Want to Set the World On Fire.*

In 1956, Harold Collins' orchestra, which was usually led by Ralph Elman, made its television debut and, in 1961, Harold conducted a rather special edition of *Sunday Night at the London Palladium* with Bruce Forsythe and Norman Wisdom (for whom Harold was MD). He even took part in a sketch in which he 'refused' to play for Norman Wisdom, declaring '...if you're in charge, I'm off!' He then climbed out of the orchestra pit and went and sat in the audience. At this point, Wisdom jumped into the pit and conducted a frenzied cacophony. Forsythe chased him out and Harold Collins was seen climbing back into the pit. This 'one from the archives' has been re-broadcast several times.

In the early sixties, the London Palladium was closed for refurbishment and the Sunday night programme was transferred to the Prince of Wales theatre, for which Harold was MD. Consequently, his orchestra was seen and heard every week for many months. During this period, however, the orchestra was not on radio. It is possible that their contract with the commercial television company precluded the orchestra from playing for the BBC, it is even more likely that the BBC, which didn't like its artists to work for the 'other side', may have given it the cold shoulder! When they did return to *MWYW*, appearances were infrequent and they were heard for the last time on 1st September 1964.

It has not been possible to establish what happened after this time, but it is believed that Harold Collins died around 1971. Over the years his orchestra had been well thought of by the BBC and, even in recent times, musicians who played for him have described his orchestra as one of the best on *Music While You Work*.

Music While You Work at 3.31 p.m. on 10th April 1962
Played by Harold Collins and his Orchestra.

Calling All Workers (Sig)	Coates
Haifa Festival	Isra
Moon River	Mancini
Felicidades	Rosada
Sous les Ponts de Paris	Scotto
Selection: *Stop the World*	Newley/Bricusse
Alcantara	Arnold

Medley: Norman Wisdom Melodies	arr. Collins
Don't Laugh at Me	
Beware	
Please Opportunity	
Vienna Dash	Strauss
Exodus	Gold
Leroy Anderson Medley	Anderson
Belle of the Ball	
Blue Tango	
Promenade	
Trumpeter's Lullaby	
Sleigh Ride	
Television Medley	
Coronation Street	Spear
This is Your Life	Turner
Dixon of Dock Green	Warner/Darnell
Birichino	Marland
Selection: *West Side Story*	Bernstein
Calling All Workers (Sig)	Coates

GERALD CROSSMAN

A popular feature of *Music While You Work* was the accordion ensemble. Several distinguished exponents of this now rather neglected instrument led their own groups through many a programme. They included Albert Delroy, Delmondi, Henry Krein, Jack Emblow and Gerald Crossman. Also popular were the accordion bands of George Scott-Wood and Primo Scala, of which more later in this book.

Gerald Crossman was born on 5th April 1920 in Upper Holloway, North London. His was a very musical family; father was a mandolin player who owned two music shops and mother was a music teacher. Three cousins also became famous. Joe Crossman played for Lew

Stone, Jack Hylton, Ambrose and other dance bands. The other two cousins were Jock Jacobson (Lew Stone's drummer) and guitarist Sid Jacobson.

Gerald Crossman took up the piano at the age of five and, after having lessons from his mother, studied at Trinity College of Music. He took up the accordion at the age of 12 and became proficient on the saxophone, clarinet and trumpet. One of his piano teachers was the well-known Edward Rubach.

In the late thirties, whilst still a teenager, Gerald Crossman played summer seasons in hotels in Cliftonville and London's Tottenham Court Road. He played with orchestras in Lyons' Corner Houses, and appeared solo in West End Theatres.

Gerald commenced his recording and broadcasting career in 1938/9 with recitals on the BBC Empire Service and with the Karl Kaylus Players, at that time directed by violinist Fred Alexander. The following year Gerald did some ENSA shows, but spent much of the time in Bournemouth with the orchestra of Plummer Roddis' Department Store Sundeck Restaurant.

Gerald joined the RAF in 1940 and three years later became RAF Central Band Sergeant Music Instructor, subsequently directing voluntary bands which included such musicians as Ernest Tomlinson and trumpeter Ronnie Hughes. After being posted to India in 1945, Gerald broadcast on accordion and piano for the Forces Radio and All-India Radio. He was Administrator/Music Instructor of the Royal Indian Air Force Band and was actually offered the illustrious post of Director of European Music, should he choose to remain in India after demobilisation; he declined this offer.

Demobilised in 1946, Gerald joined the Harry Gordon Quartet at a holiday camp in Paignton in Devon. Returning to London, he made many connections through broadcasting with the light orchestras, and through recording and film music sessions – connections that were to last for several decades.

Gerald Crossman has composed over 100 pieces of light music, the first of which, *Granada Mia* and *Marcha Espagnol*, were published in 1948. Other titles include: *A Night in Montmartre, Boulevards de Paris, Milou, Can-Can Dancers, La Vida Latina, All Hands For'ard, Banda Espanola, Poverino Mio, Tanto Gusto, The Happy Bachelor, The Albany Waltz, Nochecita, All In Step, Fantango* and many others. Gerald Crossman wrote, and played, the music for several films, including *The House of the Arrow*. In others he has brief on-screen appearances playing accordion, notably in the Morecambe and Wise favourite *The Magnificent Two*.

After the war, he continued to perform in restaurants and in Lyons' Corner Houses, playing in the orchestras of Fredric Cooper and David Java. He also played with Falkman's Apache Band and recalls how Lionel Falkman used to walk amongst the restaurant tables playing his violin. Gerald later worked aboard the Cunard liners *Queen Mary* and *Caronia*, travelling to New York, and to Buenos Aires aboard the Royal Mail ship *Andes*.

Early television appearances include playing solo accordion to the accompaniment of Eric Robinson's Orchestra in the early fifties from Alexandra Palace. Around this time he formed an accordion quartet for light music broadcasts, followed shortly afterwards by the combination that was to make him a household name in radio, The Gerald Crossman Players whose signature tune was *A Night in Montmartre*. Their first broadcast was in *Music While You Work* on Thursday 13th November 1952 at 10.30 a.m. The players consisted of three accordions, saxophone doubling clarinet/bass clarinet and violin, piano, double bass and percussion. Their contrasting repertoire included marches, paso dobles, waltzes, entr'acte numbers and selections from shows and films. Gerald arranged some pieces himself, but the majority were done by the publishers' staff arrangers (in liaison with Gerald, of course).

With so many light music periods available to the many ensembles and small orchestras that were so popular with listeners in the fifties, Gerald found himself in the studios nearly every day, playing for one or more of them. He still found time to lead his players in numerous editions of *Bright and Early, Morning Music* and various untitled, announced programmes, some with a guest artist. The players did 123 *MWYW* programmes – 24 in 1959 alone. Each programme apparently took three days to plan, so Gerald must have been under some pressure when, on one occasion, he played a 45-minute Friday afternoon show with another live edition on the following Monday. The players' three accordionists were Gerald, Albert Delroy and Ivor Beynon – alternatively, Emilio or Reg Hogarth. Pianists over the years included Billy Mayerl, Maurice Arnold, Edward Rubach, William Davies and Sidney Davey. The woodwind player was originally Frank Reidy, but later was Michael Salmons, who also played the violin.

As the arrangements were done by a number of different musicians,

The Gerald Crossman Players about to commence their first *Music While You Work* on 13th November 1952

Gerald had to spend time fine tuning them to ensure that they accurately reflected the style of the ensemble – a refined and sometimes quite delicate style. 'I didn't want it to sound like an accordion band!' Gerald told me. In addition to the Players, he had a group on Radio Luxembourg and sometimes broadcast at the piano with a trio in *Morning Music*.

Gerald Crossman has played in most of the top London hotels – Savoy, Ritz, Hilton, Dorchester, Claridge's and others – and has performed with combinations as diverse as Ted Heath, Nat Temple, Edmundo Ros, the BBC Concert Orchestra and the London Symphony Orchestra. He played for Fredric Cooper's Tipica Orchestra, in which the clarinettist was the distinguished classical player, Jack Brymer, who apparently loved doing *MWYW*. Gerald also played for Bernard Monshin, Anton, Ralph Elman, David Java, Marcel Gardner, Frank Baron, George Scott-Wood, Ronald Hanmer, Harry Davidson, Henry Krein's Montmartre Players, Bryan Smith and Jack Salisbury (for *Grand Hotel*). If that wasn't enough, he sometimes deputised in the orchestras of Sydney Thompson, Sidney Bowman, Troise, Primo Scala, Mantovani, Ray Martin and Frank Chacksfield, occasionally appearing with Phil Green, Norrie Paramor, Philip Martell, Matyas Seiber, Ron Goodwin, Peter Knight and Cyril Ornadel.

He played the piano at many American Air Force bases accompanying Roy Castle, Tommy Cooper and Bob Monkhouse. He fronted dance bands at dinner/dances after film premieres and acted as British adjudicator at world accordion championships around Europe.

The Gerald Crossman Players were heard for the last time in October 1966. Apart from one 15-minute solo interlude in 1978, Gerald has not broadcast in his own name since the sixties – a time when the BBC's axe fell upon so many long-standing broadcasters.

With the demise of radio work, Gerald spent nine years during the seventies regularly playing on P&O cruises. He also provided the accompaniment for a season of silent films at the Academy Cinema in Oxford Street and, in the 1980s, he was resident pianist at the Ritz Hotel.

In later years, Gerald has had the opportunity to entertain at Senior Citizens' Friendship Clubs, hospitals and hospices, assisted by his wife Miriam (to whom he has been happily married since 1968) with her humorous monologues.

During his long professional career Gerald has met and accompanied such notable performers as Marlene Dietrich, Sir Ralph Richardson, Sir Harry Secombe, Jack Hawkins and Charlie Chaplin. Indeed, his accordion can be heard in the sound version of Chaplin's *The Pilgrim*.

(I am indebted to Gerald Crossman for providing me with copious notes on his career, parts of which have been quoted verbatim).

Music While You Work at 10.30 a.m. on 2nd October 1961
Played by The Gerald Crossman Players

Calling All workers (Sig)	Coates
Ici On Parle Francais	Scott-Wood
What Do You Want?	Vandyke
Bonita	Steele
Annie Laurie	arr. Crossman
Tanto Gusto	Crossman
Fancy Free	Norman
Zaragosa	Baynes
Dublin Delight	Richardson

The Yodelling Mountaineer	Rogez
Selection from the film *Gigi*	Lowe
Calling All workers (Sig)	Coates

HENRY CROUDSON

Henry Croudson was born in Leeds on 13th November 1898. Upon leaving school, he became a clerk in the local branch of the Midland Bank. At the same time he served as deputy organist at St Chad's Church in Leeds.

In 1925, he decided that banking was not for him and went into music full-time, becoming organist at the local Majestic Cinema, playing for silent movies. He moved to the newly-opened Paramount Theatre in 1932 and commenced broadcasting in 1934, initially as a pianist. In 1935, he transferred to Manchester's Paramount Theatre and, in the same year, formed an Accordion Band comprising of unemployed musicians which he also used for broadcasting. It was in Manchester that he made most of his 78 rpm records on the Regal-Zonophone label, some of which had vocals by Ken Beaumont, who was subsequently to become a bandleader.

During the next few years, Henry Croudson had further moves, first to Birkenhead and then to Bedford. He also broadcast on the original BBC Theatre Organ prior to its destruction by enemy action early in the war. He was one of many cinema organists to contribute to *Music While You Work* in its early years. However, when his home in Merseyside was also destroyed by enemy action, he decided to give up the organ and move back to his home town of Leeds. There he became a publican at the Ship Inn at Briggate, very close to the Paramount Theatre, which, in common with other provincial Paramounts had now become the Odeon. It was not long before he was coaxed by the Odeon management into playing again for them.

After the war, Henry moved south, playing and broadcasting from the organs of many of the major cinemas in the London area, including the Gaumont-Haymarket, The State-Kilburn, The Dominion-Tottenham Court Road, as well as the second BBC Theatre Organ.

In the early fifties, he formed an orchestra for broadcasting (which he led from the electronic organ) called Strings in Rhythm, specialising, as the title implied, in modern rhythmic light music or, as Henry Croudson put it, 'light music with a beat'. This orchestra played regularly on *Music While You Work* throughout the fifties, as well as appearing on *Bright and Early, Morning Music* and other light music programmes.

With declining health, in 1959 Henry decided to give up regular cinema organ recitals and reverted to his occupation of publican, this time at the Red Lion in Nazeing, Essex. He took with him his Selmer Electronic Organ, with which he entertained the customers!

In common with many cinema organists, Henry Croudson was a prolific light music composer, his compositions including *Little Boy Blue, Piccadilly Promenade* and *Up North.*

The Strings in Rhythm played on *MWYW* until 1960, after which time Henry Croudson was not heard on the air, apart from a brief appearance in Robin Richmond's programme *The Organist Entertains* in 1971. Henry died on 30th November 1971, aged 73.

Music While You Work at 3.45 p.m. on 16th February 1960
Played by Henry Croudson and his Strings in Rhythm

Calling All workers (Sig)	Coates
Spanish Gypsy Dance	Marquina
Scotch And Chaser	Croudson
Medley:	
Alexander's Ragtime Band	Berlin
I Bring a Love Song	Romberg
Avalon	Rose
When Somebody Thinks You're Wonderful	Woods
When You're Smiling	Fisher/Shay
Pieremont Waltz	Green
Marigold	Mayerl
Pickin' A Chicken	Bernfield
Destiny Waltz	Baynes
Selection: *Gaytime*	Gay
Love Makes the World Go Round	
My Thanks to You	
You've Done Something to My Heart	
Let the People Sing	

Espanolita	Mondez
Unforgettable	Gordon
A Rose in Granada	Hartley
Love's Last Word is Spoken	Bixio
Roulette	Stanford
Margie	Conrad/Robinson
Trudie	Henderson
Brazilian Fiddler	Abreu
Lingering Lovers	Goodwin
Savoy Community Medley:	arr. Somers
There's a Tavern in The Town	
Who Killed Cock Robin	
Come Landlord fill the Flowing Bowl	
Some Folks Do	
John Brown's Body	
When Johnny Comes Marching Home	
For He's a Jolly Good Fellow	
Calling All workers (Sig)	Coates

SIDNEY DAVEY

Sidney Davey was born in London on 30th December 1903. His first associations with radio were in 1931 when he was working with Alfred Van Dam as pianist and arranger, later joining the Commodore Grand Orchestra under Harry Davidson. He became well-known to radio listeners in the thirties and forties playing duets with fellow pianist Arthur Dulay, who some may remember for his Cameo Orchestra.

Sidney Davey and his Players emerged in 1939, originally as a nine-piece combination specialising in light novelty numbers contrasted with popular ballads. It was essentially a salon orchestra, comprising strings, woodwind and piano. Whilst Sidney Davey conducted his Players (as opposed to directing them from the piano), he did, nevertheless, sometimes join in on second piano. This practice ceased, however, following producer reports that 'when a conductor leaves his post to play an instrument, the orchestral balance suffers and the additional colour of a second piano could be dispensed with'. It is not widely known that Sidney Davey was also an accordionist and even broadcast in that capacity as a soloist. It is, therefore, not surprising that he subsequently included this instrument in the Players, together with guitar and percussion to suit the changing styles of light music over the years.

Sidney Davey was one of the first contributors to *Music While You Work* and his ensemble provided 222 programmes in the series. During an orchestral musicians' strike in 1948 he even did one edition without the Players, simply giving a two-piano recital with the aforementioned Arthur Dulay! Other programmes featuring Sidney Davey and his Players included *Bright and Early, Morning Music, Music Box, Music All The Way, Elevenses, Uninterrupted Music* and many untitled programmes for which, in those days, the name of the orchestra was often considered sufficient.

Sidney was a versatile musician, not only arranging most of the music for his own ensemble, but also for other broadcasting orchestras. As a pianist, he played in every style from jazz to gypsy and acted as accompanist in the classical world, as well as doing cabaret work. If this wasn't enough, he broadcast regularly with Jack Mandel and the Banjoliers, Ralph Elman and his Bohemian Players and Anton and his Orchestra, his distinctive style of piano links in *MWYW* immediately identifying him.

Unlike so many of his fellow conductors, Sidney's broadcasting career did not come to a grinding halt when *MWYW* was axed. It was really a case of his being in the right place at the right time. For many years he had been pianist and arranger with Harry Davidson and his Orchestra, performing with them on hundreds of editions of *Those Were The Days* – the long-running old-time dance music programme which was started during the war and continued until the mid-seventies. As deputy conductor of the orchestra it was a logical development that, with the retirement of Harry Davidson in 1966, he should be invited to take over the series. Sidney had often deputised for Davidson, particularly in the latter years when Davidson's health was failing, and it would have been an easy task for him to take over the orchestra in its existing form, using its own repertoire, especially as much of it had been arranged by Sidney Davey anyway.

Sidney, however, did not choose the easy option and decided to form an entirely new orchestra of 25 players, with less emphasis on brass. Indeed his brass section consisted exclusively of Stan Newsome on trumpet. The BBC asked Sidney to include more 'popular standards' than formerly, but he continued to use adaptations of some of the light music arrangements which he had produced for the Players, providing that they fitted the rhythm of the dance in question. So a novelty number such as *The Portuguese Washerwoman* could quite easily be used as a *Mayfair Quickstep*. Whereas other maestros of 'old-time', such as Sidney Bowman, had adjusted the tempos of pieces to suit the dances in question, Sidney Davey avoided this by selecting only pieces that were intended to be played at the tempo of the dance being performed.

For the next ten years Sidney Davey broadcast regularly in *Those Were The Days* until, in 1976 with his wife's health failing, he decided to call it a day and informed the BBC of his intention to retire.

Sidney Davey was a courteous and friendly man who always felt that his music should 'entertain not educate'. Nevertheless, his music was always of good quality and quite delightful to hear. He died in August 1986 at the age of 82.

Music While You Work at 3.31 p.m. on 2nd June 1966
Played by Sidney Davey and his Players

Calling All Workers (Sig)	Coates
Paris Bonjour	Vallez
Bessie Larkin	Agoult
Charlie Girl	Heneker/Taylor
Chicolino	Marland
Francesco	Galbraith
Jangle Bells	Baynes
Will You Remember	Romberg
Snowman's Land	Vogel
Make the World Go Away	Cochran
Tango Negre	Phillips
Summer Holiday	Welch
Primero	Malando
To Each His Own	Evans
The Belle of Brazil	Rubach
The White Hills of Finland	Wiberg
Portuguese Washerwoman	Popp

Lavender Blue	Daniel
Square Dance Medley:	arr. Davey
Arkansas Traveller	
Turkey in the Straw	
Spitfire Reel	
Calling All Workers (Sig)	Coates

SYD DEAN

Syd Dean was born on 4th June 1907 in the village of Wellesbourne near Stratford-upon-Avon. He took up the piano at the age of ten, becoming proficient within a few years. After leaving school he worked for a while with his motor mechanic father, but his heart was in dance music and, determined to join the music profession, he answered an advertisement in *The Era* in 1926 for a pit orchestra pianist at the Boscombe Hippodrome. To his surprise, the 'pit orchestra' turned out to be a 25-piece section of the Bournemouth Municipal Orchestra directed by Dan Godfrey.

This, however, was not the area of music in which he was most interested, so he took a job with a dance band led by John Birmingham (who was later to die after falling from the balcony of his Earls Court flat). After a spell with a dance band in North Wales, Syd took the opportunity to play a season in a ballroom in Jersey where, for the first time, he realised his ambition to lead his own band. This band included alto-sax player John McCormack, who went on to lead his own band and appeared on *MWYW* from the Midlands. After two seasons Syd moved to a night club in Glasgow but, preferring ballroom work, accepted an offer at the Leicester Palais in 1934.

It seems that in those distant days nobody stayed anywhere for long and Syd was soon off to Toni's Ballroom in Birmingham, switching to the New Plaza Ballroom, Derby, in 1935 for a three year stay. He broadcast for the first time in 1936 as solo pianist in the series *Keyboard Cavalcade*. His success attracted the attention of the Music Corporation of America, which put him into Madame Tussauds,

111

London – no, not as a waxwork! Over the next two years he played at the Café Normandie (Cliftonville), the Rector's Club (opposite Jack Jackson) and then at the famous Kit-Kat Club.

A big break came in 1940 when Syd Dean not only had his first band broadcast but was invited to replace Joe Loss at the Astoria, Charing Cross Road, where his nine-piece band played opposite Jack White – already an established broadcaster. Unfortunately, war intervened and Syd spent the next four years in the RAF. Although he was able to form a small band at Bomber Command in Nottingham, he ended up on a small island in the Outer Hebrides (but without eight gramophone records!).

Although Gaumont-British (who owned the Astoria) had promised Syd his job back after the war, contractual difficulties with the band already playing there made this impossible. So, Syd Dean was sent to the Regent Ballroom, Brighton, with a 15-piece band which was a tremendous success and very popular with the dancers. He resumed broadcasting and, in 1946, did the first of his 177 *Music While You Work* broadcasts. Over the years, Syd's broadcasts (some of them from the Regent) brought several singers to fame, notably Jill Day, Dick Francis and Rita Williams. Syd also came across a vivacious young singer who impressed him to the extent that he arranged for her to be auditioned at the BBC. The young woman failed the audition and Syd, thinking that his judgement must have been in error, let her go. He must have kicked himself when she topped the Hit Parade, her name was Alma Cogan!

Syd Dean's band was so popular in Brighton that when he decided to leave in 1959, the local evening paper described him as a 'marvellous unofficial ambassador for Brighton, having publicised the resort in many ways'. He left as a result of a tempting offer from the Orchid Ballroom in Purley, but in the event only had a short stay there before moving on again!

During the following year, he opened at the newly-built Gaumont State Ballroom in Kilburn, where he fronted a nine-piece band consisting of five saxes, trumpet, piano, bass and drums. In 1962 he returned to the Astoria for a year, after which he went back to the Regent. In 1966 it was decided to demolish the Regent Ballroom, so Syd had to move down the road to the Top Rank Suite, where he stayed for a further six years.

Syd Dean specialised in 'straight' ballroom music, but, in common with other bandleaders, he had to make adjustments when fashions

112

changed – he even included a guitar in his band from 1963! Although a prolific broadcaster, Syd Dean and his Band only made a handful of records (mostly 78s), usually backing The Stargazers.

Although Syd stayed at the Top Rank Ballroom until 1972, he was finding that teenagers didn't want his music, so he left to go freelance. He said at the time: 'I'm glad to get out of it. They just don't want a band. We tried to please them but all they want are hit records'.

Syd Dean carried on with appearances and concerts for many years and ran successful dances at Hove's King Alfred Ballroom and the Corn Exchange and the Dome in Brighton. Despite his declining health he continued to do the occasional private function.

The late Chris Hayes, a musical journalist who, many years ago, provided me with much of the information in this profile, interviewed Syd in 1988, when he was planning a big band show at the Hotel Metropole, Brighton. Chris described Syd Dean as a 'dapper and handsome man, with a neat moustache and a ready smile. He possessed a smooth and pleasant personality which endeared him to people. He was genial and gracious without pomposity or conceit.' There couldn't be a more fitting epitaph!

Syd Dean died on 1st August 1993, aged 86.

Music While You Work at 10.31 a.m. on 13th September 1963
Played by Syd Dean and his Band

Calling All Workers (Sig)	Coates
Let's Face the Music and Dance	Berlin
Stepping Out With My Baby	Berlin
It's a Lovely Day Today	Berlin
The Good Life	Distel
Acapulco 1922	Allan
I remember April	Johnston
Teach Me Tonight	Chan
Souvenir D'Italie	Sigman
Rip Van Winkle	Race
I'm Confessing	Dougherty
Truckin'	Bloom
Deed I Do	Rose
You Forgot Your Gloves	Lehak
The Legion's Last Patrol	Rosso
I Love You and Don't You Forget It	Mancini

Easier Said Than Done	Linton
I'll Be Around	Wilder
These Foolish Things	Strachey
That Was the Week That Was	Grainer

JACK DORSEY

Jack Dorsey, or to give him his real name, Handel Huckridge, was born in Wrexham, North Wales. Educated at Hammersmith Central School and the Song School, Westminster Abbey, where he was a chorister, he studied the trumpet with Ernest Hall at the Royal College of Music and George Eskdale at the Royal Academy of Music. He also studied composition and orchestration with the distinguished Dr Gordon Jacob and harmony and counterpoint with Dr W.S. Lloyd-Webber.

After leaving school he joined the Band of the Grenadier Guards, where he played cornet and trumpet. He also played in theatre orchestras for shows such as *Kismet* and *The King and I*. He even had a spell playing trumpet for Bert Ambrose, and a stint with the Crazy Gang as musician and deputy conductor.

To the general public, however, Jack is best known as a musical director. In 1961 he formed a band to play at the Rank Organisation's Astoria Dance Salon in London. When he first arrived, he was surprised to find notices advertising 'Jack Dorsey and his Orchestra'. 'I am the new bandleader here, who's this Jack Dorsey?' he enquired. 'You are!' he was told. It would appear that the management did not feel that the name Handel Huckridge was very commercial, therefore they found a name that was synonymous with dance band music. Thus Handel Huckridge became Jack Dorsey, which he remains to this day, although he still answers to both names, and others that are unrepeatable (his words, not mine!).

In January 1962, Jack's energetic-sounding band, which he led on trumpet, made the first of its 37 appearances in *Music While You*

114

Work. (Jack remembers that his first encounter with *MWYW* was just after the war, when his father, also a musician, took him to the studio to attend broadcasts by Debroy Somers and his Band.) Early in 1963, the Rank Organisation Management gave Jack the opportunity to create a new 17-piece orchestra, possibly the largest band to hold a ballroom residency. It wasn't long before it was being heralded as the finest band in the country. Writing in the *London Evening News* about one of the band's television appearances, the well-known television critic James Green stated: 'This band is going to be very very big in popular music'.

As the new band was a replacement for the old, it was only a matter of time before its power-house sound was introduced to *Music While You Work*. The big band was an immediate hit on *MWYW*, although Jack's fine swinging arrangements did not initially meet with the approval of the powers that be, because some of his ideas were in contravention of the guidelines for the show – namely, that melodies should be clearly defined without frills. When Jack then arranged a jazzy version of *Calling All Workers* to close each programme, BBC officials were not pleased, to say the least, as they were very particular about the signature tune being played 'straight'. Actually, their view was somewhat hypocritical as Lou Preager had used an elaborate 'fanfare' arrangement of the tune for years. Anyway, the BBC officials backed down when Jack drew their attention to the band's high ratings.

Although Jack continued with the band for some years, it was never

Jack Dorsey and his Orchestra

115

his intention to be a palais bandleader for the rest of his life and he eventually diversified, turning his attention to the production side of the recording industry. He became A and R Manager for EMI and Pye, but fronted his own band for a number of long-playing records. Subsequently he began a 25-year association with the well-known recording orchestra *The 101 Strings*, becoming their conductor/producer/arranger as well as composing many of the pieces which they recorded. Jack also fronted his own Rose of Romance Orchestra for a series of long-Playing albums of romantic music.

When *Music While You Work* was revived for a week in 1982 as part of the BBC's 60th Anniversary celebrations, Jack Dorsey and his Orchestra were invited to contribute. The session was a veritable who's who of the dance band world!

Jack Dorsey still lives, as he has done for many years, on the South Coast in Hove.

Music While You Work at 3.31 p.m. on 22nd March 1965
Played by Jack Dorsey and his Orchestra

Calling All Workers (Sig)	Coates
Colonel Bogey	Alford
A Spoonful of Sugar	Sherman
Medley:	Strouse
Put on a Happy Face	
Kids	
A Lot of Living to Do	
March of the Gonks	Dorsey
I'll Never Find Another You	Springfield
Six-Two-Five Special	Hill
Harlem Nocturne	Hagen
Medley: *My Fair Lady*	Loewe
I'm Getting Married in the Morning	
On the Street Where You Live	
I Could Have Danced All Night	
Soulsville	Richardson
Dear Heart	Mancini
Bonanza	Livingstone
Making Whoopee	Donaldson
Soul Bossa Nova	Jones
Girls That Boys Dream About	Grainer

In the Meantime	Burch
I apologise	Hoffman
Kookie	Strevens
Medley:	
Hometown	Carr
*Wotche*r	Chevalier
Sally	Leon
Medley:	
Deed I Do	Hirsch
Truckin'	Bloom
Ida	Leonard
If You Knew Susie	De Sylva
Calling All Workers (Sig)	Coates

RALPH ELMAN

Ralph Elman and his Bohemian Players will certainly register with many older readers but sadly, because they were essentially a broadcasting orchestra, rarely venturing into the recording studio, they are unknown to the present generation and will eventually be no more than a name in old editions of the *Radio Times*. So, what better reason could there be for placing Ralph Elman and his Bohemian Players on permanent record in this book?

Raphael Elman, to give him his real name, was born on 2nd December 1907 in Mile End, London. His father, Philip, hailed from Kiev in Ukraine and was a violinist in the days of the silent cinema. Ralph's mother, Moscow-born Annie Odinoff, was a rabbi who went to the docks to receive refugees from the pogroms in Russia. Among those refugees was Ralph's father, Philip Elman, whose brother was the distinguished, and ultimately world famous violinist, Mischa Elman. With such a celebrated uncle it was hardly surprising that Ralph should take up the violin. Ralph's brother Henry became a well-known cellist.

Ralph Elman made his first broadcast with his Bohemian Players in

117

1943 and, by the end of the war, had become a regular contributor to light music broadcasts on radio. His orchestra of 14 players was a combination of strings, woodwind, trumpet, accordion, piano, electric guitar and percussion. He also broadcast as Ralph Elman and his Tzigane Orchestra. His obvious affinity for gypsy music inspired him to compose many pieces in this idiom, some written under the pen-name of Raphael such as: *Romantic Gypsies, Wild Gypsy, Laughter and Tears, Wandering Gypsies,* and most famous of all, *Gypsy Fiddler,* which Ralph regularly included in his broadcasts, as did other orchestras.

Ralph Elman and his Bohemian Players were heard in many different series over the years, including *Bright and Early, Morning Music, Café on The Corner,* various announced, untitled programmes and, of course, *Music While You Work* for which they performed 174 editions over 18 years. Despite the orchestra's title, the Bohemian Players performed a wide range of British and Continental light music with the occasional 'Romany' item.

In the late fifties, Ralph also led a sextet for a number of broadcasts. His ensembles existed essentially for radio and, in common with so many speciality orchestras, were unceremoniously axed in the mid-sixties. The Bohemian Players' final broadcast was in a series called *Swing Into Summer,* a compilation type of programme which replaced the afternoon edition of *MWYW* in 1966.

Being a much respected musician, Ralph Elman wasn't only involved with his own orchestra; he played in many others and led the orchestras of Isy Geiger, Marcel Gardner, Harry Davidson and Hugh James. In fact, Hugh James told me that he 'admired Ralph as a musician and as a man', commending his beautiful plaintive tone, which, he said, was 'so typical of someone of his background'.

In those far off days when small light orchestras were heard every day on the radio, conductors often featured compositions by their fellow bandleaders, usually on a reciprocal basis. During the sixties Ralph made a point of including, in every programme, a composition by Ron Goodwin, whose orchestra he just happened to lead and whose long playing records sometimes featured Ralph and his works.

Although Ralph Elman was not known as a recording artist, he apparently made a few 78s, although I've never come across any. In 1971, however, in what was probably one of Ralph's last professional assignments, he and his orchestra made a long-playing record of gypsy pieces, including some of his own compositions, on the Polydor label.

118

Ralph Elman spent his last years in Spain, where he died from lung cancer on 14th January 1983 whilst listening to a record of *Tzigane* by Ravel played by Heifetz.

Music While You Work at 3.31 p.m. on 6th October 1964
Played by Ralph Elman and his Bohemian Players

Calling All Workers (Sig)	Coates
Banda Espanola	Roca
Brise de Paris	Delroy
Rhumbalinda	Jupp
Man Who Plays the Mandolino	Fancuilla
This is My Prayer	Nisa
Bond Street Rag	Holland
Jay Walker	Grew
Nightingale Song	Zeller
The Red Cloak	Goodwin
Exotica	Couzens
Carriage and Pair	Frankel
Caracas	Monshin
Toytown Trumpeters	Davies
Little Venice	Busby
Wedding Dance	Newman
Carlos' Theme	Slaney
Magyar Memories	Raphael
Calling All Workers (Sig)	Coates

LIONEL FALKMAN

Lionel Falkman gave his first broadcast on 14th April 1923 from Cardiff, where he was Musical Director of the Capitol Cinema. His was the first cinema orchestra to broadcast. Like many musicians of his generation, he had gained his early experience playing for silent films, having received his musical education at the Royal College of Music and becoming an accomplished violinist. Even at the age of 12 he was leading a music hall orchestra in Abertillery, confident that as long as he stayed there he wouldn't be sent to follow his father and work in the mines. At 16 he was playing the fiddle in the Covent Garden Orchestra under Hans Richter, was first violin in the New Symphony Orchestra under Sir Landon Ronald and first violin in the Royal Philharmonic Society Orchestra. Over the next few years, he tried his hand at various types of music and formed the Newport (Mon) College of Music, at the same time working as Director of Music at the Lyceum Theatre, Newport. He later gave up the college and formed his own orchestra at a cinema in Reading, moving, in the early twenties, to the Capitol Cinema in Cardiff, where he was destined to spend the next ten years.

In the early thirties, Lionel became conductor of the Paramount Theatre Orchestra in Manchester and, from 1932 for around four years, broadcast every Friday afternoon at 2.00 p.m. on the London Regional Service. His leader was the well-known Reginald Stead and his percussionist was Thomas Kaye.

It was in the mid-thirties that Lionel formed the combination for which he is best remembered by radio listeners – Falkman and his Apache Band. Initially a septet, this orchestra soon grew to 12 players. They played in an authentic Parisian style and, not surprisingly, French music dominated their repertoire. When playing programmes requiring a wider range of light music, however, they would include pieces such as *Down South* (Myddleton), *Belle of the Ball* (Anderson), and selections from shows and films such as *Belle of New York* and *Easter Parade*.

In addition to broadcasting, in the late thirties, Falkman and his

Apache Band were to be found playing at the Lyons' Corner House, Oxford Street, London (The Brasserie).

On 16th October 1940, the Apache Band made the first of their 142 appearances in *Music While You Work,* when it was their practice to link the items with a few bars of their signature tune, which, appropriately, was *The Apache Dance* by Offenbach, played on the celeste.

In later years the Apache Band was led by Sidney Bowman and included such famous names as Bernard Monshin and Jacques Vallez, all *MWYW* bandleaders. Jacques Vallez was a Professor of Music and an accomplished cellist. He was regularly featured as soloist with the orchestra – but on the musical saw!

By way of a second string to his bow, Lionel Falkman formed another orchestra for broadcasting in the fifties. This was called The Troubadours and consisted of 16 musicians playing a wide range of British and Continental light music. Although often used in late-night programmes, it frequently appeared in *Morning Music* as well as *Music While You Work.*

The last few years of Falkman's broadcasting career were marred by illness. It was during this time that Sidney Bowman stepped in to conduct when necessary. Falkman, however, always managed to bounce back. At the close of *Music While You Work* on Saturday 13th April 1963 the announcer said 'Tomorrow, Lionel Falkman celebrates the fortieth anniversary of his first broadcast on April 14th 1923'. It was fortunate that this announcement was made because it turned out to be Falkman's last programme. He died a few weeks later.

Music While You Work at 10.31 a.m. on 13th April 1963
Played by Falkman and his Apache Band

Calling All Workers (Sig)	Coates
Marche Lorraine	Ganne
Estudiantina	Waldteufel
Blue Sapphire	Monshin
Boulevards de Paris	Michael
Valse du Diable	Basin
Heidelberg Polka	Watters
La Ronde	Straus
Sucu Sucu	Rojaz
Russian Salad	Leach

Selection from *Easter Parade*	Berlin
La Mattchiche	Borel-Clerc
Calling All Workers (Sig)	Coates

Music While You Work at 10.31 a.m. on 29th May 1958
Played by The Troubadours directed by Lionel Falkman

Calling All Workers (Sig)	Coates
Paso Bolero	Hanmer
The Merry Widow Waltz	Lehar
Music Box Polka	Binge
Portuguese Party	Vinter
Juliette	Mirros
A La Can Can	Offenbach
Selection from *Where's Charley*	Loesser
The Whistling Boy	Stewart
The Pansy	Rendine
Calling All Workers (Sig)	Coates

MICHAEL FREEDMAN

Michael Freedman was born on 31st August 1911. He took an early interest in music, playing the violin at the age of seven. At 16, he was accepting professional engagements in the West End of London.

During the Second World War he served in the Royal Air Force but, upon demobilisation, formed a ten-piece orchestra for broadcasting. This was promptly rejected by Kenneth Sydney Baynes, the man responsible at the time for *Music While You Work* and other light music programmes.

In 1947, Michael Freedman joined the Philharmonia Orchestra as a viola player and in this capacity gained immeasurable experience playing under such famous conductors as Toscanini, Beecham, Von Karajan etc. He also assisted with Walter Legge's recordings at the Kingsway Hall. Light music had become a side-line, but he again auditioned for broadcasting in 1949, this time with a 15-piece orchestra, comprising strings, woodwind, percussion and, as a nucleus, the two pianos of Edward Rubach and Robert Docker. The audition was successful and Michael Freedman and his Orchestra gave their first broadcast on 21st December 1949. For the next 17 years he broadcast regularly on the radio in such programmes as *Music for the Housewife, Morning Music, Music While You Work* (194 editions), *Continuous Performance, Music Matinee, At the Close of Day, Home To Music, Sunday Morning Melody* and, in 1961, *Strings By Starlight* – featuring the Stella Strings.

During the fifties, Michael Freedman made many light orchestral records on the Oriole label, as well as classical recordings with the London Metropolis Symphony Orchestra, whose players were largely recruited from the Philharmonia Orchestra. With this combination Michael recorded Beethoven's 5th Symphony, *Scheherazade, The Force of Destiny Overture, The Nutcracker Suite* and the *1812 Overture* amongst others. He also made recordings with the Celebrity Concert Orchestra and the Cosmopolitan Orchestra and gave concerts with the New Concert Orchestra.

An excellent LP appeared on the Oriole label made by the Michael Freedman Ladies' Orchestra, which he formed in 1956. This orchestra, led by the famous Tessa Robbins (a virtuoso soloist in her own right), gave eight radio broadcasts in 1957 with a concert at the Royal Festival Hall in December of that year. In 1958 they appeared on television on eight occasions and many will recollect their appearances in a series of 'spectaculars' entitled *The Big Parade*, in which they shared the programme with top military bands.

Apart from the Ladies' Orchestra, Michael Freedman's main broadcasting activities centred around his original light orchestra. His programmes were bright and tuneful, his motto being 'not too high for the low-brow and not too low for the high-brow'.

Although continuing to play for the Philharmonia Orchestra for some years, Michael Freedman later confined himself to conducting his orchestra, so it must have come as quite a shock when his orchestra was suddenly dropped from broadcasting in the mid-sixties, a fate which befell many orchestras at this time. Not that this was of much comfort to Michael Freedman, who now found work in the music business difficult to come by. In the late sixties, he decided to leave the music profession and start a new career as a London taxi driver. He spent hundreds of hours cycling the streets of London, memorising the names of the streets and acquiring what is known in the trade as 'The

Knowledge'. Whether the effort he put into this new career affected his health is a matter for speculation but, sad to relate, he died of cancer during the seventies after a long illness.

Music While You Work at 3.31 p.m. on 26th June 1966
Played by Michael Freedman and his Orchestra

Calling All Workers (Sig)	Coates
Frankfurt Polka	Dexter
Louissette	Vallez
Samba Rag	Lawrenson
The Maigret Theme	Grainer
Toy Town Trumpeters	Davies
Medley:	arr. Fones
It's a Hap Hap Happy Day	Timburg/Sharples
June in January	Robin/Rainer
Buttons and Bows	Livingstone/Evans
Moonlight Becomes You	Burke/Van Heuson
Tangerine	Mercer
Beyond the Blue Horizon	Harling
Aparacida	Williams
Blue Tango	Anderson
Spring Double	Marland
Nights of Gladness	Ancliffe
Ca C'est Paris	Padilla
Cuban Holiday	Phillips
Medley:	arr. Roy Green
La Ronde	Straus
Pennies from Heaven	Johnson
Dream Lover	Schertzinger
Amapola	Lacalle
Falling in Love Again	Hollonder
Great Day	Youmans
Calling All Workers (Sig)	Coates

MARCEL GARDNER

Marcel Gardner, born in the Channel Islands in 1903, was of Belgian ancestry. For many years he lived in my home town of Bromley in Kent.

He received his musical training at the Royal Conservatoire of Music, Liège in Belgium where he won first prize for violin and chamber music. He was also a member of the Conservatoire Symphony Orchestra. Over the years he was associated with many well-known recording and broadcasting orchestras, amongst which were Geraldo's orchestra and Ernest Leggett's Continental Players. At various times Marcel was also a member of the orchestras of Albert Sandler, Leslie Jeffries and Mantovani (who was then playing at the Carlton Hotel). Marcel Gardner was no stranger to the theatre; the revival of *Me and My Girl* in the eighties reminds me of the fact that he was a one-time Musical Director of the original show, starring Lupino Lane.

It was in 1947 that Marcel Gardner formed his Serenade Orchestra for broadcasting. It consisted of 11 players and, in the early fifties, was made up of the following musicians: Marcel Gardner (conductor and violin), Ralph Elman (leader), Michael Spivakovsky and Jack Greenstone (violins), David Bellman (viola), Henry Elman (cello), Jack Collier (bass), Gerald Crossman (accordion), Edward Rubach and Gordon Rodda (two pianos) and William Bradshaw (tuned percussion) – quite an impressive list of musicians, five of whom were musical directors of other broadcasting combinations. Gerald Crossman recalls that Marcel Gardner really enjoyed himself when conducting his orchestra. Apparently, unbeknown to listeners, when playing an Irish jig he would put his arms to his sides and dance on his rostrum!

Marcel Gardner's Serenade Orchestra participated in a variety of light music radio shows, including *Bright and Early, Morning Music, Continental Serenade* and *Music While You Work* to which they contributed 152 programmes. By the mid-sixties *MWYW* was practically the only remaining programme in which it was possible to hear orchestras of this type.

Despite its title, Marcel Gardner and his Serenade Orchestra played a wide range of light music and by the early fifties were boasting a repertoire of 575 pieces.

Whereas most orchestra leaders made use of professional arrangers, often in the employ of the publishers, Marcel Gardner preferred to do his own arranging. It is perhaps not well known that he made a published arrangement of the novelty *Nola* by Felix Arndt.

During the mid-fifties, BBC programme reports commented on the fact that, despite the title of the orchestra, Marcel Gardner's programmes did not appear to contain sufficient 'serenades' to justify the title! Whether or not they said anything to Gardner is not known, but the word 'serenade' ceased to be used in the title of the orchestra thereafter.

Marcel Gardner continued to broadcast regularly until the mid-sixties but, in common with so many other broadcasting combinations, his orchestra was not used after the demise of *Music While You Work*, the BBC was seemingly of the opinion that these little orchestras were 'dated'. I doubt if the feedback from listeners suggested anything of the sort. What I do know is that many listeners kept recordings which they had made of such orchestras (albeit illicitly in those days) and even today they sound delightful and not in the least dated. I am only sorry that today's young people do not have the opportunity to grow up with such lovely music!

Music While You Work at 3.45 p.m. on 16th March 1955
Played by Marcel Gardner and his Serenade Orchestra

Calling All Workers (Sig)	Coates
Viva Villa	Fonora
Dance in the Twilight	Coates
Rue de la Paix	Johnston
Serenatella	Margutti
Dance of the Three Old Maids	Porter-Brown
Kaleidoscope	King Palmer
Marechiare	Tosti
Golden Tango	Silvester
Serenata	Anderson
Selection from *White Christmas*	Berlin
Calling All Workers (Sig)	Coates

ISY GEIGER

It is perhaps surprising that Isy Geiger should have commenced broadcasting in this country at the age of 65, even more so is the fact that nearly 25 years later he was still giving public concerts; but Isy Geiger was no ordinary musician.

He was born of a family of musicians on 20th November 1886, in Yarowslav. After early tuition from his father, he continued his studies in Berlin and joined the Berlin State Opera Orchestra prior to the First World War. Around 1920, he became leader (concertmaster) of the orchestra at the Viennese Carl Theatre, where many successful Viennese operettas had received their first performances. He later settled in Vienna, where he formed his first orchestra, becoming one of Vienna Radio's most frequent and popular broadcasters. Many of his broadcasts were relayed to foreign radio stations. His success led to his receiving an exclusive contract to the Colombia Gramophone Company in Vienna (not to be confused with the Columbia record company in Britain and America).

The Italian Broadcasting Company offered him an orchestra of 30 music professors, their task being to reorganise the broadcasting of light music from their stations at Turin, Milan and Rome.

One day, when Isy was playing a Franz Lehar selection in a café, he noticed that the composer himself was sitting in the audience! Lehar called him over and suggested certain modifications to the arrangement. These were implemented and Isy was later presented with a photograph bearing the inscription: 'To Isy Geiger, the distinguished interpreter of my compositions, full of heart and soul. In friendship, Franz Lehar'. Isy Geiger treasured this throughout his life, together with an autographed score with the message: 'To my dear friend Isy Geiger, in thankful appreciation of the outstanding performances of my compositions – Emmerich Kalman'.

In March 1938, following the *Anschluss* (Hitler's march on and annexation of Austria), Isy Geiger fled from Vienna to Poland and subsequently to Britain. Having narrowly escaped capture by a German soldier, by pretending to be a foreigner (he was an Austrian citizen), he was advised to leave the country immediately. The late

Hans Geiger, Isy's son, once told me that he vividly remembered that day and still had a mental picture of his father sitting on a chair in his kitchen trembling with fear.

Isy's cellist brother Joseph had been in Britain for some time and directed a small orchestra at London's Claridge's Hotel, from where he regularly broadcast as 'Geiger and his Orchestra', even doing some early *Music While You Work* programmes. It was Isy Geiger's greatest dream that he too would have a hotel residency, but this was not to be. He did audition at the Dorchester Hotel, but as a foreigner he was not permitted to work, at least, not at first. He secured a one-off broadcast in 1943, but according to Hans Geiger this was purely for overseas listening.

The next few years were somewhat barren for Isy Geiger. As a foreigner he was not permitted to join the Musicians' Union, but, as it was necessary to be a member in order to work with other musicians, he had to be content with a spell in music publishing. This must have been frustrating for such an active musician. After the ludicrous restrictions were lifted, he formed an orchestra, Isy Geiger and his Viennese Music, and auditioned for the BBC in 1951 at the age of 65! His first broadcast was a 45-minute slot on the Light Programme on Friday 7th September at 5.30 p.m. The 17 players included Ralph Elman, Michael Spivakovsky, Max Jaffa, Charles Vorsanger, Henry Elman, Louis Mordish and Robert Keys. The orchestra was paid £65 – in total, not each!

From there on, Isy Geiger broadcast regularly, sometimes in announced programmes with guest singers but also in *Morning Music* and *Music While You Work,* which he joined in 1956. He conducted 51 editions, playing everything from *Die Fledermaus* selections to Al Jolson hits. It was a characteristic of Isy Geiger to regard every job as the most important thing that he had ever done and, being something of a perfectionist, it was not surprising that some of his musicians found him a hard task-master.

Although he enjoyed everything he did, *MWYW* was not his favourite format. To Isy it seemed rather like 'working a treadmill', churning out one piece after another. The orchestra had a unique style and its interpretations of Viennese music had a certain authenticity, which was probably only to be expected from someone whom had spent much of his life in Vienna.

Although an excellent musician, Isy wasn't the easiest of conductors to follow. The fact that he never really mastered the English language didn't help either. His son Hans, who led the orchestra in later years, said that his father often infuriated him by assuming that just because he (Isy Geiger) had thought that a piece should be interpreted in a particular way, then the musicians would automatically think likewise!

Despite his musical prowess, Isy Geiger was less adept at timing his broadcasts, which frequently overran. Indeed, I think it can be said that he was so absorbed in his music that he was almost unaware of the passage of time. As already mentioned, believing that he was ahead of time, he once crept round the orchestra inserting an extra item into the musicians' pads. But just as he reached the back of the orchestra, the red light went out – the programme was finished!

In its later years, when *MWYW* was pre-recorded, it was often recorded the day before transmission and composer Cyril Watters once recalled an occasion when he received an anxious telephone call from Isy Geiger, imploring him not to listen to a broadcast which he had just recorded, in which he had included Cyril's award-winning *Willow Waltz*. Apparently he had speeded it up because the programme was in danger of overrunning, although he wished to assure Cyril that he would include it again in his next broadcast! This was typical of Isy Geiger, a gentle and kindly man (although this fact may not have always been apparent to musicians at rehearsals!). His pianist until 1963, the appropriately named Robert Keys, described him as 'a delightful character of a man with a heart of gold. Would that more of my MD's had been like him.'

Isy Geiger was a prolific composer and arranger. Amongst his works are *Schuhplattler, Carnival Galop, Vivat Polonia, Roumanian Gypsy Dances* and countless arrangements of pieces such as *Waltzing through Old Vienna, Gay Carnival* (a selection of Viennese galops and polkas etc.), *Tales of Offenbach* and *Tel Avivia* (a brilliant selection of Israeli folk songs). In addition to broadcasting, Isy gave countless public concerts. For many years he gave Sunday performances with his 25-piece Viennese Concert Orchestra at the magnificent Concert Pavilion in Battersea Park, although the repertoire was rather more classical than is usually heard on bandstand concerts.

He continued with these concerts long after his broadcasting career ended in the mid-sixties. I have vivid memories of a week of twice-daily concerts by Isy Geiger at Victoria Embankment Gardens, London. The orchestra was assembled on the large stage, when the dressing-room door opened and a small, frail and rather serious-looking man of 87 emerged, only able to shuffle very slowly to the rostrum. The limitations of age vanished, however, as soon as Isy Geiger lifted his baton. He was completely absorbed in the music he loved. Occasionally, he would grab a violin from the orchestra and play along with the music, such was his enthusiasm. When time ran out (he never completed his concerts!) the orchestra had to stop him because they wanted to go home. I spoke to him after one of these shows and he said: 'I would willingly play all night, if they let me. I love music so much!'

Isy Geiger worked almost until his death in February 1977 at the age of 90.

Music While You Work at 3.31 p.m. on 20th February 1964
Played by Isy Geiger and his Viennese Music

Calling All Workers (Sig)	Coates
Viennese Operetta Review	arr. Geiger
Ballet Music from _Faust_, Movements 1 & 7	Gounod
Threepenny Opera Theme	Weill
Ad Infinitum	Baynes
It Happened in Monterey	Jordan
Schuhplattler	Geiger
Medley:	arr. Geiger
Port-au-Prince	Wayne
In Chambre Separée	Heuberger
The Happy Wanderer	Moller
The Dragon Fly	Strauss
Swedish Polka	Ringstrand
El Gaucho	Lockyer
Richard Rodgers Medley:	arr. Geiger
June is Bustin' Out All Over	
A Wonderful Guy	
I Have Dreamed	
I Cain't Say No	
Shall We Dance?	
The Singer not the Song	Green
Carlos' Theme	Slaney
Musical Favourites:	arr. Geiger
Glamorous Night	Novello
I Want to be Happy	Youmans
Kiss Me	Coward

Dwarf Yodel & One Song	Churchill
Stout-Hearted Men	Romberg
Door of her Dreams/Rosemarie	Friml
Calling All Workers (Sig)	Coates

HUGH JAMES

Hugh Reginald Hay James started his musical career in 1912. Whilst attending school in the day time, he played second violin in the orchestras of the Castle Electric and Gaiety Theatres in Richmond, Surrey, during the evenings for 10/6d per week.

He joined the Army under age in 1916 and fought on the Western Front at Passchendaele and the Somme until he was discharged with shell shock in 1918. Hugh then commenced serious musical study with Ferdinand Weiss-Hill (one-time master of Albert Sammons) during which time he played at the Cinema House and Picture House in Oxford Street. In the early twenties he directed the Imperial Symphony Orchestra, which was an eight-piece theatre orchestra. He also held the position of Musical Director at Horn Lane Cinema in Acton. It was around this time that he began a life-long friendship with Arthur Anton, better known to radio listeners as 'Anton', although his real name was Arthur Sweeting. Hugh happily recalled their meetings for coffee in the Lyons' Corner House during intervals at their respective cinemas in the Notting Hill Gate area.

For five years Hugh was Musical Director at the Putney Hippodrome (a variety theatre turned cinema) where, in 1926, he directed the accompanying music for *The Merry Widow*.

It was in 1936 that Hugh James, then appearing at the Rex Cinema, Stratford, first auditioned for broadcasting, playing Herman Finck's *Last Dance of Summer* from the suite *My Lady Dragonfly*. Unfortunately, the audition was unsuccessful and, despite frequent requests, the BBC declined to give him another hearing.

Upon the outbreak of the Second World War in 1939, Hugh attempted to rejoin the Armed Forces but was rejected on medical grounds. So, in 1940 he became resident Musical Director of the Chelsea Palace Orchestra, a position which he was destined to hold for nearly eight years, playing for variety acts and giving an orchestral interlude in each show.

After the war, Hugh James again applied for radio, stressing that he would particularly like to do *Music While You Work,* but again the BBC didn't want to know. He had formed a 20-piece theatre orchestra for playing in London parks and had a regular summer contract with the London County Council (later Greater London Council) and, feeling that the combination would be ideal for broadcasting, sent some of his programmes (including those for a full week at Hyde Park) to the BBC, inviting a representative to come and listen to the concerts. Finally, the BBC gave in and agreed to an audition. This turned out to be an overwhelming success; the listening panel gave glowing comments on his performance, with particular praise for the programme content. He began and ended with his signature tune *The Bandstand, Hyde Park* (Haydn Wood) and included such items as *The Arcadians* overture, *Cockney Capers, Lady of Spain* and *Montmartre.*

Thus, in the summer of 1951, Hugh James and his Orchestra took to the air with a breakfast time programme, the success of which led to several other shows in the next few months. Hugh reminded the BBC that he would like to do *Music While You Work* and, as the reports on his audition specifically commented that his orchestra was ideal for the series, his wish was granted on 4th January 1952 when he broadcast the first of 115 editions of the programme.

Hugh James continued to broadcast during the fifties and sixties, sometimes with guest artists. He was particularly associated with *Morning Music* and *Music While You Work,* having the distinction of playing the last afternoon edition in 1966.

Hugh's successful format was of tuneful light music entr'actes interspersed (in *MWYW*) with medleys and arrangements of popular standards. For *Morning Music* he would include some longer items such as overtures or movements from suites. After *MWYW* ended, he appeared in *Home To Music* and a few sessions of *Breakfast Special* in the late sixties before being axed, together with most of the other light orchestras. He regretted this, as he would have liked to continue broadcasting. He told me that he regarded it as a 'labour of love' and said: 'We, and the other orchestras, gave so much pleasure to people, yet were cast out like old clothes.' I think that many would have agreed with him; the fact that other styles of music had become popular didn't mean that older people were obliged to switch their allegiance away from the type of music that they had grown to love.

In addition to conducting his theatre orchestra, Hugh led a quartet and a salon orchestra in the London parks. He played the violin for Michael Freedman and Arthur Anton, both of whom played in his own orchestra. Other conductors for whom he played included Harold Collins, Jack Leon, Joseph Muscant, Van Dam, Raymond Agoult and, occasionally, Harry Davidson. Harry's orchestra, like his own, was led by Ralph Elman.

After broadcasting ceased, Hugh continued to play the violin in London theatre pits, as well as directing his park orchestra, until his retirement in the mid-seventies. I often attended his concerts in Victoria Embankment Gardens, London; his conducting and presentation were always professional and the orchestra responded well to his direction. His programmes covered a wide variety of light music but often included songs from the music hall, for which he had a great affection. He would go to great trouble to play requests for people, even if the orchestra hadn't played them for years. He was one of the old school – gentle, genial and polite without ever being ingratiating.

In retirement, Hugh James greatly missed conducting his orchestra, as well as the companionship of his fellow musicians. It would have been nice if Hugh could have participated in the revived *MWYW* series in 1982/83, but even if he had been invited, it is doubtful if he would have been physically up to it as, then in his mid-eighties, his health and hearing had deteriorated. He, nevertheless, listened to some of the programmes and was not always pleased with what he heard!

Hugh was saddened at the lamentable standard of much of today's popular music, which he called 'thug music'. Being a gentleman in every sense of the word, he deplored the decline in morals and good manners. Unlike many of today's entertainers, he neither drank, smoked nor swore and he was happily married for many years.

The physical limitations which beset him in his last years were a source of major frustration to him, as socialising became difficult. His intellect had not diminished and he would have liked to have been more active. His great delight was in receiving letters from enthusiasts, to whom he always replied by return of post. He said 'I like receiving letters as it gives me the opportunity to do some typing – after all, I haven't got much else to do!'

Hugh James died, aged 88, on November 6th 1986, following a short illness.

Music While You Work at 3.31 p.m. on 25th October 1963
Played by Hugh James and his Orchestra

Calling All Workers (Sig)	Coates
The Liberty Bell	Sousa
Let's All Sing Like the Birdies Sing	Evans
Tabarinage	Docker
Long Ago	Heneker
Spanish Mule Dance	Vincent
What More Can I Say	Noel
Folk Songs from Somerset	Vaughan Williams
Scarlett O'Hara	Lordan
Medley:	
All By Yourself in the Moonlight	Wallis
The More We Are Together	King
Show Me the Way To Go Home	King
Amparito Roca	Texidor
Soft Shoe Song	Jordan
Confessin'	Reynolds
Teddy Bears' Picnic	Bratton
Waltzes from *The Count of Luxemburg*	Lehar
Laughing Polka	Steurs
If I Had a Talking Picture of You	De Sylva
Salute to Jolson	arr. Hanmer
I'm Just Wild about Harry	Sissle
I Only Have Eyes For You	Warren
Avalon	Jolson
Rock-A-Bye Your Baby	Young
California Here I Come	Jolson
Calling All Workers (Sig)	Coates

FELIX KING

Felix Ferdinand King was born in Brighton on 27th March 1912. His first engagement was as pianist at the Grand Hotel, Eastbourne. In 1932, he formed a band to play at the Gargoyle Club, London but was soon to spend much of his time as pianist in leading dance bands in London, writing music for films and, indeed, playing in them! In 1935 he joined the newly-formed Victor Silvester Ballroom Orchestra and played on their first record, but left after about a year.

He then toured with Florence Desmond as accompanist, writing a number of songs for her, but it was bandleading that really interested him, so he formed a band which he took to Norway and to the exclusive Sporting Club at Monte Carlo. At this point, however, the war intervened and Felix King soon commenced a six-year spell in the Royal Air Force. When he was demobilised in 1946, Felix picked up his career where he had left off and took a band to Nice.

In 1947, Felix King, his piano and orchestra opened at the Nightingale Club, in Berkeley Square. This was a 16-piece orchestra featuring two pianos, for which Felix King composed the signature tune, *The Night and the Nightingale*. He could not use the obvious *Nightingale Sang in Berkeley Square* as this had already been adopted by a band across the road!

It was about this time that Felix King commenced his broadcasting career. Apart from his 100 *Music While You Work* programmes, he sometimes broadcast from restaurants in which his band was resident at the time. In addition he was regularly featured as solo pianist in the series *Piano Playtime*. As he possessed a suave, silky voice, Felix was allowed to present his own programmes, later developing this talent in the sixties to become a regular compère of *Housewives' Choice*.

In 1948, he and his orchestra moved to the Orchid Room, where the late Princess Margaret sometimes danced to his music. It was during this period that he did a series for Radio Luxembourg which ran for 20 months.

A residency at the Colony Restaurant began in 1950, where Felix directed a nine-piece orchestra until 1959, when he made a final move to Quaglino's Restaurant. Here his band was reduced to five and subsequent broadcasts in *MWYW* were billed as 'The Felix King Quintet'

In 1966, Felix King was invited to form a 17-piece string orchestra for *Breakfast Special,* which he directed from the piano in his expressive and distinctive style. He had already made a number of 78s for Decca in the late forties and early fifties, as well as some LPs, so it was no new experience for him when, in 1967 as a direct result of these broadcasts, he was asked to make an LP on the Fontana Special label. This was entitled *Elegance.*

According to the sleeve-notes, Felix King was an avid traveller and this enabled him to indulge in another of his hobbies – making colour movies of the places that he visited. He had been right across America, Mexico, the Caribbean and Malta, and after each trip he edited his films, adding a musical soundtrack and commentary. He joked that his friends would then ask him 'When's the premiere?' Felix King died on 13th June 1982 aged 70.

Music While You Work at 3.45 p.m. on 10th July 1958
Played by Felix King and his Orchestra

Calling All Workers (Sig)	Coates
Stairway of Love	Tipper/Bennett
Handful of Songs	Steele
Got The Sun in the Morning	Berlin
Stepping Out With My Baby	Berlin
You're Just in Love	Berlin
Time	Heneker/Norman
I Never Had It So Good	Heneker/Norman
I Am, I Am	Heneker/Norman
Twilight Time	Ram/Nevins
Espada	Dies
Brazil	Russell
Tulips from Amsterdam	Arnie
Lollipop	Ross/Dixon
I'll Follow My Secret Heart	Coward
Dearest Love	Coward
Someday I'll Find You	Coward
Who's Sorry Now	Snyder
Everything is Nothing Without You	Mann/Ripindale
These Foolish Things	Strachey

You've Done Something to My Heart	Gay
La Vie en Rose	Louiguy
All Over the Place	Louiguy
Streets of Sorrento	Osbourne
Hello Young Lovers	Rodgers
I Whistle a Happy Tune	Rodgers
Fascination	Marchetti
Under the Bridges of Paris	Scotto
Funny Face	Gershwin
Clap Your Hands	Gershwin
S'Wonderful	Gershwin
I Want to be Happy	Youmans
Whispering	Shonberger
Love Is	Lynes
I'm in Love for the Very First Time	Roberts/Woodman
Calling All Workers (Sig)	Coates

TOMMY KINSMAN

Tommy Kinsman was born in Liverpool in 1901. In his youth he learned to play the banjo, subsequently taking up the clarinet and the saxophone, upon which he became an accomplished performer. He began his bandleading career in 1928, directing what was initially called the London Frivolities Band in Western-super-Mare. For a while he played at the Florida Club, graduating to the famous Ciro's club before taking up residency at the Ritz Hotel in 1932. By the mid-thirties he was playing at the exclusive Fischer's Restaurant in Bond Street, performing for a discerning clientele. During the first ten years of the band's existence over 250 'sides' were cut for the record labels Sterno, Piccadilly, Metropole, Phonochord, Edison Bell, Winner and Octacros, for which Tommy Kinsman later became Musical Director. In addition, he recorded under pseudonyms such as The Bond Street Swingers and Eddie Harding and his Night Club Boys on the Piccadilly and Metropole labels.

During these early years the band personnel numbered between eight and twelve players. Regular broadcasting commenced on Radio Luxembourg in 1936 and Tommy Kinsman was well satisfied with his 'high society' following, avoiding the press, seeking no publicity and, therefore, not receiving any! Some of his early recordings were reissued in 1990 on a long-playing record on the Harlequin label and amongst the personnel was violinist/saxophonist Freddie Ballerini, whose own sextet often broadcast during the sixties.

Despite the large number of commercial records made before the Second World War, Tommy Kinsman is best remembered for his post-war broadcasts with his dance orchestra, playing 'strict tempo' ballroom music. He played regularly on *Music While You Work* for over 20 years, chalking up 138 programmes in the series, and very entertaining they were too! The band consisted of a full saxophone section plus brass and rhythm (the guitar and violin which he included before the war were dispensed with in later years). A memorable feature was the orchestra's two-piano team who played 'à la Victor Silvester' in a style sometimes known in the music business as 'bubble and squeak' – the second pianist being required to play an improvised 'filigree' of notes around the main melody played by the first pianist, rather in the manner of a clarinet player in a traditional jazz band.

Tommy Kinsman continued to make records after the war and, during the fifties and sixties, made more than 40 long-playing records for Oriole, Wing and Fontana. Very occasionally, a string section was used for certain tracks, as was an accordion where appropriate, but the basic sound was the same as the broadcasts: brash, bouncy and tuneful. In common with other bands, Tommy Kinsman's style had changed since the thirties and now had great appeal to London's high society, and his band become known as the 'Deb's Delight Band'. He was the doyen of dance band leaders, having fans amongst European Royalty. One of his biggest fans was the late Queen Mother!

Unlike many bands, Tommy Kinsman and his Dance Orchestra never had 'palais' residences, preferring to do gigs in London and elsewhere. They could be at Windsor Castle one day and a working-men's club the next. That they existed for about 50 years could well be attributed to the fact that Kinsman was an unassuming man who, despite his high standing in society, was quite happy to play for anyone who wanted his services; apparently he even played in people's houses. (I wish I'd known!)

Tommy Kinsman's post-war orchestra had 14 musicians and, during the sixties, played only in the longer afternoon editions of *MWYW*, which ended in 1966. The lower budget allocation for the remaining morning shows didn't allow for the use of many large bands, however, after some persuasion, Tommy Kinsman managed to secure one more broadcast before the series ended. Although the band carried on for many years after broadcasting ceased, I recall reading in the seventies that they were struggling to get work. Modern trends had meant that most of their 'society' work had dried up and they were mainly doing working-men's clubs. At that time their drummer (whose bass drum bore the autographs of monarchs of many lands) had been in the band for 22 years!

Finally, Tommy Kinsman went into the business of providing bands for cruise liners. Of course, he made sure of always fronting one himself, thus enabling him to combine work with pleasure! He also took the opportunity of playing for private parties on the Continent. In 1982, at the age of 81, Tommy decided to retire to Marbella. Sadly, he suffered a heart attack on 1st February 1984 and after a further attack on 15th March was rushed to a clinic in Malaga, where he died. He was cremated in Madrid and his ashes were scattered in the gardens of Golders Green Crematorium, as had been those of his first wife.

Music While You Work at 3.45 p.m. on 5th October 1960
Played by Tommy Kinsman and his Dance Orchestra

Calling All Workers (Sig)	Coates
Looking High, High, High	Watson
Toni's Tune	Phillips
Fings Ain't Wot They Used To Be	Bart
Sunday	Rodgers
You're Driving Me Crazy	Donaldson
Pink Elephants	Woods
Bye Bye Blackbird	Dixon
Somebody Stole My Gal	Woods
Say It With Music	Berlin
Eternally	Chaplin
How About That	Van Dyke
The Best Things in Life are Free	De Sylva
Harry Lime Theme	Karas
Dancing Time	Kern
Easy to Love	Porter

Cheek to Cheek	Berlin
Do You Mind?	Bart
La Ronde	Straus
You Forgot Your Gloves	Lehak
My Baby Don't Mean Maybe	Donaldson
Sing Baby Sing	Pollack
Ida Sweet as Apple Cider	Leonard
Glue Foot	Mercer
Cinderella Jones	Styne
Standing on the Corner	Loesser
An Apple for the Teacher	Monaco
It's the Natural thing to Do	Johnson
One Two Button Your Shoe	Johnson
The Music Goes Round and Around	Farley
Romantica	Rascel
Poor People of Paris	Monnot
Ooh La La	Calvi
Calling All Workers (Sig)	Coates

JIMMY LEACH

Jimmy Leach was born in Stockport, Cheshire on 6th November 1905. Although remembered today as an organist, pianist and composer, he actually started his working life in engineering. He subsequently moved on to stockbroking and at one time even studied dentistry! At the age of 21, however, he realised that his heart was in music and began full-time professional work with Henry Hall at Gleneagles.

In 1934 he joined Francis, Day and Hunter and started composing, soon having a big hit with *The Little Boy that Santa Claus Forgot*, which he co-wrote with Tommy Connor and Michael Carr. His next assignment was to write the Grosvenor House floor-show *The Circus of Beauty* on behalf of the Music Corporation of America (MCA), establishing what was to become an important side of his career, that of composer. Indeed, whilst he is best known as an instrumentalist,

Jimmy Leach composed a considerable number of light pieces. Titles include *Smash and Grab, Neptune's Holiday, Montego Bay, Café Sous Les Arbres, Toujour Le Vin Blanc, Russian Salad, A Bedouin in Baghdad* and *Piping Hot*. Some of these pieces were in the repertoires of the BBC Scottish Variety Orchestra and the BBC Midland Light Orchestra as well as outside orchestras. Sadly, much of his music is no longer heard, although *Piping Hot* is occasionally played by military bands. Jimmy Leach also wrote the music for the show *Someday Soon*. On the performing side, he made many records for Columbia and broadcast with Sandy Macpherson in *String Along With Sandy*.

In 1939, Jimmy Leach joined forces, as pianist, with Hammond organist Harry Farmer in a trio called Organola (signature tune *Nola*) which, by the following year had become The Organolists. They were the first band to broadcast in *Music While You Work*, on 23rd June 1940. Jimmy Leach later took over the Hammond organ, as well as the sole directorship of the group, which grew to four and eventually five players. On some of their records a violin or clarinet can be heard in the ensemble, the title of which was changed during the war to the New Organolians. By the early sixties it was known as Jimmy Leach and his Organolian Quartet, the instrumentation at this time being: Hammond organ, piano (Harry Hayward), bass, drums and guitar.

The group was regularly heard on *Bright and Early* during the fifties, on *Morning Music* during the sixties and in an amazing 256 editions of *Music While You Work* spanning 27 years, the group becoming virtually synonymous with the show. When Jimmy Leach was invited to play the 20th anniversary edition on 24th June 1960 (curiously, a day late) he wrote in the *Radio Times*: 'We made the first broadcast from Maida Vale, shortly before I went into the RAF and, until I went overseas, I came back regularly to play again. When I was stationed up North, I used to cadge lifts in Blenheim bombers to get to London on time. The music was the same as now – tuneful old favourites but few pops'. When Jimmy played the 25th anniversary edition in 1965, the BBC managed to get the day right!

The Organolians were classed as a dance band but nevertheless included rhythmic light music novelties in their programmes. The popularity of the group was no doubt enhanced by the fact that, during the course of each programme, Jimmy Leach would, on several occasions, move from the organ to join Harry Hayward at the 'top end' of the piano for medleys of familiar tunes. The effect was unusual, to say the least, as Jimmy Leach had developed a pianistic style that seemed to emulate a rapidly played ukulele! The Organolians undertook summer seasons, sometimes at Aberystwyth and were often featured on television in live summer seaside programmes, having their own spot each week – a sort of *MWYW* in miniature in which Jimmy moved from organ to piano for the duets. I can still see his beaming face as his hands shot up and down when he produced the 'ukulele effect'. He seemed to thoroughly enjoy himself!

Most of his post-war broadcasts came from Manchester and, in addition to the Organolians, he had a resident organ spot with the BBC Northern Dance Orchestra in their series *Make Way For Music*.

Jimmy Leach was one of the most popular and frequent contributors to *Music While You Work* and, having participated on the first day in 1940, it was particularly appropriate that the band should bring the series to a conclusion on 29th September 1967.

Jimmy Leach's broadcasts ceased in the late sixties. He died in 1975.

Music While You Work at 10.31 a.m on 29th September 1967
Played by Jimmy Leach and his Organolians

Calling All Workers (Sig)	Coates
Pepe the Puppet	Leach
Medley:	Trad. arr. Leach
The Lincolnshire Poacher	
A-Hunting We Will Go	
The Keel Row	
Mademoiselle from Armentieres	
St. Patrick's Day	
Charlie is My Darling	
Penny Lane	McCartney
Two Streets	Andrews
Medley:	Trad. arr. Leach
Let Him Go, Let Him Tarry	
The Wearin' o' the Green	
Men of Harlech	
The Shrimp	Rico
If I Were a Rich Man	Bock
Jamaica Walk	Norman
Beautiful Dreamer	Foster
Medley:	Trad. arr. Leach
The Fairy Princess	

Highland Laddie
Kate Dalrymple
Bonnie Dundee
The Wee Cooper O'Fife
Will Ye No' Come Back Again
Medley:

Put On Your Ta-Ta Little Girlie	Leigh
Get Out and Get Under	Kirby
Say it with Music	Berlin
Calling All Workers (Sig)	Coates

HARRY LEADER

Harry Leader was born in the East End of London on 28th January 1906. He was the son of a Russian trumpeter in the Tsar's Army who became a Professor of Music at St Petersburg Conservatoire. Anglicising the family name, Harry's father set up a grocery store after arrival in this country around the turn of the 20th century. Harry learned to play the violin from his father and, when not assisting in the family business, could be found playing for silent movies.

With the coming of jazz, Harry taught himself to play the saxophone at the age of 14. He later acquired valuable experience playing in clubs in the West End of London, as well as touring. In 1928 he was invited to join Sid Phillips' Melodians, and even took over the direction of the band during a tour of Italy when Sid Phillips had to return to London. No doubt this inspired him to form his own band, which he soon did. Initially it was essentially a combination for recording purposes and Harry made hundreds of records (often under pseudonyms) for Decca's Panachord label as well as Broadcast, Eclipse, HMV and various EMI labels. His biggest hit (recorded on Eclipse 729) was *Little Man You've Had a Busy Day*, which sold 375,000 copies. Indeed, so keen was Harry for this record to be a success he even stood in the streets of London selling it himself!

143

In the early thirties, Harry Leader played for Teddy Brown as well as for a character known as 'Jack de Yanke' at the Café de Paris. He made his first broadcast with his own band in 1934, commencing a broadcasting career spanning nearly 50 years, during which time his 'line-up' included such famous names as Norrie Paramor, Billy Amstell, Billy Bell, Freddie Gardner, George Chisholm, Nat Temple, Tommy McQuater, Steve Race, Phil Green, Kenny Baker, Johnny Gray, Bert Weedon, Ray Davies and Stanley Black.

Harry Leader's first residency was at the Hammersmith Palais from around 1939 to 1942, after which he moved to the Astoria, playing opposite Jack White until 1955. There followed seasons at Butlin's Holiday Camps until a residency was available at the Regent Ballroom in Brighton, where he stayed until well into the sixties. Harry's original signature tune was *Memories of You*, but this was later changed to *Music Maestro Please*. During his extensive broadcasting career, Harry contributed to many series that featured dance bands, as well as having his own *Harry Leader Show* on television in 1947.

Harry Leader was particularly associated with *Music While You Work*, in which he appeared 215 times. His first appearance was on the 10th August 1941 and his last on 13th June 1966. Apart, that is, from an appearance in the revival series, about which more later.

Harry was also a gifted composer who, with his wife Rona, produced over 350 songs under various aliases, his best-known composition probably being *Dragonfly*. Other compositions include *Just Fancy That, Washington Square* and *Dance, Dance, Dance*. During the sixties most of his *MWYW* programmes ended with the well-known *Tonight's The Night*, which Harry Leader maintained was also one of his compositions. If this is the case then the programme accompanying this profile has rather more than the permitted allocation of 'own compositions', but what is the purpose of a pseudonym if it is not to deceive?

Unlike many dance bands of yesteryear, many of which, to the layman at least, sounded identical, the Harry Leader Band had a very individual style, with a full, bright and beautifully harmonised sound, every note being played to its full value. This is not to say that the style did not change over the years, indeed, Harry always moved with the times, a fact that is apparent from listening to recordings of his broadcasts between, say, 1960 and 1966.

Another of Harry's claims to fame was the discovery of two leading popular singers, Clinton Ford and Matt Monro. Readers may well

144

remember the occasion of a *This is Your Life* television show featuring Matt Monro, in which Harry made a guest appearance.

By the early seventies, Harry's broadcasts were becoming infrequent and he moved down to Brighton where he continued to do gigs and to teach the flute, trumpet, saxophone and clarinet (the instrument with which he is most associated).

In 1972 Harry made an LP for strict-tempo dancing. At this time he called the band 'Harry Leader's Nu-Set' – a corny title which he even used on radio and which somehow always made me think of dentures! In 1983 he concluded his broadcasting career with a superb programme in the revived series of *Music While You Work*. I had the honour of being present and was impressed by the enthusiasm of Harry Leader, who was clearly very excited to be broadcasting after some years in the BBC 'wilderness'. He rallied his musicians, saying: 'Come on lads, let's enjoy ourselves, just like we used to in the old days.' Well, Harry certainly did! He was dancing on the rostrum in one piece and the overall broadcast had a sparkle which put some of the other bands to shame.

Sadly, it was to be his last broadcast and he died on 20th January 1987.

Music While You Work at 10.31 a.m. on 17th December 1965
Played by Harry Leader and his Band

Calling All Workers (Sig)	Coates
Dance, Dance, Dance	Roberts
In The Middle of Nowhere	Kaye
Three O'Clock in the Morning	Robledo
Lonely Girl	Hefti
Strong Love	Silver
Dream on Little Dreamer	Burch
Jubilee Hayride	Dale
Dragonfly	Wain
Slippery Samba	Cugaro
Sweet Beginning	Bricusse
Hot Line	Reed
Post Horn Beat	arr. Leader
Just Fancy That	Leader
Tonight's the Night	Primo
Calling All Workers (Sig)	Coates

REGINALD LEOPOLD

Of all the artists which I have chosen for these profiles, Reginald Leopold is perhaps the odd one out, because his orchestra never appeared in the original series of *Music While You Work* although, as one of the best violinists in the world of light music, Leopold participated in countless editions and, as we shall see later, his orchestra played for the 1983 revivals.

Reginald Leopold was born on 20th May 1907. At the age of 11 he won a scholarship to the Trinity College of Music, London, where he studied the violin. His first professional work was at the Trocadero Restaurant, London; he later played with Carroll Gibbons and the Savoy Hotel Orpheans, Hugo Rignold, George Melachrino and Eugene Pini. He made his first broadcast from Savoy Hill in 1927 with Jack Payne. In the early thirties he was lead violinist for Fred Hartley and his Quintet, a group which also utilised the talents of another famous violinist, Sidney Sax, who, when Hartley emigrated to Australia in the fifties, took over the group, renaming it The Harlequins, a contraction of Hartley Quintet!

In 1932, Reginald Leopold formed his own orchestra at the Dorchester Hotel and it was here that he met his wife, Jeanne. In the forties, he joined the London Studio Players. This was a BBC house orchestra which, in addition to broadcasting in its own right, combined to form ensembles of different sizes, amongst which were Edward Rubach and the Novelairs, The Casino Orchestra (Reginald Kilbey), The Tunesmiths (Sidney Bright), Melody on Strings (Max Jaffa), The Grinzing Players (Charlie Katz) and Reginald Leopold and his Players. The latter combination was highly acclaimed by the BBC as one of the best small orchestras on the air. Like Fred Hartley, Reg Leopold had a reputation for meticulous rehearsals and has been described as a strict disciplinarian by those who worked for him, although my own impression of him (having attended several of his broadcasts) was that he was a gentle and benign man, but I only saw him during the later years of his career!

When not directing his own players, Reg Leopold could be found leading the London Theatre Orchestra and the London Light Concert Orchestra, both of which were based on the London Studio Players,

146

which he led in a delightful series called *Strings By Starlight*. This series was so successful that it spawned several long-playing records, the conductor being the well-known cellist, Reginald Kilbey.

In the mid-forties, Leopold started two orchestras from within the London Studio Players, namely The Majestic Orchestra and the Southern Serenade Orchestra, but when he temporarily left the 'Unit' (as the London Studio Players were known) these orchestras were handed over to Lou Whiteson, who continued to direct them for many years.

Reginald Leopold will always be remembered for his 17-year association with *Grand Hotel*, directing the Palm Court Orchestra (another Unit combination) and even announcing the items. He followed a series of illustrious predecessors which included Albert Sandler, Tom Jenkins, Jean Pougnet and Max Jaffa.

Pain in his left hand forced Reginald Leopold to give up playing the violin, which he finally sold. Fortunately, his wealth of conducting experience enabled him to form an orchestra consisting of strings, with piano (Robert Docker), celeste (Dennis Gomm) and accordion (Henry Krein). The instrumentation was suggested by the BBC and produced a most attractive sound; however, Reg Leopold always thought it a 'silly instrumentation'. Silly or not, it kept him on the radio many years longer than most of his contemporaries. The orchestra, which was led by George French, or sometimes Tessa Robbins, was the only light orchestra broadcasting regularly by the mid-eighties, the BBC Regional Light Orchestras having all been axed. Most of the orchestra's music was especially arranged by Robert Docker.

The orchestra was long associated with the Sunday morning programme *Melodies For You* and with *Among Your Souvenirs*. During the season of BBC Light Music Festivals, this latter programme was sometimes recorded in the foyer of the Royal Festival Hall in the presence of an audience, as were editions of *Grand Hotel*.

In 1983, Reg Leopold contributed two editions to the revived series of *Music While You Work*, the recordings of which I had the pleasure of attending. He even put in *Ragamuffin* by Rixner as an unprogrammed request for me, having arranged for the first violins to be missing their parts for the scheduled piece – a very kind gesture on his part!

At the end of 1985, without any explanation, Reginald Leopold was dropped from *Melodies For You*. At this point Reg said he thought that he ought to take the hint and retire. Early in 1986, however, he was asked to play for Charlie Chester's Sunday afternoon show, but he was distinctly worried: 'They want me to do sixteen weeks – no selections – just short light pieces. Obviously we can't play pieces like *Valse Triste* for 'Cheerful' Charlie Chester! I don't think the repertoire can stand it!' To his relief, the series turned out to be only of four weeks' duration and the final item *Scrub, Brothers, Scrub* brought Reginald Leopold's broadcasting career to a conclusion. He told the BBC that at the age of 79 he didn't want any more broadcasts and wished now to take life easy in his home town of Brighton.

Rather touchingly, the BBC paid tribute to him on his 80th birthday with a programme of his favourite pieces, played by his orchestra, under the direction of Barry Wordsworth. The show was personally presented by Reginald Leopold – a fitting conclusion to a distinguished career. He died on 26th February 2003, aged 95.

Music While You Work at 12.02 p.m on 27th May 1983
Played by Reginald Leopold and his Orchestra

Calling All Workers (Sig)	Coates
Tabarinage	Docker
Masquerade	Loeb
Swedish Polka	Alfven
Country Wise	Turner
At the Dance	Coates
Happy Times	Bottcher
Swedish Rhapsody	Alfven/Faith
Flowers of Edinburgh	Hartley
Anna Lisa	Rogers
Calling All Workers (Sig)	Coates

BERNARD MONSHIN

Of the many 'speciality orchestras' featured on radio since the Second World War, Bernard Monshin and his Rio Tango Band must surely be amongst the best remembered and most popular.

Born in the East End of London on 2nd July 1914, Bernard Monshin took up the violin at the age of five, winning an open scholarship to the Royal Academy of Music at 14. He formed his first band at the Kit Kat Restaurant in 1931 playing opposite such famous names as Roy Fox and Joe Loss. At a mere 17 years of age he was London's youngest bandleader. Calling his group Renaldo's Tango Band, Bernard soon commenced broadcasting, but was forced to drop the name after just one broadcast following a complaint by one Gerald Bright (Geraldo) that the name could be confused with Geraldo's Gaucho Tango Band! For a short while he changed the name to D'Monshin's Tango Band before reverting to his own name. Incidentally, Bernard told me that the European origin of his name was Mondscheine meaning 'moonshine'.

During the mid-thirties, Bernard Monshin toured the country with his tango band, playing in variety theatres until 1937, when he was invited to take the band to Reykjavik, Iceland, for a year. Weekly broadcasts were made from the Hotel Borg until 1938, when the band returned to London to become the resident tango and Latin-American orchestra at the newly-opened Casini Club in Regent Street.

The Second World War meant a break in Monshin's career and from 1940 to 1944 he served with distinction in the Royal Air Force. After the war he re-formed his orchestra for radio under the title of Bernard Monshin and his Rio Tango Band, a 14-piece orchestra of strings, two pianos, two accordions (played by Henry Krein and Gerald Crossman), guitar and percussion. In 1951, as part of the Festival of Britain celebrations, the band gave concerts on London's South Bank, as did several other broadcasting light orchestras. It was around this time that Bernard Monshin formed his Concert Tango Orchestra, which varied in size according to requirements (and no doubt BBC budgets), numbering anything from 19 to 34 players. Inevitably, its size meant that the orchestra was not used as frequently as the smaller combination. The Rio Tango Band, however, was quite adequate and not only had one of the most original styles on the air, but it also had a freshness and sparkle, the like of which is rarely heard today. They didn't just play tangos, of course, although there were usually three or four in a programme. The full range of Latin rhythms was used: sambas, paso dobles, beguines, joropos, rumbas, cha-chas and boleros, plus the occasional waltz or novelty number for contrast.

In the fifties, at the suggestion of Bernard Monshin, the BBC commissioned a series of Sunday morning shows entitled *Tango Time*, for which Bernard wrote the signature tune. The series was a great success, considerably boosting the listening figures for this time. The orchestra's normal signature tune was *Hear My Song, Violetta* and when it broadcast programmes of continuous music, such as *Music While You Work,* a few bars of this were played on the celeste between items.

It must not be overlooked that, in addition to his talents as a violinist and conductor, Bernard Monshin achieved considerable success with his Latin-American compositions, amongst which were *Fascinating Tango, Bravo, Bravo, Mi Linda, Caracas, Tango Time, Blue Sapphire, Last Tango* and *Tango Yvonne*, which was dedicated to his daughter.

Bernard Monshin told me the story behind one of his pieces, a joropo entitled *Caracas*, composed under the nom-de-plume of Antonio Alma. One day he was sitting in his car, waiting for his wife to return from shopping, when a tune came to him in its entirety. He hurriedly took a piece of manuscript paper and jotted it down. That evening he took it to a club where he was appearing with a small group and, together with the pianist, hastily produced an arrangement. During the evening the group played it several times and within a fortnight it received its first broadcast with the Rio Tango Band.

Bernard Monshin participated in many light music programmes over the years including *Melody Hour, Café On The Corner, Serenade In The Night, Tango Time, Morning Music, Breakfast Special* and of course *Music While You Work*, for which the Rio Tango Band played 146 editions. Bernard also vividly recalled a broadcast which took place around 1964, when he was asked to provide an experimental stereophonic broadcast of light music using the Concert Tango Orchestra. Nineteen musicians took part in this broadcast, which could only be heard in stereo by tuning in to television's BBC2 as well

150

as the radio. The programme consisted of 25 minutes of continuous music with celeste links.

Although Monshin was not known as a recording artist, he did record one EP for Pye/Nixa and an LP for the Oriole Record Company. I am told that there were a few 78s, but I have yet to encounter them. As a violinist, he played in the orchestras of Isy Geiger, Anton, Lionel Falkman and in Wynford Reynolds' Raeburn Orchestra. It was in 1958 that Wynford Reynolds became seriously ill and Bernard Monshin offered to conduct the orchestra so that their dates were not lost to another combination. Consequently, Monshin conducted the Raeburn Orchestra for a number of editions of *Marching and Waltzing* and a couple of *MWYW* programmes prior to Reynolds' untimely death later that year.

The Rio Tango Band continued to broadcast until the late sixties, their final appearance being in an early Sunday morning programme. This programme was badly edited and some of the rehearsal was actually heard on air, including re-starts and Monshin's instructions to the orchestra! The announcer found this amusing but it made for a rather inauspicious final broadcast. Although the Rio Tango Band didn't broadcast again, Bernard Monshin continued to broadcast with what the BBC considered to be a more commercial style of orchestra, which he used in *Breakfast Special, Roundabout* and a series called *Time For Latin Tempo* that incorporated studio dancing in a similar manner to Sidney Bowman's *Time For Old Time*. The Bernard Monshin Latin-American Orchestra, which by now had been augmented with woodwind and brass, continued to broadcast until the mid-seventies.

Fortunately for Bernard Monshin, he had another string to his bow in the form of orchestral management, otherwise known as 'fixing'. For some years he had successfully provided orchestras for television and films, and one of his last assignments was a James Bond film.

During the 1983 season of *Music While You Work*, Bernard organised and played in the Geoffrey Brand Orchestra and it was at one of these sessions that I persuaded him to approach the Producer with a view to getting his own orchestra back on radio. He went into the control box saying, 'I'm Bernard Monshin and I haven't broadcast for seven years.' Apparently the Producer's reaction was to wrap a newspaper round his head. The message was obvious – he didn't want to know! Sadly, Bernard Monshin never succeeded in getting his orchestra back on the air. He died in March 1988 aged 73.

Music While You Work at 3.31 p.m. on 22nd October 1963
Played by Bernard Monshin and his Rio Tango Band

Calling All Workers (Sig)	Coates
El Pandero	Lanjean
Port-au-Prince	Wayne
The Proud Matador	Moran
Callela	Douglas
I Lost My Heart in Budapest	Ninaly
My Heart in Portugal	Caste
Portuguese Party	Vinter
Crepuscule	Bianco
Cheeky Chico	Woods
Sway	Ruiz
Morning Glory	Reynolds
Baion de Santos	Jupp
Fascinatin' Tango	Monshin
Under the Linden Tree	Felix
La Mattchiche	Borel-Clerc
Carnival	Bonfa
El Novillero	Rubach
Calling All Workers (Sig)	Coates

RONNIE MUNRO

Ronald George Munro was born in London in 1897. He started to play the piano at the age of eight. Initially, he took lessons from his mother but was later taught by Charles Woodhouse. At 17 he went to study at the Guildhall School of Music, under Joseph Speight. From 1915 to 1918 he served in the Army, but upon demobilisation decided on a career in music. He started as pianist in Moody's Club in Soho, also playing in other West End clubs as well as the Bow Palace and Lyons' Corner Houses. In 1923, he joined the Emlyn Thomas London Band, which played in cinemas and theatres, followed in 1926

152

with a spell at Jade's Club in Golden Square (formerly the Little Club). Around this time, Ronnie Munro was becoming increasingly busy as an arranger and won arranging contests sponsored by the *Daily Sketch* and *Melody Maker*. An arrangement of *Carolina* resulted in an engagement with Debroy Somers and the commencement of his recording career. In 1926 he had a recording contract for his own band with Parlophone, becoming the label's Director of Dance Music, a job he did for some years. This was the beginning of a 13-year relationship with EMI. Ronnie also recorded for HMV, Regal Zonophone and Columbia. He used a variety of pseudonyms on record, including: The Roof Garden Orchestra, The Merton Orchestra, Parlophone Syncopaters, West End Players and many others. The hand-picked personnel for these recordings included Max Goldberg, Carroll Gibbons, Ted Heath, Freddie Gardner, George Evans and Jack Simpson.

Ronnie Munro became Musical Director of HMV's house orchestra (The New Mayfair Orchestra), composing and arranging extensively for Jack Hylton, Lew Stone, Percival Mackey, Henry Hall and Ambrose, whose signature tune *When Day Is Done* was orchestrated by Munro in an elaborate concert style. The thirties was possibly the busiest period of Ronnie Munro' s career as, in addition to playing with several bands, he arranged music for films, being Musical Director for British National Pictures throughout the period.

Ronnie Munro's big break as far as broadcasting was concerned came late in 1940 when he was appointed conductor of the newly formed Scottish Variety Orchestra (the prefix BBC wasn't used until after the war). He was soon broadcasting several times a week and making records with the orchestra. One of his most popular shows was *Sunday Serenade*, which ran for several years. Ronnie stayed with the Scottish Variety Orchestra until 1944, when he handed the baton over to Kemlo Stephen, although he continued to play in *Sunday Serenade* with his own orchestra, usually broadcasting from wherever the orchestra happened to be located at the time.

It is evident from information available to researchers at the BBC Written Archives Centre that Ronnie Munro's departure from the Scottish Variety Orchestra was far from smooth. He had arranged hundreds of pieces for the orchestra and had come to regard them as his own property. Furthermore, he intended to continue to use them in *Sunday Serenade* with his own orchestra, so he took them away with him. Unfortunately, the BBC was adamant that the arrangements were not his property and could only be used with prior permission. A BBC representative therefore went to his home and reclaimed them! After some negotiation, Ronnie Munro was finally loaned three weeks' supply of scores, by which time he was expected to have written new arrangements for the series! *Sunday Serenade* continued under Ronnie's direction until 1946. On one occasion his car was broken into outside his home and all his arrangements for the following day's broadcast were stolen. Undeterred, Ronnie sat up all night rewriting them so that the broadcast could go ahead. (Anybody who has ever written out an orchestration, complete with band parts, will realise that this was an enormous and seemingly impossible task.)

After Ronnie Munro's *Sunday Serenade* ended (reverting to the BBC Scottish Variety Orchestra), he got a few broadcast dates with his dance band, but a row blew up during a *Music While You Work* rehearsal when a sound engineer told the saxophone section that they were playing too loudly. The musicians, including Ronnie Munro, took exception to this interference, declaring it to be 'nonsense and out of order'. The engineer then went into the next studio to find a colleague who would back him up. In this hostile atmosphere the ensuing broadcast did not go well. At one point the pianist was playing one tune with the saxes playing another and they virtually ground to a halt in the signature tune, apart from one trumpet which managed to keep going. Possibly as a result of this incident, Ronnie Munro's dance band ceased to be offered broadcasts and when he enquired in 1950 as to the reason, he was curtly told that the Light Programme was not in the market for his kind of show.

Although 'off the air', Ronnie Munro's band continued to tour the country, playing five summer seasons at the Butlin's Holiday Camp in Ayr and, in 1949 and 1950, visiting Eire, where his became the first British band to broadcast on Radio Eireann. As far as I can ascertain, he didn't resume broadcasting for the BBC until the mid-fifties.

At this point, let us pause to review Ronnie Munro's talents as a composer. He wrote several popular songs, including *All Over Italy* and the curiously titled *Gertie the Girl With the Gong*; however, he is surely best-remembered for his light orchestral compositions, such as *Punch and Judy Polka, Miss Pony Tail, Estorella* (paso doble)*, The Musical Typist, Ski Waltz, Fly Away Peter, Summer Promenade* and *Galapagos*.

On the recording side, Ronnie Munro made a number of records on the Decca *Music While You Work* label, with both the Scottish Variety

Orchestra and what was termed his 'waltz orchestra'. Decca subsequently reissued a number of Strauss waltzes from these 78s on one of their first long-playing records.

Picking up his broadcasting career, Ronnie Munro formed a light orchestra in 1956 which, initially, consisted of strings, woodwind, clavioline (later organ), harp, piano and rhythm. At this time he was using different-sized combinations for different programmes, including his eight-piece salon ensemble, Harmony Music, and orchestras of 12 or 17 players. He later standardised to one 17-piece orchestra specialising in tuneful, rhythmic light music. The orchestra consisted of strings, organ, piano and rhythm; the organ, usually played by William Davies. It had a most attractive sound, the combination of organ with strings giving a warm, friendly effect.

In 1962 Ronnie Munro formed a 'more economical group'; his idea being to use variable percussion effects produced by the two percussionists and the second guitar. Electronic organ was again present, with Munro on piano. Never was the phrase 'kitchen sink department' more apt, as the players appeared to be rattling and banging everything except each other! He wanted to call the group 'his Combo' but the BBC insisted on the more formal title of Ronnie Munro and his Sextet.

For a time the sextet's broadcasts alternated with those of the orchestra but Munro, worried that the sextet could actually threaten the existence of the orchestra, asked the BBC if the group could be used in *Morning Music,* keeping the orchestra for *MWYW*. The BBC's response was to axe the orchestra, the small group obviously being more economical from their point of view. Actually, by 1965 there were eight players in the group, although it was a long time before the billing changed from 'Sextet' to 'Music'. Over the five years of the group's existence, Ronnie Munro made several changes to both the style and instrumentation. In its final form, it comprised two saxophones (doubling flutes), musette accordion (played by Albert Delroy), piano, bass, percussion and two guitars (one, a bass guitar played percussively).

Ronnie Munro had been a stalwart contributor to *MWYW* over the years, appearing with most of the combinations which he had directed, namely the Scottish Variety Orchestra (91 performances), Dance Band (10), Harmony Music (1), Light Orchestra (52) and Sextet (28).

During the sixties Ronnie Munro had played piano and organ on cruises from Southampton to South Africa, so when broadcasting completely dried up in 1967, he and his wife decided to emigrate to Johannesburg. Once there, he re-formed his orchestra for broadcasting, and eventually became Head of Light Music for SABC.

He retired in 1975 and died on 3rd July 1989, having been blind for the last seven years of his life.

Music While You Work at 3.31p.m. 5th June 1962
Played by Ronnie Munro and his Orchestra

Calling All Workers (Sig)	Coates
Amparito Roca	Texidor
The Willow Waltz	Watters
The Happy Gondolier	Pockries
Medley:	
Taboo	Lecuona
Tico Tico	Abreu
Anna	Roman
Wonderful Land	Lordan
Oh Dear! What Can the Matter Be?	arr. Munro
Jeannie	Stanford
Swedish Rhapsody	Alfven
Exodus	Gold
Petite Mechante	Munro
Berlin Melody	Gaze
Small Town Parade	Norman
Covered Wagon	Leslie
Piccolino	Berlin
_Ay Ay Ay_	arr. Munro
Pianissimo	Alstone
Primera	Stanford
Dream of Olwen	Williams
Round the Ring	Elroy
Calling All Workers (Sig)	Coates

JACK NATHAN

Jack Nathan was born in London in 1910. Upon leaving school he took up a position as Assistant Secretary in a manufacturing company in the City, with a view to becoming an accountant. In 1932 he started doing gigs with a quintet at a road-house called the Spider's Web on the Watford By-Pass. The group included Ivor Mairants, Les Lambert and Harry Gold, three musicians who were destined to be associated with him for many years to come. The Spider's Web engagement came to an end after six months and, coincidently, Jack lost his day job in the same week!

As music was clearly in his blood, he decided to make it a career and joined Jack Padbury's band (together with Harry, Ivor and Les) at the Prince's Restaurant in Piccadilly. In October of 1932, Roy Fox, who was moving to the Café Anglais from the Monseigneur, offered all four musicians jobs in his band.

To be playing in one of Britain's foremost bands within a few months of joining the profession was no mean achievement and was undoubtedly recognition of Jack's pianistic skill. During his six years with Roy Fox, Jack also used his talents as an arranger, being ultimately responsible for two-thirds of the band's arrangements. In 1936, he arranged a concert version of *Whispering*, which he subsequently conducted on a recording by the Roy Fox Band.

In 1938, Jack joined Canadian bandleader Billy Bissett at the Café de Paris, leaving in 1939 to form his own band at an exclusive club called La Suiva. In October 1940, he joined the RAF, leading a station dance band and conducting a military orchestra.

Upon demobilisation in 1946, Jack Nathan played in the Harry Hayes Band at Churchill's Club prior to returning to Roy Fox for a short spell as pianist/arranger at the Milroy. He then joined the London Coliseum Orchestra under the direction of Reginald Burston for the musical *Annie Get Your Gun*.

It was in 1947 that Jack Nathan re-formed his own nine-piece band. For a while he was resident at Churchill's Club, moving on to The Nightingale and the '96' Restaurant. Within a few months of their formation, Jack Nathan and his Band started broadcasting and, in

1948, joined the regulars in *Music While You Work*, appearing 146 times during the ensuing two decades.

In 1950, Jack took an 'All Star' band to the Edmundo Ros Club, where he stayed for six years. He was a superior dance band pianist with a unique style which is difficult to describe; it was a bold, positive style, skilfully using the left hand to achieve much variety of expression. Curiously, the band's arrangements exactly reflected his piano style, with 'push' and vitality.

After Jack Nathan's band left the Edmundo Ros Club, they alternated between the Pigalle and Churchill's for 18 years, after which time they moved to the Stork Club in Streatham. Although the band stayed there until the club's closure in 1981, Jack did not. Having had a minor motor accident in 1980, he was taking tablets for a stiff shoulder. Unfortunately, these had alarming and unexpected side-effects, resulting in Jack suffering an internal haemorrhage. He spent a year in hospital, where he had four major abdominal operations. He was lucky to recover but remained a far from well man. Nevertheless, he continued to perform as a solo pianist several evenings a week for many years.

Quite apart from his *Music While You Work* appearances, Jack Nathan broadcast in many other programmes over the years. He had a quintet in the early morning series *Bright and Early* and gave regular recitals in *Piano Playtime,* occasionally doing live late-night broadcasts from Churchill's with his band.

Jack was well regarded at the BBC, whose executives knew that he could always be relied upon to organise his broadcasts efficiently, many of which were introduced by his signature tune *Happy Listening,* written by Jack in 1947. Another of his compositions, *Dizzy Daisy,* was recorded by him as a piano solo in 1938. I am not aware of any recordings by his regular band but he did make some long-playing records for EMI in the late sixties with a 'big band', the first of which was entitled *If Glenn Miller Played the Hits of Today*. Around this time, Jack also directed a string orchestra for a number of *Breakfast Special* sessions.

Less known was the fact that Jack Nathan also wrote a number of film scores, collaborating with Basil Kirchen on *The Abominable Dr Phibes, The Shuttered Room, The Strange Affair* and *I Start Counting.* In 1984 he wrote an arrangement of Jewish folk songs for the Reginald Leopold Orchestra to broadcast in *Melodies For You.* Jack Nathan died early in 1990, a modest, cultured and charming man, highly respected as a musician and as a person. He left a widow, former

Television Topper Patricia Worth, to whom he had been married for 36 years. They had three children.

Music While You Work at 3.31 p.m. on 8th December 1965
Played by Jack Nathan and his Band

Calling All Workers (Sig)	Coates
She Loves Me	Hock
In the Chapel in the Moonlight	Hill
Medley:	
Ain't We Got Fun	Whiting
Lulu's Back in Town	Warren
Rose of Washington Square	Hanley
Yesterday	Lennon/McCartney
Charlie Girl	Henneker
White Christmas	Berlin
Medley:	
Aren't You Glad You're You	Van Heuson
Taking a Chance on Love	Duke
Here It Comes Again	Reed
Hey Good Looking	Williams
Almost There	Shayne
Winter Wonderland	Bernard
The First Time It Snowed	Worth
A Walk in the Black Forest	Jankowski
Francesca	Galbraith
I Could Have Danced All Night	Lerner/Loewe
Medley:	
June is Busting Out All Over	Rodgers
Have You Met Miss Jones	Rodgers
Aqua Marina	Gray
Hello Dolly	Herman
Medley:	
When I Take My Sugar to Tea	Norman
Cool, Cool, Cool of the Evening	Carmichael
Hit the Road to Dreamland	Arlen
Calling All Workers (Sig)	Coates

CECIL NORMAN

Cecil Norman was born in Oldham, Lancashire, on 29th September 1897. His father and mother were in the variety profession, as a double act billed as Otto and Olga, although there is evidence in the form of old newspaper cuttings that his father had been a blacksmith and his mother a mill hand. Cecil, whose real name was Cecil Law, was regarded as a child prodigy. At the age of eight he won a piano competition at the Preston Musical Festival and was considered very gifted, and possibly (for his age) the finest pianist of his day. By the age of 11 he was playing concertos, at 15 he appeared at London's Aeolian Hall!

As a result of incessant practice, however, he developed neuritis in the right hand, forcing him to give up the piano for a couple of years. According to a note in his file at the BBC Written Archives Centre, he took up the saxophone for a while (although the accuracy of this is questionable) and joined Jack Hylton's Band. Returning to the piano, Cecil decided to specialise in dance music, this being less likely to aggravate his condition.

He later formed a band with his saxophonist brother, Leslie, and played at the Criterion, Café de Paris and the Carlton. After this he went to America to work with Ray Noble and Rudy Vallee. Having played with many well-known bands, he toured extensively with Howard Jacobs in 1937, visiting Australia, New Zealand and Honolulu.

Returning to Great Britain, he played for Jack Jackson at the Dorchester and George Melachrino at the Café de Paris, accompanying many famous stars. One night in October 1941, in the middle of an air raid, he received a call from Billy Ternent, asking him to join the BBC Dance Orchestra, a position which he gladly accepted. Later in the war he moved on to join Victor Silvester's Ballroom Orchestra, which incorporated two pianos – the other piano was played by Pat Dodd. The duo made a number of records on the Decca *Music While You Work* label.

When Pat Dodd left the orchestra, he was replaced by Ernest Wilson. By now, the two pianos had become such a popular part of the Silvester orchestra that it was suggested they should broadcast in their own right. Thus, in 1945, Cecil Norman and the Rhythm Players were born – a five-piece combination of two pianos, guitar, bass and percussion (the latter doubling on xylophone and later vibraphone). In 1945, they made the first of their 466 appearances in *Music While You Work* and were soon to become one of the most popular bands in the series. Indeed, Cecil directed more editions than any other bandleader. They played a mixture of popular medleys and light music novelties, one of which was always a Cecil Norman 'original'. Some readers may recall pieces like *Green Turtle* and *Up with the Lark* (appropriate for Cecil, who had to rise at 5.00 a.m if he was playing *Music While You Work!*). Other titles included *Macapa, Small Town Parade, Tulip Chimes* (inspired by a trip to Holland), *Fancy Free, The Jazz Drum Major, Keyed Up, Blue Moonlight, Jamaica Walk, Tampico, Blues in a Hurry* and *Chateau of Dreams*. Actually, whilst many of these would sound familiar to the older listener, the titles probably mean little as *Music While You Work*, like some other programmes, was unannounced.

In 1959 there was a series called *The Composer at the Piano* in which different pianists played 30 minutes of their own compositions. Cecil Norman was one of those asked to contribute and he played many of the above-mentioned pieces, this time announced. Cecil Norman was featured in many different series during the fifties and sixties, either with the Rhythm Players or as a solo pianist. These programmes included *Piano Playtime, Kings of the Keyboard, Music Box, Bright and Early, Morning Music* and *Play it Again* – a sequence of uninterrupted melodies in which Cecil Norman and Eddie Macauley (who had replaced Ernest Wilson as second pianist) were joined by other well-known soloists such as Jack Emblow, Tommy Reilly, Leslie Baker and Jackie Brown. This programme later became part of *Morning Music* and was re-titled as *Good Morning Music*.

Cecil was reportedly devastated when *Music While You Work* was taken off – it ended on his 70th birthday, although the Head of the BBC Popular Music Department, Kenneth Baynes, did send him a tape of his final programme, by way of a souvenir. Some consolation! The Players did the occasional session in *Breakfast Special* over the next couple of years before finally being dropped. Cecil's final broadcast was in 1970 when he appeared as a soloist in a series entitled *Concert Grand* (formerly *Kings of the Keyboard*). He played his own composition *Keyed Up*.

Although Cecil made few records in his own name, at least after the 78 era, he did briefly come out of retirement in 1974 to make an LP of strict-tempo dance music on the Decca Eclipse label entitled *In the*

Style of Charlie Kunz – a daft and frankly insulting title for a record by a pianist who was known for his own style, never attempting to sound like anyone else!

Cecil Norman moved to Worthing in 1971, a decision he later regretted, feeling rather detached from his friends. He never really recovered from the death of his wife Betty, his 'biggest fan', in 1981 and spent the rest of his life in his cold, dark flat, living off Meals On Wheels. With negligible income, he had to sell his piano in order to live and had to appeal to such distant relatives as he had to pay his electricity bill. A lonely old man, dreading every winter, he was barely able to look after himself but refused offers to go into a home for the elderly. He died on 8th February 1988, aged 91.

Music While You Work at 10.31 a.m on 7th October 1958
Played by Cecil Norman and the Rhythm Players

Calling All Workers (Sig)	Coates
Friends and Neighbours	Scott
I'm Sorry I Made You Cry	Clesi
Come Dancing	David
Blue Moonlight	Norman
Twilight Time	Ram
Return To Me	Lombardo
Near You	Craig
Ad Infinitum	Baynes
All the Nice Girls Love a Sailor	Scott
Fall in and Follow Me	Scott
I Do Like to be Beside the Seaside	Kind
Put Me Amongst the Girls	Murphy
Hello, Hello, Who's Your Lady Friend	Godfrey
Take Me Back to Dear Old Blighty	Scott
Fiesta	Coles
Father's Doing Fine	Smart
Little Serenade	Ferrio
Sugar Moon	Wolfe
Calling All Workers (Sig)	Coates

LOU PREAGER

The qualifications Doctor of Psychology, Doctor of Metaphysics and Licentiate in Chromotherapy are not the usual credentials of a palais bandleader; however, they were certainly the credentials of Lou Preager, who was at one time a Director of the Park Royal Hotel in Brighton, owner of Harmony Book Publishing Company, Managing Director of an art production factory, founder of the Golden Bell Record Company, Managing Director of Tele-Variety Ltd., owner of Radius Film Productions and Director of Lou Preager Productions. He was also a practising psychologist and a Fellow of the British Federation of Psychologists. Oh yes, he was also a bandleader!

Lou Preager was born in London on 12th January 1906. Whilst still at school, he played the piano in light orchestras and dance bands. After leaving school at 16, he spent several years in a chartered accountant's office and with a solicitor in an advertising agency. I recall him once saying on radio that he regarded these years as the wasted years of his life!

At the age of 19 he became a professional – in the capacity of musician, comedian and stage manager in touring revues. He played in West End clubs, and joined the Maurice Handford Band at the Piccadilly Hotel, giving his first broadcast with the band in 1928. In 1931, the Monseigneur Restaurant wanted a tango band, so Lou joined a combination fronted by Eugene Pini. Curiously, despite the billing of 'Eugene Pini and his Tango Orchestra', Lou Preager always insisted that he was the Musical Director.

It was during this period that Lou met Billy Reid and together they formed the Billy Reid Accordion Band. As Lou Preager did not know how to play the accordion, Reid gave him an intensive three-day course! Lou then joined the Gene Louis Band at Selfridges, playing for tea-dances in the afternoons but directing a Continental-style band in the Mayfair Restaurant in the evenings.

It appears that nobody ever did anything for long in those far-off days and 1933 found Lou Preager leading an 11-piece band at Ciro's but transferring within weeks to Romano's in the Strand, issuing his first gramophone record in 1935. The band's appropriate signature tune at that time was *Let's All Go Down The Strand.* Lou's Accordion Serenaders were also broadcasting around this time.

In 1937, Lou took a band on tour, taking up a residency in Bangor until the outbreak of war. Despite immediately offering himself for service, he was told to continue entertaining. He therefore formed a show band, which he took to France. Having been machine-gunned on route, however, the band was immediately sent back to England for its own safety.

After a spell of ambulance driving, Lou joined the Intelligence Corps in 1941, but, whilst training for a commission in Scotland, he was involved in a serious motor accident (ironically, whilst off-duty) and his right arm was smashed. It was only after eight months' intensive hospital treatment that he was able to get his arm reasonably straight.

He was invalided out of the Army in 1942 but was soon fit enough to form a 14-piece ballroom orchestra at the Hammersmith Palais, where he was destined to stay for nearly 18 years. He started broadcasting regularly as 'Lou Preager and his Correct Tempo Ballroom Band' (as it was initially called). He sometimes broadcast live from the Hammersmith Palais in such shows as *Saturday Night at the Palais,* as well as doing studio sessions with singers such as Paul Rich, Edna Kaye and Rita Williams. He began a long association with *Music While You Work* in 1942, playing quickstep medleys interspersed with other dance rhythms – the hotter, big-band-style numbers being reserved for other programmes.

Many readers will remember his distinctive, somewhat martial arrangement of *Calling All Workers*, making effective use of fanfares on the trumpets with the melody played underneath on the saxophones. Although his signature tune was now *On the Sunny Side of the Street,* he normally closed his *MWYW* programmes with *Whispering,* featuring tenor sax and piano and gradually speeding up to link with *Calling All Workers*. He did 96 editions.

Whilst at the Hammersmith Palais, Lou played opposite Harry Leader and Phil Tate. The latter was playing for the revival series of *MWYW* in 1982 when it became apparent that the band was tight on time. One musician called out: 'Let's do a Lou Preager and speed it up', and another musician interjected 'That's right – let's play *Whispering*'!

One of Lou's biggest broadcasting successes was a song writing contest called *Write a Tune for £1000.* The 52 programmes took place during the years 1945, 1947 and 1950 and produced a number of successful tunes, notably *Cruising Down the River*, which made a fortune for a couple of spinsters, Nellie Tollerton and Eily Beadell. Nowadays, there's the Eurovision Song Contest, about which the less said the better!

Lou Preager and his Orchestra were featured frequently on television, with *Palais Party* on ITV in 1955 and later with the very successful *Find a Singer*, for which Lou wrote the script, shared the presentation and was involved with the production, as well as conducting the band! In 1959, he decided that it was time for a change and his orchestra moved to the Lyceum in The Strand. He was regularly featured on television's *Come Dancing* in the days when this programme came simultaneously from two ballrooms, each in the region of the competing teams. In later years Lou appeared as an adjudicator.

In 1962 ill health caused Lou Preager to retire. Internal operations in 1955, 1961 and 1962 affected him for the rest of his life. During his career he had won several trophies, including, on three occasions, the Carl Allan Award for the best palais band.

Lou left London and went to live in Slough, where he bought the local Carlton Ballroom. After a heart attack in 1967, however, he sold the ballroom, settling down to a quiet life playing golf, billiards and snooker.

Over the years, Lou Preager made records for Panachord (some as Don Luiz and his Tango Band), Regal Zonophone and Columbia. Some of his Columbia 78s were reissued on a President LP. Lou also recorded as Lou Preager's Mink Tone Music – strict-tempo ballroom music in the which the brass section used mutes lined with mink! This might sound like publicity talk, but Lou actually cut up his wife's discarded mink coat so that the mutes could be lined with it. This created quite a distinctive sound which he used for *Music While You Work*.

In the fifties, Lou Preager was well-known as a disc-jockey introducing *Housewives' Choice* and his own *Record Serenade, Meet My Friends, Platter Playtime* and *Listen With Lou*.

Lou Preager was a complex man, intense and serious and, apparently, not one to suffer fools gladly, but he was also known to be gentle, generous and kind-hearted. As I mentioned earlier, he had impressive qualifications as a psychologist and, so I'm told, practised faith healing. Quite an extraordinary man! He died on 14th November 1978 at the age of 72.

Music While You Work at 3.45 p.m on 28th November 1960
Played by Lou Preager and his Orchestra

Calling All Workers (Sig)	Coates
Fings Ain't Wot They Used to Be	Bart
An Apple for the Teacher	Burke
If I Had a Talking Picture of You	De Sylva
Amapola	Lacalle
Always	Berlin
What'll I Do?	Berlin
Goody Goody	Mercer
This Can't Be Love	Rodgers
The Continental	Conrad
Romantica	Rascel
Cindy Lou	Shepherd
Bell Samba	White
Let Yourself Go	Berlin
Change Partners	Berlin
Cheek to Cheek	Berlin
My Little Corner of the World	Pockriss
The Touch of Your Lips	Noble
The Very Thought of You	Noble
Sicilian Samba	Lewis
Galway Bay	Colahan
Along Came Caroline	Stephens
How About That?	Worth
I've Got a Pocketful of Dreams	Burke
Sweet Sue	Harris
I'm a Dreamer, Aren't We All?	De Sylva
Singing Piano	Evans
Feel So Fine	Lee
Bon Sante	Elman
Spooky	Deane
Love Look Away	Rodgers
You Are Beautiful	Rodgers
There's a Blue Ridge Round My Heart	Bryan
I Can't Give You Anything But Love	Gaskill
Pardon Me, Pretty Baby	Rose
Truckin'	Bloom
Ida	Leonard

166

Button Up Your Overcoat	De Sylva
Why Do I Love You?	Kern
You're the Cream in My Coffee	De Sylva
Whispering	Schonberger
Calling All Workers (Sig)	Coates

REG PURSGLOVE

Many purveyors of dance music have subsequently, or simultaneously, become associated with light orchestral music. The names of Percival Mackey, Ronnie Munro and Jack Coles immediately come to mind. Another musician whose career followed a dual path was Reg Pursglove, remembered by radio listeners in the fifties and sixties for his Albany Strings.

Reginald Pursglove was born on 21st November 1902, and, having become proficient on the violin, commenced his professional career with Moss Empires as sub-leader and conductor. He later joined the Savoy Group, playing for Carroll Gibbons's band, The Sylvians, and the Orpheans under Debroy Somers. After a spell with Howard Jacobs's band at the Berkeley Hotel, he joined Ray Starita in 1928 for a two-year engagement at the Ambassadors Club. He formed his first band in 1930, playing at Quaglino's Restaurant and at the Embassy Club. Throughout the 1930s he did freelance work for such bandleaders as Ambrose, Ray Noble and Carroll Gibbons. In 1931 he landed an engagement at the exclusive Malmaison Restaurant in Stratton Street, Mayfair, but for some reason, probably contractual, for this engagement and on early records, he called himself 'Gene Arthur and his Band'.

Reg Pursglove and his Orchestra adopted the signature tune *Love is in the Air* by Richard Whiting. This also became the title of a series which the orchestra did for the BBC in 1939, Pursglove's 'sweet' style being ideal in view of the 'love' theme of the show. He was, however, required to use extra strings and a harp.

It is difficult to be precise when describing the instrumentation of Reg Pursglove's broadcasting combinations, as they varied according to the requirements of the show or series. When Reg Pursglove and his Orchestra started doing *Music While You Work* in 1940, the instrumentation was three saxes, four rhythm, trumpet and violin (nine players), and this appears to be the line-up on their many recordings for Decca's special *MWYW* label. After the war the orchestra was augmented to 26 players for a while, having five saxes, strings, two pianos and a full brass section. As Pursglove was once again doing theatre pit work, this combination would have been ideal.

During the war years, another combination called The Music Makers had been regularly heard on the air. Initially there was no credit given to the Musical Director in *Radio Times,* but it was indeed Reg Pursglove, and his name was eventually attributed to it.

The Music Makers originally consisted of six players but was later increased to eleven and heard regularly for some years. The larger orchestra had ceased to broadcast by the late forties and Reg had formed yet another orchestra, this time for the BBC Music Department, playing light music. He called it the Albany Players. It is evident from the BBC files that the Variety Department didn't take kindly to 'their' musicians playing under the auspices of the Music Department or the Light Music Department (formed in the mid-fifties). Playing for two departments obviously doubled potential broadcasting opportunities, but was seen in some quarters as unfair to those conductors who specialised in one area of music. In fact, in 1949, Kenneth Sydney Baynes told Reg Pursglove that he would not be offering the Music Makers any more *MWYW* programmes, as he deemed them 'unsuitable' for the series. I must say that it had taken him a long time to come to that conclusion and one can only speculate as to whether Pursglove's contract with the Music Department might have been the real reason! When Reg complained, however, he was told that as the Corporation was still employing his Albany Players, the BBC was fully satisfying its obligations to him.

After some persuasion, Reg Pursglove managed to secure a broadcast with the Music Makers in December 1949 but the BBC deemed that 'it lacked guts and was not sufficiently audible in factories'. Apart from one dance music date in 1951, Reg's career was now entirely in the light music field.

The 18-piece Albany Players ceased broadcasting in 1951 and Reg Pursglove formed a combination of eight to twelve players called The Muted Strings. Its title and style made it most suitable for late-night broadcasts, and although used occasionally in *Morning Music*, it was

168

not getting broadcasts as frequently as Reg Pursglove would have liked. In 1954, the BBC pointed out that its title was tending to limit its use and advised him to rename it The Albany Strings. He took their advice and so was born a highly attractive 11-piece light orchestra which appeared in a wide variety of programmes over the next 14 years.

Reg Pursglove had already done 142 editions of *Music While You Work* with his dance orchestra and the Music Makers. On 1st June 1959, The Albany Strings made the first of 75 appearances in the series.

For the purposes of *MWYW* the programmes were, of necessity, light. The Albany Strings, however, was a versatile orchestra with skilled personnel and when used in other series, played more serious music, some of it specially written for string orchestra. Those who remember listening to this orchestra will recall its clear, refreshing sound. No guitars, no drums, just strings and a piano.

With the demise of *MWYW* in September 1967, and the corresponding reorganisation of radio, Reg found that many of the series in which he had participated were no more. He had been contributing to *Breakfast Special* for some time but the BBC suddenly decided that he didn't provide the sort of music wanted for the show. So what sort of music did the BBC want? Whatever it was, the versatile Albany Strings could have provided it! In 1969, Reg Pursglove asked the BBC why it was that he had been given 23 broadcasts in 1966 but just one in 1967. The BBC conceded that Pursglove was justified in being aggrieved that after 30 years on the air, he should suddenly be dropped even though the standard of his orchestra's performances had in no way diminished. The problem was that suitable 'slots' were no longer available. After some discussions, the orchestra was given a few sessions as holiday relief for the BBC's London Studio Players, in which the orchestra was augmented to 22 players, but this proved to be its swan-song. Reg Pursglove died on 15th March 1982, aged 79.

Music While You Work at 3.45 p.m. on 30th October 1959
Played by Reg Pursglove and The Albany Strings

Calling All Workers (Sig)	Coates
Colonel Bogey	Alford
I'll Be Around	Wilder
Five Minutes with Joyce's Waltzes	arr. Hartley

Here's to Love	Mougeot
Serenata	Anderson
Sweden in Springtime	Lindberg
The Westminster Waltz	Farnon
Regency Rondo	Rubel
The Very Thought of You	Noble
Fiddlers' Bugle Call	Martin
Selection: *The Dancing Years*	Novello
Miss Melanie	Binge
Killarney	Balfe
Sicilian Samba	Herbert
Honouring the Haggis	Agoult
Spanish Gypsy Dance	Marquina
Calling All Workers (Sig)	Coates

WYNFORD REYNOLDS

Wynford Hubert Reynolds was born in Ebbw Vale in 1899. After studying the violin in Cardiff, he joined the Army during the First World War. Upon his return to civilian life he studied violin, viola and composition at the Royal Academy of Music, later becoming musical director of a cinema, like so many of his contemporaries, gaining his early experience playing for silent movies. He later joined Sir Henry Wood as a violinist in the famous Queen's Hall Orchestra.

It was as a member of a string quartet that he made his first broadcast from Savoy Hill. Subsequently he played viola in many broadcasting combinations, including those of Fred Hartley, Reginald King and Jack Payne.

During the thirties he directed his own orchestra at the Spa, Felixstowe, his signature tune being his own composition *Spa Song*, which was later re-titled *Cocktail of Happiness*. Other delightful compositions from his pen include an exhilarating Viennese waltz entitled *Morning Glory* and novelties such as *Twinkletoes*.

170

By the late thirties, Wynford Reynolds and his Orchestra were broadcasting regularly. This orchestra, which specialised in light, tuneful novelties and medleys, initially comprised 11 players but was later increased to 13. Around this time, Wynford Reynolds also joined the staff of the BBC as a producer.

When *Music While You Work* commenced in 1940, Wynford Reynolds and his Orchestra were early contributors, appearing nine times in the first year. In 1941, the BBC created the post of *Music While You Work Organiser* and appointed Wynford Reynolds to take on this task. As part of his work would involve the selection and allocation of contributing orchestras to the programme, he was not permitted to appear with his own orchestra whilst he held this appointment. He might have been seen to have an unfair advantage over other contributors, and there was the potential for difficulties to arise when dealing with disciplinary matters. In any case, he was kept busy visiting factories around the country, advising managers on suitable receiving equipment, ascertaining the views of the workers on the suitability of contributing bands, and even listening to programmes in prevailing conditions to establish their audibility above factory noises.

Although independent of the BBC, the Decca Record Company produced some 420 records on their special *Music While You Work* label, the majority of which were produced by Wynford Reynolds, whose own orchestra was well represented. Many of the recordings from this series have now been released on compact disc.

Wynford Reynolds relinquished his appointment as *MWYW* Organiser in 1944 and his orchestra resumed broadcasting in the series. After the war, he continued to participate in various light music programmes including *Bright and Early*, *Morning Music*, *Uninterrupted Music*, and *Time For Music*. He also had a 19-piece combination called The Raeburn Orchestra, his pseudonym as a composer being Hugh Raeburn. This larger orchestra was also featured in *And So To Bedtime* and *Time for Music*. The two orchestras collectively appeared in 109 editions of *Music While You Work*. Many will recall the Raeburn Orchestra's long association with *Marching and Waltzing*.

Other combinations directed by the Maestro were The Wynford Reynolds Players and the 29-piece Wynford Reynolds Concert Orchestra, which was mostly used in breakfast-time programmes.

Unfortunately, in 1956, Wynford Reynolds was told by the BBC that his original 13-piece orchestra was 'dated' and had 'outlived its usefulness'. The BBC disliked his use of three saxophones at a time 'when the public had become accustomed to the sound of five saxophones', which (in their opinion) gave 'an aura of the early thirties'. It would seem that his style was considered redundant!

Graciously, the BBC told Wynford Reynolds that he could continue broadcasting with the Raeburn Orchestra. This he did until being taken seriously ill in 1958. At this time the orchestra was contracted do a series of *Marching and Waltzing* as well as some *MWYW* programmes. Violinist/conductor Bernard Monshin, who played in the orchestra as well as being its 'fixer', told me that he offered to conduct the scheduled programmes himself, 'to prevent the broadcasts being lost to another orchestra'. Consequently, quite a number of the Raeburn Orchestra's programmes were conducted by Bernard Monshin.

In August 1958, Wynford Reynolds informed the BBC that he hoped to return to broadcasting the following January and that, in the meantime, he was working on new arrangements in his hospital bed. Sadly, his optimism was ill-founded, as he died in October 1958, aged 59.

Music While You Work at 10.30 a.m. on 21st April 1956
Played by Wynford Reynolds and his Orchestra

Calling All Workers (Sig)	Coates
Begorrah	Martin
Rip Van Twinkle	Nelson
Medley:	Friml arr. Reynolds
Chansonette	
Indian Love Call	
Every Little While	
Only a Rose	
Flirtation Waltz	Heywood
Medley:	arr. Reynolds
The Poor People of Paris	Monnot
Love is the Tender Trap	Van Heuson
Robin Hood	Sigman
The Royal Tango	Monshin
Theme from *The Threepenny Opera*	Weill
Throw Open Wide Your Window	May
Medley:	arr. Reynolds
I've Got a Pocketful of Dreams	Burke/Monaco

An Apple for the Teacher	Burke/Monaco
Great Day	Youmans
Guanta le Gusta	Ruis
Valse Royale	Reynolds
Calling All Workers (Sig)	Coates

Music While You Work at 10.31 a.m. on 24th May 1958
Played by The Raeburn Orchestra
Conductor: Wynford Reynolds

Calling All Workers (Sig)	Coates
Marching Strings	Ross
Westminster Waltz	Farnon
The March Hare	Green
La Petite Valse	Heyne
Stringing Along	Reynolds
The Gay Nineties	arr. Gray
Pepita	Versey
Selection: *Where's Charley*	Loesser
Calling All Workers (Sig)	Coates

BILL SAVILL

Bill Savill was born in London on 15th March 1910. In the thirties he played drums for Teddy Brown, fulfilling many engagements at night-clubs such as The Mitre, Golden Square, and 50-50. When war came he joined the RAF and, having attained the rank of Sergeant, was instrumental in forming the dance orchestra of RAF Fighter Command, which he directed until 1944. He also provided the resident band at the Officers' Club, Grosvenor House, between 1942 and 1946. It was with this band, a sextet, that he made his first broadcast in 1943. In fact, he made over 100 *Services Calling* broadcasts, as well as appearances at

173

the Allied Club, Piccadilly, and at St James's Palace. If this wasn't enough, he was also Musical Director for a show called *This is the Gen* at the Phoenix Theatre, West London.

After demobilisation, he formed a civilian orchestra which gave its first broadcast on the Light Programme in 1946. He soon established his own highly distinctive style with this 14-piece dance orchestra, consisting of strings, saxes, piano and rhythm. Familiar names such as Eric Rogers, Neville Hughes, Reg Leopold and Neil Richardson played in the orchestra over the years, the latter being responsible for many of the arrangements.

Bill Savill continued to fulfill engagements at the Dorchester, Claridge's and Hyde Park Hotels and at the Royal Albert Hall. He became very much associated with London's high society, playing for private functions, hunt balls, and charity balls such as the Royal Caledonian Ball, Queen Charlotte's Debutantes' Ball, and the Westminster Appeal for the Blind Ball to name but a few. There were also numerous engagements for RAF associations and Masonic and Rotary functions. In 1951, Bill Savill was awarded the Jack Hylton Cup for Musical Directors.

On radio, Bill Savill and his Orchestra were particularly associated with *Music While You Work* and between July 1946 and September 1967 appeared on no less than 308 programmes, sometimes doing as many as 20 editions in a year. They were the last ballroom orchestra to appear in the series – just nine days before its demise in September 1967. No doubt much of their appeal was due to their individuality of style and the fact that they were one of the few post-war dance orchestras to use a string section instead of brass.

From 1957 onwards, they produced a series of superb LPs for Decca, which were not only perfect for dancing but also ideal for listening. The orchestra was augmented from 14 to 19 musicians for these records – a few extra strings were added, as was a trumpet, but this was used most discreetly and the overall sound was very similar to the broadcasts.

After *MWYW* finished, Bill Savill's broadcasts became infrequent, with occasional appearances in *Breakfast Special* until the late sixties. For some time, Bill had arranged the provision of orchestras in his own name for private functions and he continued to do this for many years after broadcasts ceased. He died on 3rd March 1995.

Music While You Work at 3.31 p.m. on 18th March 1963
Played by Bill Savill and his Orchestra

Calling All Workers (Sig)	Coates
Let's Face the Music and Dance	Berlin
I Whistle a Happy Tune	Rodgers
You're the Cream in My Coffee	De Sylva
Lonely	Bilk
The Best Things in Life are Free	De Sylva
Button Up Your Overcoat	De Sylva
Good News	De Sylva
I'll Follow My Secret Heart	Coward
Some Day I'll Find You	Coward
The Night Has a Thousand Eyes	Wayne
Bushel and a Peck	Loesser
If I Were a Bell	Loesser
Guys and Dolls	Loesser
Slightly Out of Tune	Jobim
I Get Along Without You Very Well	Carmichael
Globetrotter	Meek
The Street of Linden Trees	Geller
Pied Piper	Race
The Last Time I Saw Paris	Kern
I Love Paris	Porter
C'est Magnifique	Porter
Soul Bossa Nova	Jones
Betty Dear	Agoult
Alley Cat	Bjorn
Surrey with the Fringe on Top	Rodgers
Out of My Dreams	Rodgers
People Will Say We're in Love	Rodgers
Broken Date	Phillips
Together Wherever we go	Styne
Everything's Coming Up Roses	Styne
Dancing with My Shadow	Wood
My Hat's on the Side of My Head	Wood
We'll All Go Riding on a Rainbow	Wood
Calling All Workers (Sig)	Coates

175

PRIMO SCALA

Nearly half a century after his death, the name of Primo Scala is still remembered by lovers of accordion music and his recordings are still being reissued on compact disc. Yet there was never a person of that name, Primo Scala being one of several pseudonyms of pianist Harry Bidgood (son of the march composer, Thomas Bidgood).

Harry Bidgood was born in London in 1898, receiving early musical education from his father prior to attending the Royal College of Music. He commenced his professional career just after the First World War as pianist with De Groot at the Piccadilly Hotel, London. In 1926 he started directing recording sessions for Vocalion, which, in 1928, began to issue the famous 8-inch Broadcast records. Harry directed a 'house band' for these records, known as Harry Bidgood and his Broadcasters. Other studio bands under his direction included: The New York Nightbirds, Ciro's Club Band, The Manhattan Melody Makers, Al Benny's Broadway Boys, The Riverside Dance Band and Nat Lewis and his Dance Band.

When accordion bands started to become popular in the early thirties, Harry Bidgood saw the potential and formed a band for Eclipse called Don Porto' s Novelty Accordion Band. He also recorded (in 1935) as Rossini's Accordion Band for the Crown label, which sold in Woolworth's stores. It was under the alias of Primo Scala and his Accordion Band, however, that he was destined to become most famous.

There are various theories as to the origin of the name Primo Scala. It has often been suggested that 'Primo' came from a heavyweight boxer named Primo Carnera and that 'Scala' came from Emilio Scala, winner of the Irish Sweepstake, although it is more likely to have to have derived from Scala Records, once part of Vocalion, for which Bidgood recorded. Primo Scala's success on record was such that he assumed this identity for the rest of his career; furthermore, the band began to take on public engagements and by the late thirties was regularly heard on the radio. By January 1941, Primo Scala and his Accordion Band was appearing on *Music While You Work,* soon becoming one of the most frequent and popular contributors, partly because accordions came over well in the factories. During the next 16 years the band played 296 editions. In the war years, the BBC was anxious not to be accused of employing Italians. As mentioned in Chapter One, this created a problem when using artists with Italian pseudonyms or stage-names. So, Harry's band became 'Primo Scala's Accordion Band directed by Harry Bidgood'. There was even an accompanying paragraph in the *Radio Times* stating that he had 'taken over' the band before the war!

For broadcasting, the Primo Scala band consisted of four accordions, two pianos, bass, drums and guitar (doubling Banjo). In the early years, a violin was sometimes included. Pictures of the band sometimes show about eight accordions but this was probably just for stage use.

After the war, Primo Scala's Accordion Band dropped the appendage 'Directed by Harry Bidgood' but continued to play regularly in *MWYW* as well as *Bright and Early* – a programme on similar lines which made for a delightful way to start the day at 6.30 a.m.

By the fifties, Harry Bidgood had decided to make his 'sound' more commercial (at least on records) and, having dispensed with the violin, he added trumpet and saxophone for a series of records in which the band was joined by the Keynotes. Personally, I preferred the style and instrumentation which he used on the radio.

By 1956, Harry Bidgood's health was beginning to deteriorate and some of his broadcasts were directed by guitarist Ernest Penfold, whom many will remember for his South Sea Serenaders. Harry Bidgood died on 16th November 1957 at the age of 59.

During the sixties, some of Harry's later 'Keynotes' recordings were reissued on an LP. Another LP was produced in 1962, purporting to be Primo Scala and his Accordion Band but it bore no resemblance to the band. Not surprising, since it was a group of session musicians assembled for the occasion under the direction of Ivor Raymonde. Happily, in the 21st century many original recordings of Primo Scala are now being made available on compact disc, ensuring the preservation of these happy sounds for another generation.

Music While You Work at 10.30 a.m. on 12th June 1956
Played by Primo Scala and his Accordion Band

Calling All Workers (Sig)	Coates
Pickin' a Chicken	Bernfield
Please Hold Me Tightly	Morris
Zambesi	Carstens

177

Band of Gold	Taylor
Vanity Box	Bidgood
Rock and Roll Waltz	Allen
Theme from The Threepenny Opera	Weill
Cookie	Mortimer
My September Love	Evans
I Love the Sunshine of Your Smile	Macdonald
Come Next Spring	Steiner
The Dummy Song	Brown/Rose
You Can't Be True To Two	Hoffman
Napolitana	Troise
Calling All Workers (Sig)	Coates

GEORGE SCOTT-WOOD

As another leading accordion band leader, it is logical that George Scott-Wood's profile should follow that of Primo Scala, but in all honesty, it is because he comes next alphabetically!

George Scott-Wood was born in Glasgow on 27th May 1903. He studied the piano from the age of five with Miss Hoffman, Crossland Hirst and Philip Halstead (a pupil of Leschetizky). He performed his first concerto, Beethoven's Third in C Minor, at the age of 16, winning awards at the Glasgow and Edinburgh Music Festivals. He also won (with his brother) the famous Marchant Cup for Chamber Music. In 1925, George toured the USA, making many concert appearances.

His career in popular music started sometime during the twenties when he played with a Glasgow University Band called the Five Omega Collegians, touring and recording with them until their disbandment in 1928, at which time he joined Jay Whidden's Band for a two-year spell as pianist and arranger.

In 1930 he became Director of Light Music for Parlophone (under Oscar Preuss) and subsequently for the other three EMI companies – HMV, Regal-Zonophone and Columbia – a post which he held until 1939. The thirties was a decade in which George Scott-Wood really

178

established himself in a big way. Apparently, he made more records than anyone else in Britain, either directing one of his own combinations or accompanying famous artists, often under pseudonyms or anonymously. He conducted accompaniments for an impressive list of performers which included Richard Tauber, Sir Harry Lauder, Beatrice Lillie, Larry Adler, Gracie Fields, Vic Oliver, Stanley Holloway, Max Miller, Evelyn Laye and Ivor Novello, to mention but a few of the 80 or so artists he backed! He recorded about 20 sides with the New Mayfair Dance Orchestra in 1935 after Ray Noble left for America.

It was in 1934 that Scott-Wood's Six Swingers came into being. This was a rather superior jazz group which really caught the public's attention during its seven-year existence and produced over 50 recordings. George was later described as 'the pioneer of swing music in this country'. In the 1938 *Daily Mail* radio popularity poll, the Six Swingers were voted top of radio entertainment, with all other dance music grouped together in seventh place.

Apart from his considerable talents as a virtuoso pianist, arranger, conductor and composer (of which more later), George Scott-Wood was regarded as one of the country's leading piano-accordion exponents. This instrument has, unfortunately, gone out of fashion in recent decades and I know of people who do not even regard it as a proper musical instrument! Nevertheless, over the years there have been, and still are, many brilliant exponents of the instrument. George Scott-Wood was the author of the first ever comprehensive accordion tutor, published in 1930; indeed, he is credited with having introduced the piano accordion to Great Britain, becoming its first professional exponent.

Having spent some years singing Spanish tangos to his own accordion accompaniment, it isn't surprising that his interest was such that in 1934 he became MD of the London Accordion Band, a Regal-Zonophone house band. By 1940, he had formed his own accordion band. This, initially, had nine accordions but, after the war, it reduced to four accordions, bass, drums, guitar and Hawaiian guitar (later vibraphone), with George directing operations from the piano. It always surprises me that accounts of George Scott-Wood's career concentrate on the Six Swingers with little reference to his work with accordions, which, after all, represented a much larger part of his career.

From 1943 to 1947, George topped theatre bills as a solo pianist, travelling extensively up and down the country. He spent much time visiting garrison theatres, hospitals, factories, remote camps and action stations.

By the end of the war, George Scott-Wood and his Accordion Band resumed regular broadcasting and were featured in *Accordion Club, Bright and Early* and, of course, *Music While You Work*, to which they contributed 214 programmes. As a piano soloist George was often featured in *Piano Playtime*. Even the BBC had to admit that George was an excellent musician and an ingenious arranger – on one occasion I can recall him being described as a 'master craftsman of many years' standing'.

He re-formed his Six Swingers briefly in 1950, but it did not achieve its former success. He also suggested to the BBC that he should be allowed to form a 23 piece theatre orchestra, using his accordion band as a nucleus, but the idea fell on stony ground, as did his suggestion that he should adopt an Italian alias! (Perhaps he had in mind the success of Primo Scala?)

For many years, popular music at the BBC was handled by the Variety Department (dance music) and the Light Music Department (light orchestras and groups). Despite his long association with dance music, George had always been sympathetic to light music and in 1946 had applied, albeit unsuccessfully, for the position of Head of Light Music at the BBC.

Although contracted to the Light Entertainment Department, successor to the Variety Department, George had often included items of light music in his programmes, so in 1957 he applied for an audition with the Light Music Department for a slightly smaller combination which would specialise in this repertoire. The new seven-piece ensemble – George Scott-Wood and his Music – gave its first broadcast in early 1958, the instrumentation being three accordions, piano, guitar, bass and percussion. For a while he continued broadcasting on *Music While You Work* with the nine-piece accordion band, no doubt hoping to reap the benefits of being contracted to two departments. As stated previously in these profiles, this was not deemed a satisfactory situation by the departments concerned or, indeed by the BBC. So by 1959 all of George's broadcasts, including *MWYW*, were given by the seven piece group, which also played regularly in *Morning Music*.

George was a prolific composer. In 1938, he recorded his *Dainty Debutante,* a brilliant piano feature, with his salon orchestra. The Accordion Band recorded his *Flying Scotsman* and *Corn on the Cob* in 1950. Other Scott-Wood 'specials' included *London Caprice, Ici on parle*

180

Francais, Deb-on-air, Song without Words, A Landler for Sandler, Holiday for Accordions, Cuba Boogie, Penny Farthing Polka, The Laughing Seine, Conchita' s Song, Happy Fingers, El Cochero, Rumbaba, Amontillado and *Champagne Galop* from his suite *Carnival of Bacchus, Sirocco, Clip-Joint, Fab,* and his famous signature tune, *Shy Serenade.*

Nowadays, some of George Scott-Wood's vintage recordings are appearing on compact disc, including several volumes of the International Novelty Orchestra (house band of Regal-Zonophone) for which he was reliably believed to have been the Musical Director (albeit anonymously).

George Scott-Wood and his Music could always be relied upon to provide a bright, tuneful programme – immaculately played. It included such virtuoso personnel as Gerald Crossman and Henry Krein. They played in *MWYW* right up to the end in 1967 and were then dropped from broadcasting until making a brief come-back in 1970 and 1971 on the *Sam Costa Show.*

George Scott-Wood, who was married with two children, died on 28th October 1978 at the age of 75.

Music While You Work at 10.31 a.m. on 5th October 1960
Played by George Scott-Wood and his Music

Calling All Workers (Sig)	Coates
Lady of Madrid	Evans
Arrividerci Roma	Rascel
Tinkle Box Samba	Rubach
Silly Little Tune	Pockriss
Brazil	Barroso
Ici on parle Francaise	Scott-Wood
Caravelle	Owen
Tom Pillibi	Popp
A Media Luz	Donato
Angry	Mecum
Bonita	Steele
Small Town Parade	Norman
Calling All Workers (Sig)	Coates

IAN STEWART

It is unusual to associate the role of a dance band leader with that of a distinguished career in the Army. Such was the case, however, with Ian Stewart, whose strict-tempo pianistic style was a feature of radio for many years.

Ian Edward Stewart was born in December 1908 of a Scottish father and an American mother, spending most of his early life in Seaton, Devonshire. He was a chorister at Salisbury Cathedral and spent three years at St Edwards, Oxford. A pupil of Herbert Howells, Ian Stewart became organist at Chalfont, Somerset, at the age of 18. In complete contrast, he had also formed his own band in Seaton, which he called the Geisha Dance Band. He began his professional career in a rather humble way playing the piano for a marionette show on the beach at Margate. This led to an engagement touring with the musical *So this is Love* – initially as pianist but later as Musical Director. Next, Ian Stewart turned his hand to music publishing, a venture which occupied him for five years prior to his going to the USA where he frequently broadcast for NBC.

Returning to London in 1935, Ian Stewart was reintroduced to dance music by his idol, Carroll Gibbons, joining the Savoy Hotel Orpheans as Deputy Leader and second pianist in the years leading up to the Second World War.

His military career commenced as a territorial with the London Scottish and ended as a Brigade Major with the 17th Indian Division, he received a meritorious award of MBE in Burma in 1945. When demobilised in 1946, he immediately formed his own band at the Berkeley Hotel, London. Although he had done some pre-war work in radio, Ian Stewart, his piano and his orchestra began regular broadcasting in 1947.

Ian's admiration for Carroll Gibbons was such that, initially, he deliberately emulated his style but soon realised that he would be more successful if he had his own way of playing. He therefore evolved a quite distinctive staccato style, making use of repeated notes to great effect, which immediately identified him. With the premature death of Carroll Gibbons in 1954, Ian Stewart took over the band, reviving the name of Savoy Hotel Orpheans. For radio purposes, he used a combination of piano, bass, guitar, drums, saxophone (doubling clarinet) and accordion; the group was called Ian Stewart and his Quintet. The guitar was omitted from the group in the early sixties.

The band broadcast regularly in *Bright and Early, Morning Music* and *Music While You Work*, playing 264 editions over 20 years. As a solo pianist he was a frequent contributor to the 15-minute series *Piano Playtime*. Having a cultured voice, he was one of the few pianists who was allowed to introduce his own programmes. His signature tune for these programmes was his own composition, *Story of a Song*.

As well as broadcasting, Ian Stewart made many records for Decca, Parlophone and Fontana, including a series called *Hits For Six* – each featuring six hits of the day. He would have been hard put to find six playable tunes in the charts of today!

Like Carroll Gibbons before him, Ian Stewart's name became synonymous with the Savoy Hotel, where he played until his retirement in 1978, the occasion being celebrated with a live television performance in an early evening magazine programme.

An elegant and articulate man, Ian Stewart had all the attributes of the soldier that he once was. Indeed, at the BBC he was known as 'The Colonel'. Some diners at the Savoy, however, found him a little aloof. Whereas some bandleaders would push their own personality, Ian was very reserved. 'I'm just not an extrovert', he said. 'I was never a table-hopper – perhaps I should have been, I might have done better and been more famous!'

Although he played requests, he did not always play them immediately. He once recounted the story of a drunken diner who repeatedly asked for the same tune. In desperation, the irate diner slapped a pound note on the piano, snarling 'I suppose you are waiting for a tip'. Stewart said 'I flicked it off. It was very satisfying seeing him have to pick up his own note!'

Ian Stewart played for Churchill, the Macmillans at Number 10 and for the Royal Family, the late Queen Mother being a devoted fan. When playing for informal gatherings he was warned not to make the dances too long. The procedure, however, was to keep on playing whilst a member of the Royal Family was on the floor. Ian Stewart recalled: 'The first time I went there, I was about to stop as the Queen left the floor when somebody whispered, "There's somebody else coming on." This went on for ages. Eventually, a perspiring Duke of

Edinburgh came over: "Give it a break, old man. I can be lumbered as much as anybody else!"'

Ian Stewart died on 30th July 1989 after a long illness, aged 80.

Music While You Work at 10.31 a.m. on 1st October 1965
Played by Ian Stewart and his Quartet

Calling All Workers (Sig)	Coates
S'posin'	Denniker
Ida, Sweet as Apple Cider	Leonard
When You've Got a Little Springtime	Woods
When Somebody Thinks You're Wonderful	Woods
Tears	Uhr
Elizabeth	Katscher
A Lot of Living To Do	Strouse
I Left My Heart in San Francisco	Cory
Sugartime	Echols
Am I Wasting My Time	Bibo
Thank Heaven For Little Girls	Loewe
Who Can I Turn To?	Bricusse
Toot Toot Tootsie	Kahn
Almost There	Keller
Whistle and Flute	Woods
Second Hand Rose	Hanley
The Way You Look Tonight	Kern
Volare	Modugno
Ain't She Sweet	Ager
I Whistle a Happy Tune	Rodgers
We'll All Go Riding on a Rainbow	Woods
Calling All Workers (Sig)	Coates

EDDIE STREVENS

Edwin Cyril Strevens was born in London. As a child he studied the violin at the Guildhall School of Music, winning a scholarship to the Royal Academy of Music.

During the war, Eddie served in the Duke of Cornwall's Light Infantry and as it was no secret that he was a brilliant jazz violinist, he was often asked to play at camp concerts. His musical ability soon came to the notice of the bandmaster of the regiment's military band who was anxious to make use of his skills. The only problem was that the 'hot fiddle' is not traditionally associated with the military band, so Eddie was given a saxophone and told to learn how to play it! This he quickly did and joined the band.

Back in civilian life, he continued to play the saxophone, although his first love was still the violin. He played in the bands of Ronnie Munro, Harry Parry and Roy Fox, but his longest association was with the orchestra of Geraldo, for whom he had a high regard.

It was in 1956 that Eddie Strevens formed his own band, and passed a BBC audition. In 1959, he made the first of 89 appearances in *Music While You Work,* playing both violin and saxophone, supported by accordion, piano, bass and drums. Initially, he also included a guitar but he soon dispensed with this on broadcasts.

Eddie Strevens and his Quartet played regularly in *Morning Music, Breakfast Special, The Sam Costa Show, Music Through Midnight* and many other programmes. Eddie Strevens also enjoyed some success as a composer with titles such as *Easy Come, Easy Go, Playtime for Poodles* and *Getting With It.*

Although, in common with so many combinations, Eddie Strevens and his Quartet ceased to broadcast in the late sixties, he continued to fulfil public engagements for many years. He fronted a group on P&O transatlantic cruises and played for cabaret, variety shows and dances. In 1978, he made a long-playing record on the Halcyon label which featured his skills on the violin throughout.

It has not been possible to establish what Eddie Strevens' activities have been in more recent years or, indeed, whether he is still alive. If he is, it is likely that he will have been retired for some years.

Music While You Work at 10.31 a.m. on 2nd December 1965
Played by Eddie Strevens and his Quartet

Calling All Workers (Sig)	Coates
Little White Lies	Donaldson
Diga Diga Doo	Fields/McHugh
Rosetta	Hines/Woods
Yesterday	Lennon/McCartney
Whistle and Flute	Woods
Getting With It	Strevens
I Left My Heart in San Francisco	Cross/Cory
Eros	Deane
Medley:	
Close Your Eyes	Pethers
A Nightingale Sang in Berkeley Square	Maschwitz
Tonight's the Night	Primo/Secton
I'll Be Around	Wilder
Let's Kick	Moorhouse/
	Mansfield
Soulsville	Richardson
Going To Town	Heath
Medley:	Berlin
Be Careful It's My Heart	
I've Got the Sun in the Morning	
I've Got My Love To Keep Me Warm	
Calling All Workers (Sig)	Coates

PHIL TATE

Phil Tate was born in Bramley, Yorkshire, on 28th April 1922 and was educated at West Leeds High School. He developed an early interest in music, taking up the violin at the age of eight. He concentrated on classical music until the outbreak of war, when he joined the Royal Air Force as a radar mechanic. In 1943 he was transferred to welfare and was then able to form his own orchestra of service musicians. After demobilisation he formed a civilian orchestra which included most of his wartime players.

In 1948 he accepted an appointment as Musical Director to the Folkestone Corporation and broadcast both from Folkestone and London. Regular broadcasting commenced in 1950, when he gave the first of his 144 *Music While You Work* programmes. This was with a small band which he was then directing at the Hammersmith Palais (opposite Lou Preager) – a residency held by both bandleaders for many years.

Phil Tate subsequently decided to form a larger orchestra for broadcasting and, knowing that the BBC specifically encouraged bands to sound 'different', he set about creating his own particular 'sound' – a blend of three flutes, five saxophones and clarinet with two pianos, trumpet and rhythm. This produced a warm, friendly sound with the same spine-tingling effect as the famous Glenn Miller sound, yet in no way was this an imitation of this or any other style.

Phil Tate's orchestra was a firm favourite on radio during the fifties and sixties. He even compèred his own breakfast-time series featuring his orchestra and quintet, which he led on clarinet. By this time, television audiences had come to know him as the resident musical director for the various beauty contests sponsored by Mecca and leading up to the Miss World Contest in the Royal Albert Hall each November.

For their broadcasts, the band specialised in strict-tempo dance music and its success led to a contract with Oriole Records and the issue of many 78s and 45 rpm records as well as some long-playing records. Phil Tate and his Orchestra had already been captured on celluloid in the early fifties when they appeared in the film *Green Grow the Rushes*. It is for radio, however, that Phil Tate is best remembered, and for the 16 years he played regularly in *Music While You Work*. As his programmes were largely in medley form, he often got through about 40 pieces in a 45-minute programme!

By the sixties, Phil Tate had moved from the Hammersmith Palais to the Ilford Palais and, around 1964, he made some minor changes to the instrumentation of the orchestra and to the style of the programmes by introducing some longer arrangements. He replaced the second piano with a guitar (presumably to facilitate the playing of some current 'pops'). The blend of flutes and saxes was retained.

When the Ilford Palais residency ended, Phil Tate decided that a permanent orchestra was no longer viable and he disbanded, but regular broadcasting continued in *Breakfast Special* with a slightly smaller combination known as Phil Tate's Windjammers, which had a distinctive but quite different style.

In 1982, when the BBC brought back *MWYW* for one week, Phil Tate was asked to reconstitute his orchestra in the style for which it was best remembered. This he did, restoring the second piano and using only arrangements from the original series. The success of this week (and in particular, Phil Tate's broadcast) led to a resumption of the programme in 1983, and Phil again took part. The BBC assumed that he would want to use the Windjammers, but Phil insisted on using the full orchestra as before. So, despite what was shown in the *Radio Times*, and even incorrectly announced on air, what was broadcast was Phil Tate and his Orchestra!

By this time, Phil had been out of regular music-making for some while, although he was still conducting for the annual Miss World Contest. His main occupation now was as Managing Director of Mecca Agencies, a joint position with Ivor Rabin (Oscar Rabin's son).

In 1990, the BBC celebrated the 50th Anniversary of *Music While You Work* with a further week of programmes and, once again, Phil Tate took part. It was 40 years since his first appearance on the show and this broadcast was destined to be his swan-song.

Music While You Work at 3.45 p.m. on 2nd January 1961
Played by Phil Tate and his Orchestra

Calling All Workers (Sig)	Coates
I'm in a Dancing Mood	Sigler
Dancing With My Shadow	Woods
My Hat's on the Side of My Head	Woods
My Little Corner of the World	Pockriss
Whispering Tango	Munro
You Turned the Tables on Me	Alter
El Pandero	Baker
Red Sails in the Sunset	Kennedy
Dreamin'	De Vorzon
Everything's in Rhythm With My Heart	Sigler
One, Two, Button My Shoe	Burke
Just in Time	Styne
Snowcoach	Stanford
Paradise	Brown
Isn't This a Lovely Day	Berlin
Easter Parade	Berlin
Madeleine	Addison
Cindy Lou	Shepherd
Love Walked In	Gershwin
The Love Nest	Hersch
I've Got My Eyes on You	Porter
Romantica	Rascel
Rustlin'	Russell
Cuban Fiesta	Ellis
To Each His Own	Livingstone
High Tide, Low Tide	Race
Rosalie	Porter
You're the Cream in My Coffee	De Sylva
There's a Small Hotel	Rodgers
Don't Blame Me	McHugh
Try a Little Tenderness	Woods
Somebody Loves Me	Gershwin
Once in a While	Edwards
Kickin' Up the Leaves	Bart
Mountain Greenery	Rodgers
Ain't She Sweet	Green

You Forgot to Remember	Berlin
Rosemarie	Friml
Bye, Bye, Baby	Robin
Calling All Workers (Sig)	Coates

NAT TEMPLE

Nat Temple was born in Stepney, East London, on 18th July 1913, one of four brothers. He took up the saxophone and clarinet and, prior to becoming a bandleader, played with many of the leading bands, including those of Ambrose, Geraldo and, occasionally, Lew Stone, but is probably most associated with Harry Roy, for whom he has nothing but praise. Many of the clarinet solos on Harry Roy's recordings were performed by Nat Temple.

He served in the Grenadier Guards for much of the war, playing with their regimental band in North Africa and Italy. It was a fact that musicians serving in the Forces sometimes took 'time out' to do gigs with ad hoc bands – a situation which led to questions being asked in Parliament! Nat certainly took the opportunity to play sessions with many well-known bands, notably Geraldo from 1941, forming his own band in 1944. Early vocalists included Benny Lee and Frankie Vaughan. Nat also accompanied Lita Rosa, David Whitfield, Anne Shelton, Julie Andrews and many others.

His broadcasting career started in 1946, when he formed the Nat Temple Octet. He later broadcast as 'Nat Temple, his clarinet and woodwind' (or Woodwindettes). By 1950, the Nat Temple orchestra was broadcasting regularly. It usually consisted of about 12 players, although it was sometimes augmented with strings, if required.

During the late forties it was commonplace for a dozen or more programmes of dance or light music to be broadcast each day (a far cry from the present time) and this enabled Nat to broadcast frequently, filling many an instrumental half-hour with his orchestra, as well as playing for variety or light entertainment programmes such as *Breakfast with Braden, Bedtime with Braden* (and their sequels), in which he often participated in the repartee between Bernard Braden and Barbara Kelly. There were, however, a number of other situation comedy series in which Nat not only provided the music but acted as stooge to the main stars as well! Apart from appearing on other people's programmes, he also had his own series called *Enchanted Rhythm*.

Nat Temple's many television credits during the fifties included *My Wife Jacqueline* and *Barbara with Braden*. My first memories of him, whilst still a child, were on children's television in programmes such as *Crackerjack, Telebox* and *Jack-in-the-Box*, when Nat and the band involved themselves in comedy routines. I still recall my surprise when hearing them on *Music While You Work* and realising, for the first time, that they were not just a comedy band!

Nat Temple once told me that it was sometimes suggested that he should forsake music for comedy – the implication being that he was a better comedian than he was a musician. In fact he was, and still is, a very good musician. He composed a number of pieces such as *Burma Road* and *Nattering Around,* both of which he recorded with a combination called Nat Temple and his Club Royal Orchestra. He also wrote his signature tune *Canzonetta*, which I don't believe he recorded with his own band, but a Parlophone recording by Geraldo and his Orchestra featured Nat as a solo artist. The piece was also recorded by Eric Winstone, Lou Preager, Joe Loss, Reg Leopold and Phil Green. There was even a recording by the distinguished clarinettist Reginald Kell with Monia Liter's Twentieth Century Serenaders.

Nat Temple and his Orchestra played regularly for radio and television throughout the fifties and continued with *Music While You Work* until 1966. When this series was revived in 1982 as part of the BBC's 60th Anniversary celebrations, Nat Temple's band was the first to be featured and Nat was shedding tears of emotion by the conclusion! He made further appearances in 1983 and subsequently in *Music All the Way*.

I had the privilege of attending several of Nat Temple's *MWYW* programmes and recall him telling me on the phone that he was under pressure to include more modern material, so I suggested a piece called *We'll Meet Again* – no, not the Vera Lynn hit but the title tune for a then current television drama series set in the Second World War, played in the style of Glenn Miller. As Nat did not know of it, I sang a few bars down the phone which he then sang to his wife. He then exclaimed, 'My wife knows it and says it's good – so we'll use it!' A few weeks later he played it in *Music While You Work*.

I clearly recall sitting on a hard stool in the cramped Studio 5 at Maida Vale, literally only a couple of feet behind Nat Temple – keeping as still as possible for fear that a creak would be heard over the air, when suddenly, in the middle of the actual broadcast, Nat turned round to me and mouthed the words, 'Is it alright?' I gave him the 'thumbs up' sign and he nodded appreciatively before resuming playing his baritone saxophone!

Nat Temple has never been associated with a particular ballroom as, over the years, his band has played mostly for private and corporate functions. He did summer seasons for Butlin's, university balls, Christmas parties at Windsor Castle plus many appearances at top London hotels. He also ran an entertainment agency and, even in his eighties, was providing bands for functions. A compact disc was issued by *Evergreen* magazine to coincide with Nat Temple's 90th birthday in July 2003.

Music While You Work at 3.41 p.m. on 29th September 1965
Played by Nat Temple and his Orchestra

Calling All Workers (Sig)	Coates
Selection: *Mary Poppins*	Sherman
March of the Mods	Carr
Make It Easy On Yourself	Bacharach
A Walk in the Black Forest	Jankowski
Granada	Lara
What's New, Pussycat?	Bacharach
Lollipops and Roses	Velona
Selection: *West Side Story*	Bernstein
That's the Way	Blakely
Girl from Ipanema	Jobim
I Love You and Don't You Forget It	Mancini
Catch Us If You Can	Clark
Happy Days and Lonely Nights	Rosa
Among My Souvenirs	Nicholls
Sunny Side of the Street	McHugh
My Old Man	Collins
Calling All Workers (Sig)	Coates

BILLY TERNENT

Many bands of the past attempted to create their own style, some more successfully than others. Perhaps one of the most distinctive styles of all time belonged to Billy Ternent. Indeed, the phrase 'that unmistakable sound' will always be synonymous with him on broadcasts and records.

Billy Ternent took up the violin at the age of seven and his first job was with a trio at a North Shields cinema when he was 12. At 16, he was conducting a cinema orchestra on a circuit run by George Black. He made his first broadcast with a sextet from a tea-room in Newcastle, later playing at the famous Kit-Kat Club in Piccadilly. It was probably his long spell with Jack Hylton and his Orchestra (1927 to 1939) that really brought him to the public's attention, during which time he acted as Deputy Conductor and principal arranger. Many well-known bandleaders were better managers than they were musicians – some bands even regarded their conductor as a liability! Not the case with Frederick William Ternent, who was a fine and much respected musician who could, and sometimes did, play every instrument in the orchestra. This was very useful to Jack Hylton, who was able to use him whenever a player was off sick.

In September 1939, Billy Ternent was appointed conductor of the BBC Dance Orchestra or 'The Dance Orchestra' as it was then called. He conducted the first *ITMA* broadcasts with Tommy Handley, worked on *Variety Bandbox*, and had a weekly slot on *Music While You Work*. When he resigned from this post in 1944, he handed over the baton to Stanley Black, who conducted the band until its demise in the early fifties.

At this point Billy Ternent formed a new band with which he went on tour. The band's signature tune was *She's My Lovely*, from the musical *Hide and Seek*. This, however, attracted some complaints due to the fact that the opening glissando, to some people, sounded like the start of an air-raid warning! Nevertheless, it remained the signature tune of Billy Ternent and his Orchestra for many years to come. The original

1943 Decca recording featured the singing of actor/guitarist Ken Beaumont, who was later to find fame on the radio with his sextet.

The secret of Billy Ternent's success was the combination of the superb musicianship of both leader and players, coupled with having created one of the most distinctive styles in broadcasting. It was a seemingly old-fashioned style, using a tenor-dominated saxophone section with a strong vibrato (perhaps reminiscent of Guy Lombardo) and a trumpet section which was frequently required to play muted passages with rapid triple tonguing – a sort of 'stuttering' effect – possibly inspired by the American band, Shep Fields and his Rippling Rhythm. The overall effect, however, was original and required a musical expertise far above that of the average palais player; indeed, the top session men Billy used found the arrangements to be very challenging.

The late Roger Moffat, best known for his humorous presentations of the BBC Northern Dance Orchestra, often compèred Billy's programmes in later years. On one occasion he told Ternent on air, 'You are very old-fashioned.' 'No I'm not,' Ternent retorted, 'I'm very modern!' Actually, this was in some ways quite true because even though the arrangements (penned by Ternent himself) alluded to styles of the past, they were highly complex – even sophisticated.

Roger Moffatt was in the habit of engaging Billy Ternent in conversation during the broadcasts – most of it was scripted but not always. Indeed, some of his ad-libs displeased the BBC and eventually cost him his job.

On one occasion Roger Moffatt said to Billy Ternent, 'Hey Bill – I hear that they're taping these broadcasts down at the Foreign Office! You know when your lot go "uh uh uh uh,uh uh,uh,uh" – all staccato like on the trumpets? Well, they think you're transmitting coded messages to a foreign power!'

Despite the 'holocaust' in radio music when, in the sixties, most dance bands and light orchestras were unceremoniously dumped by the BBC, Billy Ternent and his Orchestra survived, broadcasting regularly until the mid-seventies.

Billy Ternent, who was born in Newcastle on 10th October 1899, died on 23rd March 1977, but this amiable Geordie can still be remembered through his legacy of 78s and long-playing records (now available on CD), spanning a long and distinguished career.

Music While You Work at 3.30 p.m. on 13th March 1950
Played by Billy Ternent and his Orchestra

Calling All Workers (Sig)	Coates
You Forgot to Remember	Berlin
My Thanks to You	Gay
Kiss Me Sweet	Drake
Long Long Ago	Brown
The World is Waiting for the Sunrise	Lockhart
Best of All	Dewar
Boa Noite	Warren
A Rose in a Garden of Weeds	David
Lovers Lane Has Everything	Denson
The Harry Lime Theme	Karas
Is It True What They Say About Dixie	Lerner
Calling All Workers (Sig)	Coates

TROISE

Pasquale Troise was born in Naples in 1895 and took up the clarinet at an early age, graduating to the school band at the age of seven. It was several years later that he began learning the banjo, mandolin and guitar, becoming a proficient performer in all three instruments.

Troise came to this country in the early twenties and in 1926 joined the London Radio Dance Band directed by Sidney Firman and subsequently Jack Padbury. After a spell with Jack Padbury's sextet at the Cosmo Club, Pasquale Troise decided to form his own band – the Selecta Plectrum Mandoline Orchestra. He secured a recording contract with Decca and made a number of records, including *The Bohemian Girl* Selection and *Rendezvous* by Aletter.

It was hardly surprising that by the early thirties the somewhat cumbersome title of the band had changed to Troise and his

Mandoliers and, having joined the variety theatre circuit, the band toured the country, commencing with the Plaza, Haymarket. Their phenomenal success on the halls was due, in no small measure, to the energetic enthusiasm of their leader. During the thirties, the Mandoliers cut over 60 sides for Rex, Regal and Regal-Zonophone with items as diverse as the *Zampa Overture* (Herold) and the *Spanish Gypsy Dance* (Marquina). When on stage, the mandoline players doubled on banjos, and the resulting combination became Troise and his Banjoliers. Some years ago Jimmy Perry presented a television series called *Turns* which used rare archival clips of artists from the past and both the Banjoliers and Mandoliers were featured.

When *Music While You Work* was introduced in 1940, Troise was an obvious choice as a dispenser of bright and cheerful music and made his first appearance in September of that year. After four performances by the Mandoliers, however, it was decided that the Banjoliers were more suited to the programme, banjos apparently being more audible than mandolines in noisy factories. So, all subsequent appearances were by Troise and his Banjoliers, the Mandoliers being used in other programmes. During the forties, the Banjoliers made a number of recordings on the Decca *Music While You Work* label.

In addition to his skills as a mandoline player and conductor, Troise was a prolific arranger and composer. Titles include *Festive Romance, Jolly Archers, Here they Come* and, most famous of all, a tarantella entitled *Napolitana,* which was actually a selection of Neapolitan songs. Other medleys arranged by Troise include *Tally Ho!, Gems of Stephen Foster* and *Songs of Old England.* Another feature of his *MWYW* programmes was a medley of current pops arranged by Billy Cater-Smith and later Antony Fones Jnr. The same tunes were used for several consecutive broadcasts and then replaced when they were no longer of plugging value to the publishers. As already mentioned, publishers would finance the cost of arrangements, providing that they were played an agreed number of times during their currency in the playlist. This, apart from reducing bandleaders' arranging costs, was beneficial to publishers but understandably frowned upon by the BBC, whose Charter did not permit advertising or 'plugging' in any form, but, in practice, most bandleaders did it and seemingly got away with it. No doubt the BBC turned a blind eye, providing that there was no obvious bias towards any one publisher or composer.

During the fifties, Troise sometimes broadcast with a combination called Troise and his Serenaders, or as Troise and his Continental

Music. This combination of 19 players was basically the Mandoliers with the addition of a small string section. Early in 1957, Troise fell ill and the Banjoliers were conducted by Jack Mandel, a respected violinist who played for such famous names as Harry Davidson and Ralph Elman (even taking over the direction of their orchestras when they were indisposed). Mandel had been taught banjo and mandoline by Troise in the thirties and had played for him ever since.

Sadly, on 21st March 1957, Troise died. He had commanded tremendous respect from the music profession as well as from the BBC. Senior executive H. Campbell-Ricketts once said: 'I've never known him do other than a good broadcast.' The popularity of the Banjoliers was such that the BBC was determined that they should be kept together and, within just a few days of Troise's death, negotiations took place with his widow, which resulted in the appointment of Jack Mandel as permanent conductor. It was agreed that, initially, a hire fee would be payable to Mrs Troise for the use of the library. For a time, the Mandoliers and Continental Music continued to broadcast on *Morning Music*, but they were eventually dropped, as the Banjoliers were proving to be more popular. Their instrumentation was piano, bass, drums, accordion and eight banjos in varying sizes and pitches. Jack Mandel kept faithfully to the Troise style of programming for some years, although he tended to use fewer medleys in relation to individual pieces.

When the BBC integrated their Light Music Department into their newly-formed Popular Music Department, Jack Mandel introduced more dance music into the repertoire, although he dispensed with the *Popular Pot-pourri* which had virtually become a medley of current film and television themes and show tunes, there being little in the charts that was stylistically suited to the band. Although, in common with other combinations, they had become more commercial, they still played a repertoire superior to other banjo bands, most of which specialised in the popular song repertoire/minstrel tunes etc. The Big Ben Banjo Band had become popular but even their conductor, Norrie Paramor, admitted that he had only formed it for a joke and had been surprised at its success.

For me, the Banjoliers had that bit of extra class, their superb playing and fine arrangements of a wide range of music made them unique in broadcasting. Their personnel changed very little over the years – classical mandoline player Hugo D'Alton, Billy Bell and Terry Walsh were all there to ensure stability, with accordionist Emile

Charlier or Albert Delroy and pianists such as William Davies and Sidney Davey.

The Banjoliers hold the record for the most *Music While You Work* programmes, Troise and Jack Mandel having led 258 and 217 respectively. After the series finished, the Banjoliers continued to broadcast until being axed by the BBC in the early seventies. Some years later the Mandoliers' library was revived in *Friday Night is Music Night*, using a combination called The Mandolin Men. The revival was short-lived, however, and the library subsequently went to a school which had its own mandoline orchestra.

Jack Mandel was asked to reform the Banjoliers in 1982 to do a *Music While You Work* as part of the BBC's 60th Anniversary Celebrations. This turned out to be the band's final broadcast. Jack Mandel retired to Israel, where he died a few years later.

Music While You Work at 3.45 p.m. on 2nd March 1956
Played by Troise and his Banjoliers

Calling All Workers (Sig)	Coates
March: *El Capitan*	Sousa arr. Troise
Yodelling Strings	White
The Shifting Whispering Sands	Hadler
Whistling Rufus	Mills
Medley: *Tunes of Today*	arr. Fones
Robin Hood	Sigman
Someone on Your Mind	Houck
Young and Foolish	Hague
The Military Polka	Thomas
Sway	Ruiz
Song of the Mountains	Ortelli/Pigarelli
Medley: *Popular Pot-Pourri*	arr. Cater-Smith
Hey, Mister Banjo	Morgan/Malkin
Meet Me on the Corner	Hart
Twenty Tiny Fingers	Tepper/Bennett
Summertime in Venice	Icini
Go on By	Hamblen
Arrividerci Darling	Rascel
Old Pianna Rag	Phillips
Calling All Workers (Sig)	Coates

LOUIS VOSS

Louis Voss was born in London on 12th January 1902 and studied violin and piano from an early age. He was 'discovered' whilst playing at a school function at the age of 12 and subsequently studied at the Guildhall School of Music where he gained many prizes and scholarships, including the AGSM.

In the twenties, Louis directed cinema orchestras, accompanying silent films until the arrival of 'talkies', whereupon he turned his attention to café and restaurant work where, as violinist and conductor, he specialised in gypsy, Viennese and Hungarian light music.

During the thirties and forties, the Louis Voss Grand Orchestra made many records for Bosworth's and also recorded under the title 'West End Celebrity Orchestra'. The Grand Orchestra was led by no less than Alfredo Campoli. By the mid-thirties, Louis Voss was broadcasting regularly, at first under the pseudonym of Luigi Voselli and his Hungarian Orchestra, but later using his own name. The orchestra comprised three violins, viola, cello, harp, accordion, bass and drums.

When the war came, Louis Voss secured exemption from military service on account of his being 'one of J. Lyons' key men'. For a while he continued to broadcast, under his own name rather than Luigi Voselli, as the BBC at this time did not like to be seen to be employing Italians, even though, in his case, it was only a pseudonym! He did get called up in 1942, however, and served in the Royal Air Force. Whilst it was hoped that he could still give the occasional broadcast (he was actually given contracts), it was presumably felt that winning the war was a greater priority and the arranged programmes were conducted by Lionel Falkman.

In 1946, Louis Voss returned to broadcasting with several different combinations – the Bioscope Orchestra, The Tyroleans and Louis Voss and his Players, which consisted of three violins with flute, cello, bass, piano and accordion. The six-piece Tyroleans, as well as broadcasting in their own right, also became a featured spot in the orchestra best remembered by radio listeners – The Kursaal Orchestra – a 21-piece light orchestra comprised of strings, woodwind, accordion and percussion, which specialised in novelty numbers, Continental tunes and show selections. The bass player switched to tuba for the Tyrolean style pieces, many of which came from the pen of Louis Voss. Most of the repertoire was specially arranged for the orchestra by publishers' 'house arrangers' who, at that time, included Ernest Tomlinson and Cyril Watters. I recall Cyril telling me how helpful Voss was with the arrangements – the scores being clearly marked with his instructions as to which instruments were to be used in each passage. He favoured a delicate sound, making much use of the combination of piccolo, glockenspiel and bass clarinet, contrasting with a luxurious string sound. Chords were 'punched out' with a combination of accordion, woodwind and sometimes tuba. The origin of the title 'Kursaal Orchestra' is somewhat obscure, possibly being inspired by the Kursaal at Interlaken in Switzerland. Kursaal is a German word literally meaning 'cure room' or 'spa', evolving into 'Winter Gardens' in later years. According to the Oxford English Dictionary, it is pronounced 'Koorzahl' – not 'Kurzle', as Southend folks would have it!

For more than 20 years, Louis Voss broadcast in programmes such as *Café on the Corner, Morning Music, Dancing Round the World, Remember These, Music Mixture, Marching and Waltzing* and *Music While You Work*, to which The Kursaal Orchestra contributed 149 editions.

Apart from being a violinist and conductor, Louis Voss was also a prolific composer. Amongst his compositions are *Alpine Fairy Tale, Masquerade in Madrid, Conversation Caprice,* and *Piccaninny Puppets.* Most of his pieces were written under the name of Stefan Rogez, his son being Roger and his daughter, the well-known soprano and actress Stephanie Voss. It was to her that Louis dedicated one of his earlier pieces, *Stefanka.* I wonder if his composition *Antonella* was dedicated to fellow conductor Arthur Anton, in whose orchestra Louis Voss sometimes played?

By the late forties Louis Voss was one of the BBC's most frequent broadcasters, yet he still found time to do theatre work, becoming MD for a musical entitled *The Kid from Stratford* starring Arthur Askey, which toured the country before settling down at the London Hippodrome. In 1953, he was contracted to do 'holiday relief' for BBC Staff Orchestras and for a five-week spell he was broadcasting about four times a week in programmes that included *Commonwealth of Song* and *Mid-day Music Hall.* Louis Voss was well respected, both by the

BBC and by his fellow musicians and he continued to broadcast, either with the Kursaal Orchestra or a larger combination called The Louis Voss Light Orchestra, until 1967, when the axe fell on most of the outside orchestras. Unbeknown to listeners, however, Voss broadcast for some time as conductor of the Sydney Thompson Old Time Orchestra. Thompson, being a dancer rather than a musician, merely managed his orchestra and announced the items, leaving the conducting to Voss. It always struck me as the height of discourtesy that no mention of this fact was made, either on air or in the *Radio Times*. If Louis Voss was annoyed by this, he never said anything. According to a former producer, he was 'too much of a gentleman to complain'. Louis Voss died on 14th March 1980 at the age of 78.

Music While You Work at 3.31 p.m. on 3rd January 1964
Played by Louis Voss and his Kursaal Orchestra

Calling All Workers (Sig)	Coates
Tartan Patrol	Ewing
Maigret Theme	Grainer
Medley:	arr. Papworth
Valentina	Christine
Valencia	Padilla
Ooh La La	Jessel
Peg O' My Heart	Fisher
Heidelberg Polka	Watters
A Garden in Granada	Lewis
Antonella	Rogez
Mexican Serenade	Coles
Song of Alassio	Charles
Jangle Bells	Baynes
Happy Hurdy Gurdy	Carmichael
Selection: *The Sound of Music*	Rodgers
Maria's Tarantella	Green
La Cannebiere	Agoult
Perfidia	Dominguez
The Happy Mountaineer	Schlapfer
Medley: *Souvenir D'Italie*	arr. Fones
Chella Lia	Taccani
Kiss me, Kiss Me	Casadel
Souvenir D'Italie	Luttazzi

Summertime in Venice	Icini
Torero	Carosone
Calling All Workers (Sig)	Coates

JACK WHITE

Jack was born Eugene Joseph White, in Liverpool, on 2nd December 1905 and, at the tender age of three, he played the concertina at his grandfather's funeral! He played this instrument throughout his childhood, even doing gigs – singing to his own accompaniment. He had no intention of turning professional, therefore upon leaving school he became a motor mechanic. His enthusiasm for music remained, however, and he took up the drums, later learning the alto-saxophone, tuition for which was paid for by his mother. At the age of 19 he formed his own 'family band', having taught his father to play the drums and his brothers Jay and Tom to play saxophones. In 1926, the band won contests organised by *Melody Maker* and in 1928 was awarded the Jack Hylton Trophy, sponsored by Jack Hylton at the Embassy Ballroom, Liverpool. There was a local school called St Francis College and Collegiate School, thus the band became known as Jack White and his Collegians. The band turned professional in 1929, appearing at the Rialto Ballroom in Liverpool, its original signature tune being *Collegiate*. In later broadcasting days, Jack changed his theme tune to *Out of Nowhere*. After a long spell at the State Café, Liverpool, the band performed at the Plaza Ballroom, Manchester, the West End Ballroom, Birmingham, the Regent Ballroom, Brighton, and in 1935, the Hammersmith Palais. The original quintet had increased to six and then eight players.

When Jack's father died in 1930, the band's personnel were reshuffled and Tom became the drummer, a position which he held throughout Jack White's career. In an age when musicians were constantly moving from one band to another, it is truly amazing that several of Jack's 1935 band were still with him 20 years later.

In 1936, Jack White started what was intended to be a six week spell at the Astoria Dance Salon in London, whilst Joe Loss was away on tour, but he was retained as second band and remained there (apart from a few years' break for war service) until November 1957 – probably the longest residency in dance band history. By 1936, Jack White was broadcasting regularly and in late 1937 commenced recording for Parlophone and later, Regal-Zonophone. The title 'Collegians' was dropped in 1940 when they became No. 1 band opposite Syd Dean, at the same time increasing their personnel to 12.

In 1941, Jack and his two brothers were called up, Jack joining the RAF on 12th May 1941. The band continued for some months and did quite a few editions of *Music While You Work* under the direction of Jack Lennox before disbanding. Jack White was now in the Central Band of the Royal Air Force, eventually forming a ten-piece band which, believe it or not, actually included five of his Astoria musicians, amongst whom was his brother Jay. Soon after the war, Jack White and his Band re-established themselves as No. 1 band at the Astoria, playing opposite Harry Leader. Regular broadcasting resumed and, whilst Jack contributed to many different programmes, he is probably best remembered for *Music While You Work*, for which the band played 309 editions between 1940 and 1966. Available documentation shows that he had a very enthusiastic and loyal following amongst his listeners and by the mid-fifties was doing more broadcasts than any other bandleader in the country. His popularity was well justified as his brass section had a terrific 'punch', tempered with a beautiful, warm mellow saxophone section. The arrangements were stylishly done by Jack himself and the musicians always sounded as if they were enjoying themselves.

A distinctive feature of the band was the unorthodox percussion style of Jack's brother Tom, particularly when using the wire brushes – and it didn't always meet with the approval of BBC producers, who were probably looking for a more modern sound. The fact was that Jack didn't care for the modern trends in pop music and made little attempt to emulate them. In fact, the band's style in the sixties retained many of the characteristics of their records made in the 1930s.

It was unfortunate that the frequency of the band's broadcasts, which was based on their popularity, attracted a certain amount of professional jealousy from bandleaders who had become famous in a wider sphere of dance music (big band swing etc.) but were not getting as many broadcasts. Jack White never tried to compete with anybody, he didn't try to recruit 'star' players, his only concern being that the musicians he used would give a polished performance of the repertoire. This fact, coupled with the obvious rapport between leader and players, must have accounted for the incredible stability of personnel over the years.

In November 1957, Jack White finally decided to leave the Astoria, hoping to get another residency elsewhere, but none was forthcoming and the band ceased to exist on a full-time basis. Despite this, broadcasts continued, for which he used most of the Astoria personnel, supplementing them with session men when required. BBC policy was such that full-time bands were given priority over those that were 'got together' just for radio and, as Jack now came into this category, his appearances became less frequent and, during the sixties, were confined to *Music While You Work*.

Many will recall, with affection, the annual Christmas edition which consisted of community songs and music hall tunes. The musicians joined in, singing and cheering during some of the numbers, creating a wonderful atmosphere. Even in their 'normal' broadcasts Jack White's band sometimes forgot that they were on the air. I can recall sometimes hearing the sound of whistling and, on one occasion, a shared joke followed by raucous laughter!

Jack White's final broadcast was given on 23rd December 1966 and, being the cheerful Christmas show, was a fitting finale to his career. He then moved to the South Coast and set up a successful printing business.

A sad epilogue to the story is that Jack White, depressed at the way tuneful dance music had given way to crude 'beat and shout' pop music, chose to erase his career from his mind, destroying all his memorabilia and not wishing to meet anyone who might bring back memories. Apparently, in old age, he even refused to admit to having ever been a bandleader! Jack White died on 25th June 1988 at the age of 82.

Music While You Work at 3.45 p.m on 5th April 1961
Played by Jack White and his Band

Calling All Workers (Sig)	Coates
Button Up Your Overcoat	De Sylva
My Heart Stood Still	Rodgers
You're the Cream in My Coffee	De Sylva
Sailor	Scharfenberger
You're Driving Me Crazy	Donaldson

Are You Lonesome Tonight	Turk
Lulu's Back in Town	Warren
Avalon	Jolson
Chicago	Fisher
Till	Sigman
Pepe	Wittstatt
Just as much as ever	Singleton
Shine	Mack
Shepherd of the Hills	Nicholls
Pardon me Pretty Baby	Kalges
Mistakes	Nicholls
Samba Rag	Laurenson
Friendly Street	Cleaver
Hap Hap Happy Day	Tinberg
This is the Missis	Brown
Here Comes Cooke	Gordon
Passing Breeze	Stanford
Marry Me	Jacks
Eternally	Chaplin
If You Knew Susie	De Sylva
Goodbye Blues	McHugh
I'm Gonna Lock My Heart	Eaton
Cherry Blossom Lane	Leslie
We're Gonna Dance	Barell
Someone is Thinking of You	Powell
You are my Sunshine	Davis
Sugartime	Phillips
Calling All Workers (Sig)	Coates

And the Christmas Special ...

Music While You Work at 10.30 a.m. on 23rd December 1955
Played by Jack White and his Band

Calling All Workers (Sig)	Coates
Jolly Good Company	Raymond
Twelfth Street Rag	Bowman
Destiny	Baynes
The Veleta	Morris
Lily of Laguna	Stuart
Little Dolly Daydream	Stuart

John Brown's Body	Trad.
You Made Me Love You	Monaco
St Bernard's Waltz	Swallow
The Gay Gordons	Bonheur
The Lambeth Walk	Gay
Hello, Hello,Who's Your Lady Friend?	Godfrey
I Do Like to be Beside the Seaside	Glover
Man Who Broke the Bank at Monte Carlo	Gilbert
The Campbells Are Coming	Trad.
Knees Up Mother Brown	Weston
I Belong to Glasgow	Fyffe
If You're Irish	Glenville
Through the Night	Trad.
The Lincolnshire Poacher	Kennett
On Ilkley Moor Baht 'At	Trad.
Lassie from Lancashire	Murphy
Up from Somerset	Sanderson
Sussex by the Sea	Biggs
Blaydon Races	Trad.
Maybe it's Because I'm a Londoner	Gregg
Here's a Health Unto Her Majesty	Trad.
John Peel	Trad.
Calling All Workers (Sig)	Coates

When I commenced this chapter dealing with the careers of a selection of *Music While You Work* contributors, I did not expect it to become the lion's share of the book. The fact that it has is probably all for the better, as many of the artists featured have had little written about them until now, despite having been household names on radio for decades. Regardless of this, many did not see themselves as stars, merely as working musicians earning their living. Hugh James, in one of his last letters to me wrote: 'I was well-known to fans of my *MWYW* and Park programmes, but if you went into the street today and asked people if they had heard of Hugh James, the answer would be – No!'

It will be apparent to afficionados of *MWYW* that many major contributors have not been profiled in this book. Apart from the obvious limitations of space (this is not intended to be an encyclopaedia), the main reason is the lack of available information.

Light orchestra leaders, in particular, were curiously remiss in providing career information to magazines and books that dealt with music and musicians. Sadly, it has to be admitted that the editors of such publications would be unlikely to seek them out unless they were prolific recording artists such as Mantovani. So, I would like to round off this chapter with such limited information as I possess about a few of the 'notable omissions'.

Our front cover is adorned with a picture of **ANTON AND HIS ORCHESTRA** broadcasting from the Camden Theatre, London. Anton, who was a violinist, was born Arthur Sweeting but, when working in theatres in the 1930s, was advised to find himself a more imposing name. So, Anton he became! During the latter half of the 1930s he was the conductor of the Paramount Theatre Orchestra in Tottenham Court Road, London, from where the orchestra gave a weekly broadcast as well as making many records for HMV, often accompanied by the cinema organist Al Bollington. Some of the broadcasts came from the Brixton Astoria, so, on those occasions, the orchestra was re-titled the Paramount Astoria Orchestra. Anton later formed his own orchestra specifically for broadcasting and gave the first of his 252 *MWYW* broadcasts in 1946. He and the orchestra took part in many other series, including *Bright and Early, Morning Music* and *Marching and Waltzing*.

Arthur Anton was also a reserve conductor for the BBC Regional Light Orchestras and conducted the BBC Scottish Variety Orchestra and the BBC Northern Ireland Light Orchestra in countless broadcasts. In 1965 he was Musical Director for the London show *Charlie Girl*. After retiring from the music business he and fellow conductor Joseph Muscant became joint Presidents of the Vintage Light Music Society, which was run by the late Stuart Upton, a man greatly respected for his unique and encyclopaedic knowledge of the world of traditional light music. Arthur Anton died in March 1980, but many of his early records have now been issued on a series of CDs.

The aforementioned **JOSEPH MUSCANT AND HIS ORCHESTRA** were also *MWYW* regulars between December 1948 and Muscant's retirement in 1959, playing 51 editions in that series alone. Like Arthur Anton, he had enjoyed considerable success during the thirties. He gave classical violin recitals in his young days but turned his attention to light music in 1929 when he was appointed Musical Director at the Commodore Theatre, Hammersmith directing the famous Commodore Grand Orchestra. From 1930 this orchestra broadcast for an hour every Saturday lunchtime as well as making more than 50 commercial recordings for Decca, Regal-Zonophone, Edison Bell and the Broadcast label. In 1934, Harry Davidson took over the conductorship of the Commodore Grand Orchestra, although he was later to become famous with his own orchestra in the long-running series *Those Were The Days*. Joseph Muscant moved on, taking up a similar position with the Troxy Broadcasting Orchestra – a position which he held for some years. After the Second World War, he formed his own orchestra, playing summer seasons at resorts such as Paignton and Broadstairs, broadcasting regularly in *Morning Music* and other programmes. He died in December 1983 aged 84.

HARRY FRYER AND HIS ORCHESTRA is another combination associated with the early years of *Music While You Work*, but their broadcasts are probably only remembered by a few. Harry Fryer was born in 1896 and started his musical career by playing the piano in a cinema in Sunderland. In 1923, he joined the Gaumont British Picture Corporation, for which he worked for over 12 years, ending up as Musical Director for the Tivoli Music Hall in London's Strand. Here he adopted the signature tune *I'll See You Again* from Noel Coward's *Bitter Sweet*, for which he was the conductor during its London run. Harry Fryer later succeeded Louis Levy at the Shepherds Bush Pavilion, from where he gave over 200 broadcasts. After touring various Paramount theatres for three years, he took his orchestra to the Chiswick Empire in the late thirties. He later broadcast frequently from the Tudor Restaurant, Kingston-on-Thames. Harry Fryer and his Orchestra made a number of records on the Decca *Music While You*

Work label, several of which have been re-released on CD; these complement Harry's 142 appearances on the series. It is probably true to say that the Harry Fryer Orchestra was on the air more than most during the war. They had a fortnightly placing in *MWYW* as well as appearing regularly at other times. By 1946, they were also heard every week in *Morning Music*, so Harry's death, at the early age of 50 on 24th November 1946, must have come as quite a shock to the BBC. The orchestra carried on for some years under the able direction of Fred Alexander, however, re-titled the Portland Light Orchestra.

THE RICHARD CREAN ORCHESTRA, like that of Harry Fryer, was a major radio contributor during the Second World War. Richard Crean was born in Dublin in 1879 and was educated at the Royal Irish Academy, becoming a teacher of piano and organ, as well as voice production. He became Chorus Master of the Thomas Quinlan Opera Company, touring many countries. Upon returning to England he took over as Chorus Master at Covent Garden under Julius Harrison and Adrian Boult. He then turned to variety, initially at the Ilford Hippodrome, but in 1930 he took up the position of conductor of the London Palladium Orchestra, one of the major light orchestras of pre-war days, with which he recorded and broadcast until the mid-thirties. At this time he formed the Richard Crean Orchestra, which he conducted for the rest of his life, apart from a period in 1941/2 when he was the conductor of the newly-formed BBC Midland Light Orchestra. Although he made some appearances in *Music While You Work* with the MLO, it is for his 208 appearances in that series with his own orchestra that he is particularly remembered, along with *Morning Music* and other programmes. Richard Crean made many records on the Decca *Music While You Work* label, some being reissued on an LP. In recent years a few recordings have appeared on CD. Richard Crean died in November 1955, having just prepared a *MWYW* programme. The final broadcast went ahead under the direction of Reginald Kilbey.

VAN DAM AND HIS ORCHESTRA presented 140 shows for *MWYW* and certainly qualify for a special mention in this section. Alfred Van Dam was born in London on 1st March 1902. After studying at the Guildhall School of Music, he joined the Carl Rosa Opera Company at the age of 17 and, at 19, began a 12-year association with Gaumont-British, conducting orchestras on their circuit. After a spell at the Trocadero, Elephant & Castle, Van Dam was appointed Musical Director of the famous State Orchestra at the Gaumont State Cinema in Kilburn. Broadcasting began in 1931 and Alfred Van Dam and the State Orchestra were regularly heard on the air over the ensuing decade. As already mentioned, during the war, Van Dam tried to establish a 25-piece light orchestra in the Royal Air Force to provide entertainment for RAF personnel as and where required. When Van Dam failed his medical examination, the whole idea fell through, but the musicians who had already joined the RAF with a view to forming the orchestra had to remain there for the duration. Van Dam formed a new orchestra in 1943 and had a long association with the Golders Green Hippodrome. He had appeared eight times on *MWYW* with the State Orchestra and went on to play a further 132 editions over the next 15 years. In common with several other theatre orchestras, the Van Dam Orchestra ceased broadcasting in 1958, at a time when the use of conventional orchestras in the theatre was diminishing. The BBC was also rationing the appearances of such combinations, which were larger and more expensive than many of the other ensembles in use. Believe it or not, there is even a BBC memorandum advocating minimal use of theatre orchestras in the hope that they would disband. Many duly obliged! Van Dam died in 1973.

RAYMOND AGOULT AND HIS PLAYERS were a popular ingredient in *Music While You Work* from the mid-fifties onwards, but little is known about the man behind the music – even to his own musicians! I have to admit that whilst I met Raymond on a number of occasions, I never found out much about him. The fact that he spoke only broken English (he apparently hailed from Alsace) didn't exactly help. It was in 1954 that Raymond Agoult came to the attention of the BBC, mainly through his work in the theatre; the BBC was seeking a new conductor for their Scottish Variety Orchestra and Raymond Agoult was considered to be 'head and shoulders', musically speaking, above others under consideration. However, it was difficult to entice musicians away from lucrative work in London to work in the provinces, so the job went to Michael Collins. The BBC subsequently invited Agoult to form a light orchestra for use in *Morning Music* and *Music While You Work*.

Although initially made up of 20 players, the orchestra was soon reduced to 16 musicians and re-titled Raymond Agoult and his Players. It consisted of strings, woodwind, piano, percussion and a

French horn which featured prominently. The Players had a highly distinctive style; most of the arrangements, which were often quirky and full of humour, were penned by the maestro. For example, if a piece happened to have a French title, such as *Ça C'est Paris*, Raymond Agoult could not resist inserting fragments of the *Marseillaise* and the *Can Can!* His arrangement of *Calling All Workers* had a piccolo and xylophone motif running through it which was apparently made up by using Raymond's initials – R.A. in Morse code. This certainly gave a new meaning to the term 'signature tune'! Raymond Agoult was a prolific composer, his best-known titles being *La Canniebiere, Honouring the Haggis, Madame Guillotine* and *Betty Dear*, which was dedicated to his wife. When the Players ceased to broadcast in the mid-sixties, Raymond Agoult continued to be heard on the air conducting the BBC Radio Orchestra. During the seventies he formed a military band for programmes such as *Brass and Strings* and *Friday Night Is Music Night*. It was called Raymond Agoult and his Master Band and featured the maestro's rumbustious and tongue in cheek arrangements.

I think it was about 1982 when I spotted Raymond Agoult walking in London's St James's Park. By an extraordinary coincidence (and this really is the truth), I just happened to have with me a cassette player and a tape of one of Raymond's 85 *MWYW* broadcasts. So, I crept up behind him and switched on the player. He listened in silence for a few minutes before bursting forth 'My sound! My sound! I never thought that I would hear it again!' Needless to say, he asked for a copy of the tape because, in common with many musicians, he had never thought to record any of his broadcasts. Raymond Agoult died on 20th July 1992.

FREDRIC COOPER AND HIS TIPICA ORCHESTRA made the first of their 143 appearances on *MWYW* in 1951, playing tuneful light music with the emphasis on Latin-American rhythms. Little is known about Fredric Cooper other than the fact that he was a violinist leading an orchestra at the Lyons' Corner House in London's Coventry Street back in the late thirties when he would 'table-hop', playing requests for the restaurant's customers (whether they wanted it or not!).

Accordionist Gerald Crossman played with the Tipica Orchestra throughout its existence, together with other distinguished musicians such as trumpeter Bill Shakespeare and the famous classical clarinettist Jack Brymer, who apparently loved doing *MWYW*. Several of the 14 players in the orchestra found themselves doubling on percussion during the Latin numbers. According to the *Radio Times*, a tipica orchestra is one whose repertoire is always typical of its country of origin, but, as Fredric Cooper sometimes played current pops as rumbas and sambas, I do not think that he was governed by that definition! Fredric Cooper is thought to have retired to the West Country, but if he is still alive, he has certainly disappeared into the mists of time.

Another violinist, **JACK SALISBURY AND HIS SALON ORCHESTRA**, joined the *MWYW* regulars in 1948 and played 148 editions. Whilst his orchestra-leader brother, Arthur Salisbury, enjoyed success as a Musical Director at the Savoy Hotel in London, Jack had a long association with the De La Warr Pavilion at Bexhill, where he stood in front of his orchestra playing his violin in true Palm Court style. Indeed, Jack's orchestra sometimes deputised for the BBC's Palm Court Orchestra in *Grand Hotel*. They also participated in a wide range of programmes including *Bright and Early* and *Morning Music*. When light music programmes became more commercial in the sixties, Jack Salisbury's rather traditional style went out of favour with the BBC and his broadcasts decreased in frequency – a pity as he always maintained a high standard. Long into his retirement, Jack continued to play the violin and could often be heard playing in his Bexhill home; in fact he became known locally as the 'Mozart of Bexhill'. Jack Salisbury died in February 1997.

HAROLD GELLER AND HIS ORCHESTRA first appeared in *Music While You Work* in 1946, initially as a nine-piece ensemble, led by the maestro on violin and broadcasting regularly until 1952. After a break from radio, Harold Geller returned in 1955 with a new style and instrumentation. The orchestra (now increased to 14 players) comprised strings, saxophone (doubling flute), accordion, piano, guitar, bass and drums – plus the distinctive sound of a mandoline, played by the well-known Hugo D'Alton. Harold Geller's Orchestra returned to *MWYW* late in 1958 and played a total of 52 editions. They would undoubtedly have done more but for the fact that they were extensively used in other programmes such as *Morning Music*, for which they provided some 115 editions between 1961 and 1965. They had an attractive and quite sophisticated style and despite being officially classed as a dance orchestra, their instrumentation enabled them to include contemporary light music in their repertoire. During the sixties the orchestra was resident at the London's Kensington Palace Hotel. Harold's daughter Roslynn became quite well-known as a broadcasting and recording artist, playing the harp with her trio.

Harold Geller, who was born in Sydney, Australia, and came to this country as a child, was a prolific composer. Amongst his compositions are *El Toreador, Kibbutzim, Street of Linden Trees, Dancers of El Paso* and *The Green Cockatoo*. He also wrote a mandoline concerto for Hugo D'Alton which was broadcast by the BBC Concert Orchestra under Geller's direction. Radio work had dried up in the early seventies and Harold Geller emigrated to the United States a few years later. He died in Las Vegas on 26th February 2005 aged 89.

THE JACK EMBLOW SEXTET was regarded by some senior BBC producers as the best small group on radio, led by one of the most skilful accordionists in the country. Jack Emblow was born in Lincoln on 27th June 1930. He started learning the piano at the age of nine, switching to the accordion two years later. At 15 he was part of a stage act with jazz pianist Eddie Thompson and, at 17, he auditioned with the BBC. In addition to solo broadcasts, he played with a variety of

groups during the fifties and had a three year spell at the Berkeley Hotel in Piccadilly, playing for Ian Stewart. The Jack Emblow Sextet made its radio debut in *MWYW* in 1956 and for about five years was one of the mainstays of the programme. Increasing demands for the band's services in other programmes rather limited their appearances in the series in later years, their superb arrangements, smooth sound and flawless playing making them suitable for any time of day. They did about 500 broadcasts, of which 54 were in *MWYW*. Jack also played in many other groups, his distinctive style making him immediately recognisable. Although generally regarded as Britain's top jazz accordionist, the self-effacing Jack Emblow doesn't agree, preferring to be regarded as an 'all-rounder'. For more than 40 years he provided the accordion accompaniment for the Cliff Adams Singers in *Sing Something Simple* and during the seventies formed the French Collection for radio and records, leading the group on the French Musette accordion – an instrument that he does not particularly like! He much prefers his straight-tuned Excelsior accordion, which has a special tone chamber, enabling him to achieve his famous mellow tone. For many years he contributed to the incidental music for the television series *Last of the Summer Wine*, and also played the theme for the comedy series *'Allo 'Allo*. Jack Emblow was elected Honorary President of the National Accordion Organisation of the Untied Kingdom in 2002.

HAROLD C. GEE AND HIS MARITZA PLAYERS did not play in *Music While You Work* until 1961, but gave 51 performances. By no means new to radio, Harold C. Gee had been a regular broadcaster since the thirties. For many years he gave live performances from his home town of Bournemouth, sometimes providing orchestral concerts, but on other occasions playing the violin in late night recitals, often accompanied by the organ. As the title 'Maritza Players' was inspired by Emmerich

214

Kalman's gypsy operetta *Countess Maritza*, and the orchestra's signature tune was *Play Gypsy* from that same operetta, it will be apparent that the ensemble was formed to specialise in the gypsy music that was very much in vogue in the thirties. Harold C. Gee, who even called his house *Maritza*, discovered quite early on that, by coincidence, there was another violinist called Harold Gee performing in the Bournemouth area. So, to avoid confusion, he asked the BBC to insert a 'C' into his name – apparently his middle name was Cecil. Fellow musicians called him Harold Squeegee! Our front cover depicting Anton and his Orchestra shows Harold sitting next to accordionist Gerald Crossman. One possible reason why the Maritza Players were so late joining the *MWYW* team was that gypsy music was not considered very suitable for the programme, so Harold C. Gee played mostly familiar standard light music in the series, but with plenty of tangos and paso dobles to reflect the idiom. While the musicians were changing their music between pieces, the pianist would play a few bars of *Play Gypsy* leading into the next number. Harold C. Gee died in 1973 (my thanks to his son Brian for this information). My last memory of him is an appearance he made in a Benny Hill television show as a violin-playing tramp – not the most auspicious way to end a distinguished career!

THE ALBERT CAZABON ORCHESTRA is probably best remembered by listeners to *Morning Music* but their other broadcasts did include 23 editions of *Music While You Work*.

Albert Cazabon was born in 1883, the son of French violinist Alphonse Cazaubon. He began playing the violin, aged four, under his father's tuition and was regarded as a child prodigy – giving his first recital, aged nine, at London's Queen's Hall. He received musical training at the Guildhall School of Music and later in Paris. He studied composition under Gustav Holst (composer of *The Planets*).

After touring the British Isles as a violin soloist, supplementing his earnings with orchestral playing, he then turned his attention to conducting, working with the London Symphony and Bournemouth Symphony Orchestras, amongst others. He arranged music for the theatre and later for silent films, becoming Director of Music at the Everyman's Theatre, Hampstead for some years.

In 1927 he went to Australia, spending nine years in Sydney as Director of Music at the Prince Edward Theatre, following a recommendation from Basil Cameron. In 1930 he conducted the Hungarian March from Berlioz's 'Damnation of Faust' for Columbia – the first recording of a symphony orchestra to be made in Australia. He made commercial recordings of his own compositions for violin and piano and wrote the *Song of the Great Bridge* for the opening of the Sydney Harbour Bridge in 1932. He was awarded a Jubilee Medal by King George V in 1935 for services to music in Australia.

Returning to England in 1937, he broadcast with the Albert Cazabon Trio and later with his orchestra, making his first appearance in *Music While You Work* in 1941. His orchestral compositions include *The Jesters, Fjell Melody*, and *Giocoso*. He also produced many orchestral arrangements, theatre scores, violin solos, piano pieces and comic songs, broadcasting frequently until his retirement in the mid-fifties. He died in 1970.

Last but not least, **JACK LEON AND HIS ORCHESTRA** appeared regularly on *Music While You Work* from the earliest days of the programme. Judah Leon Aronoff (to give him his birth name) was born in Kiev in 1905 but moved with his family to Antwerp the following year. He came to London in 1914, becoming a British citizen in 1929, having changed his name to Jack Leon. Although trained as a violinist, he gave this up in favour of conducting. His early dance band records, of which he made many, served as a prelude to the light orchestral performances that were to dominate his career. He recorded extensively for 'Mood Music' libraries and his recordings with the New Concert Orchestra are now becoming available to a new generation by way of compact disc.

Jack Leon's theatrical connections included the London Casino and the Theatre Royal, Drury Lane, for which he was Musical Advisor. He also had a long association with the Prince of Wales Theatre, London as Musical Director.

He moved to Glasgow in 1956 to take up the appointment of conductor of the BBC Scottish Variety Orchestra, a position he was destined to hold for ten years, broadcasting several times every week. He retired (albeit very reluctantly) from the BBC in 1966 and soon reformed his own orchestra for broadcasting. Early in 1967 he was

216

given a series of broadcasts in *Breakfast Special*. Sadly, after completing only a few recordings he collapsed in the street in Glasgow having suffered a heart attack from which he died, aged only 61, on 10th March 1967.

Jack Leon was a perfectionist and was regarded by some as a 'hard task-master,' but his daughter Miriam remembers him only as a kind and loving father from whom she was parted at the tender age of eighteen.

With 324 editions of *Music While You Work* to his credit, Jack Leon conducted the most light orchestral programmes in the series.

That concludes my review of a selection of the principal contributors to *MWYW*. I recall a conversation with an elderly musician a few years ago when I remarked that it was sad that most of the legendary names in light music were now dead – to which he replied 'They're not dead. Whilst you and I remember them they'll never die!' How right he was; perhaps this book will further ensure their immortality.

Chapter 5

The Contributors

This section is divided into light orchestras, dance bands, cinema organists, brass and military bands and is, to the best of my knowledge, a complete list of all contributors to *Music While You Work* between June 1940 and September 1967. I have tried to list contributors in the order that they first appeared on the show, except for those artists who directed more than one ensemble over the years; in these instances they are grouped together. For example, Ronnie Munro directed the Scottish Variety Orchestra during the war, a dance band in the late forties, a light orchestra in the fifties and early sixties, a small salon ensemble called Harmony Music and finally a sextet in the sixties. You will, therefore, find the dance band on the separate listing for dance bands and the light music combinations listed together under 'Light Orchestras and Groups' – apart from the Scottish Variety Orchestra, which is listed separately with its different conductors over the years. Sounds complicated, doesn't it? This is the most extreme example, as most musical directors only had one band or orchestra. More than 60 bands only appeared once, illustrating the BBC's wish to use only the most suitable. Others made just a handful of appearances. Where a band or orchestra made a significant contribution to the series, the approximate number of programmes performed is given in brackets – I say 'approximate' because the BBC sometimes made last-minute changes which came too late to be reflected in the *Radio Times*. Also, during the early weeks there were several programmes billed as 'An orchestral concert conducted by...', the orchestra being unspecified. It can be reliably assumed that these were the **BBC Northern Orchestra** or the **BBC Scottish Orchestra**.

Light Orchestras & Groups

Geiger and his Orchestra (live from Claridge's Hotel)
Guy Warrack (an orchestral Concert)
Leonard and his Orchestra (formerly Jack Leonardi)
Jan Berenska and his Orchestra (82)
BBC Theatre Orchestra (Stanford Robinson/Reginald Burston/Harold
    Lowe)
BBC Orchestra – Section A (Sir Adrian Boult)
Toni and his Orchestra (from the North Pier Blackpool)
The Caravan Players (Rae Jenkins)
The Boulevard Players (Director unspecified, probably David Wise)
Maurice Johnstone (an Orchestral Concert)
Jack Hardy's Little Orchestra
BBC Salon Orchestra (Jean Pougnet and Leslie Bridgewater) (37)
Arthur Dulay and his Cameo Orchestra (132)
Harry Fryer and his Orchestra (142)
Jack Leon and his Orchestra/London Casino Orchestra (221)
London Palladium Orchestra (Debroy Somers)
Sidney Davey and his Players (222)
Jack Frere and his Orchestra/London Coliseum Orchestra (Jack Frere)
    (13) Reginald Burston (59)
Weston-Super-Mare Municipal Orchestra
Gideon Fagan (an orchestral concert)
Joseph Lewis and his Orchestra
BBC Orchestra – Section C (John Ansell)
Wynford Reynolds and his Orchestra (87)
The Raeburn Orchestra (Conductor Wynford Reynolds) (24)
Sam Rogers and his Orchestra
Lewisham Hippodrome Orchestra/Harold Collins and his Orchestra (228)
John Reynders and his Orchestra (100)
Clifford Greenwood and his Orchestra
Harry Davidson and his Orchestra (109)
Charles Windsor and his Manchester Hippodrome Orchestra
The Kenilworth Octet
The Entr'acte Players (Sidney Crooke)
BBC Variety Orchestra (Charles Shadwell)
Troise and his Mandoliers ⎫
Troise and his Banjoliers ⎬ (475)
The Banjoliers (Directed by Jack Mandel) ⎭

Frank Walker and his Miniature Orchestra
Irish Rhythms Orchestra (David Curry)
Sydney Phasey and his Orchestra
Alfred Van Dam and his State Orchestra
Van Dam and his Orchestra (132)
Reginald King and his Salon Orchestra
Falkman and his Apache Band (142)
The Troubadours (Directed by Lionel Falkman)
Victor Fleming and his Orchestra
Harry Engleman's Quintet
Mantovani and his Orchestra
Fred Hartley and his Sextet/Music
Bristol Hippodrome Orchestra
Yasha Krein and his Gypsy Orchestra
Louis Voss and his Orchestra/Hungarian Orchestra
Louis Voss and his Kursaal Orchestra (142)
Charles Ernesco and his Sextet
Jack Wilson and his Versatile Five
The Lockier Grosvenor Octet
Ernest Leggett and the Continental Players
Scottish Variety Orchestra
    (Conductors: Ronnie Munro (91), Kemlo Stephen (54), Jack Leon
    (103))
Gilbert Stacey and his Sextet
Alexander Lerner and the Finsbury Park Empire Orchestra
Albert Cazabon and his Orchestra (23)
Dudley Hippodrome Orchestra (Harry Pell/William Hand) (23)
Michaeloff and his Mazurka Orchestra
The J.H. Squire Celeste Octet
William Rees and the St Anne's Pier Orchestra
London Studio Players (Albert Sandler)
Tivoli Theatre Orchestra (Clifford Jordan)
Sidney Kaplan and his Orchestra
Torquay Pavilion Light Orchestra (Ernest Goss)
Frank Stewart and his Orchestra
The Dulcet Strings (Frank Stewart)
The Casino Orchestra (Rae Jenkins)
A.J. Powell and his Banjo Octet
De Wolfe and his Orchestra
BBC Midland Light Orchestra (61)

Walter Barry and the Burnley Palace Theatre Orchestra
The Richard Crean Orchestra (208)
George Steele and his Orchestra/Birmingham Hippodrome Orchestra
John Blore and his Orchestra (83)
BBC Revue Orchestra (Mansel Thomas/Alan Crooks/Frank Cantell)
    (29)
Norman Brooks and his Orchestra
West Country Studio Orchestra (Norman Brooks)
Royal Artillery Theatre Orchestra
Eugene and his Orchestra
David Java and his Orchestra (67)
Orchestra of the Royal Corps of Signals
Owen Walters and his Orchestra (65)
Harry Pell and his Orchestra (25)
Leeds Grand Theatre Orchestra
BBC Scottish Orchestra (Iain Whyte)
BBC Northern Orchestra (Charles Groves)
Oxford New Theatre Orchestra (William Brightwell)
Morrisons' Engineering Works Orchestra (W. Reynolds Payne)
    (which became Reynolds Payne and his Orchestra) (61)
BBC Theatre Orchestra (Harold Lowe)
Anton and his Orchestra (252)
The Masqueraders (Eric Robinson)
Jan Hurst and his Orchestra (48)
Bunny May and his Orchestra/Filmay Light Orchestra (W. Bunny
    May) (45)
Charles Tovey and his Theatre Music
Vernon Adcock and his Light Orchestra
Butlin Light Orchestra (John Thorpe)
    (which became The Regent Orchestra – John Thorpe) (111)
Marcel Gardner and his Serenade Orchestra (152)
The Bobby Howell Orchestra (91)
Portland Light Orchestra (Fred Alexander) (33)
Fred Alexander and his Players (90)
Ralph Elman and his Bohemian Players (174)
Sidney Bowman and the Promenade Players (151)
The Billy Mayerl Rhythm Ensemble
The Rendezvous Players
Rene Pougnet and Tony Fones (Two Pianos)
Arthur Dulay and Sidney Davey (Two Pianos)

Bernard Monshin and his Rio Tango Band (146)
Jack Salisbury and his Salon Orchestra (148)
Joseph Muscant and his Orchestra (51)
Arthur Salisbury and his Orchestra
The Edward Griffiths Orchestra
Percival Mackey and his Orchestra
Fredric Cooper and his Tipica Orchestra (143)
Jack Coles and his Orchestre Moderne (51)
Norman Whiteley Trio/Quintet/Norman Whiteley and his Sextet
Bertram Willis and his Orchestra
Birmingham Hippodrome Orchestra (Frank Hagley)
Michael Freedman and his Orchestra (94)
Hugh James and his Orchestra (115)
Cyril Ornadel and his Orchestra
Strings in Rhythm (Henry Croudson) (45)
The Gerald Crossman Players (123)
Louis Mordish and his Players
Criterion Light Orchestra (Charles Mackerras/Michael Collins)
Harry Acres and his Orchestra
Lionel Monte and his Orchestra
Raymond Agoult and his Orchestra/Players (85)
The Albert Delroy Sextet (61)
Michael Collins and his Orchestra
Isy Geiger and his Viennese Music (51)
Ronnie Munro and his Orchestra (52)
Ronnie Munro and his Harmony Music
Ronnie Munro and his Sextet/Music (28)
BBC Northern Ireland Light Orchestra (David Curry) (69)
Charles Mackerras conducting his Light Orchestra
Reg Pursglove and the Albany Strings (75)
George Scott-Wood and his Music (60)
Ralph Wilson and his Septet (37)
The Bryan Rodwell Quartet
Maurice Arnold and his Sextet (27)
    (taken over from Norman Whiteley, who emigrated to Australia)
Eddie Carroll and his Music
Les Perry and his Players
Delmondi and his Quartet (32)
The Mandolin-Minstrel Band (Eric Wilson-Hyde)
Harold C. Gee and his Maritza Players (51)

The Sidney Sax Strings
Sidney Sax and his Music
Ronald Hanmer and the Marimberos
Jacques Vallez and his Players/Septet
Charles Smitton Quartet
George Blackmore Sextet
Cyril Watters and his Players
Henry Krein and his Quartet
BBC Scottish Radio Orchestra (Iain Sutherland/Sidney Bowman) (26)

Dance Bands & Groups

The Organolists
Jimmy Leach and the New Organolians ⎫ (256)
Jimmy Leach Organolian Quartet ⎭
Geraldo and his Orchestra (28)
Don Felipe and his Cuban Caballeros
Billy Hardy and his Band
Henry Hall and his Orchestra
Gaby Rogers and his Band/Serenaders
Eddie Carroll and his Dance Orchestra
Reg Pursglove and his Orchestra/Music Makers (125)
Joe Loss and his Band
Teddy Foster and his Band (21)
Billy Reid and his Accordion Band
Josephine Bradley and her Ballroom Orchestra
Sidney Lipton and his Band
Debroy Somers and his Band (128)
George Scott-Wood and his Band/Accordion Band (154)
Billy Ternent and the Dance Orchestra/His Orchestra (130)
Percival Mackey and his Sophisticated Players/Band/Orchestra (104)
Victor Silvester and his Ballroom Orchestra (264)
Herman Darewski and his New Rhythm Orchestra
Jack White and his Collegians/Band (309)
George Melachrino and his Orchestra
Jack Simpson and his Sextet/Band/Septet (180)
Jack Payne with his Band/Orchestra (27)
Primo Scala's Accordion Band (Directed By Harry Bidgood) ⎫ (296)
Primo Scala and his Accordion Band ⎭

224

Van Straten and his Music (22)
The Swingtette (directed by Dennis Moonan)
Oscar Grasso and his Orchestra/Music
Hal Tauber and his Orchestra
The Roland Powell Octet
Mantovani and his Dance Orchestra (47)
Peter Rush and his Band
Al Collins and his Dance Orchestra/Orchestra/Band (36)
George Elrick and his Band
Eric Winstone and his Accordion Quintet ⎫
The Eric Winstone Sextet/Quintet ⎬ (118)
Eric Winstone and his Accordion Band/Band/Orchestra ⎭
Billy Mayerl and his Band/Grosvenor House Dance Orchestra (28)
Melville Christie's Dance Band/Orchestra (42)
Harry Roy and his Band
Harry Leader and his Band (214)
Jack Jackson and his Orchestra/Band (33)
Felix Mendelssohn and his Hawaiian Serenaders
Charlie Kunz and his Rhythm
Lou Preager and his Band/Correct Tempo Ballroom Band/Orchestra
   (96)
Phil Green and his Band (41)
Stan Atkins and his Band (47)
Johnny Rosen and his Band
The Music Makers
Nat Allen and his Band/Orchestra (82)
Tommy Rogan and his Orchestra
Robin Richmond and his Sextet ⎫
The Robin Richmond Trio/Quartet ⎬ (104)
Robin Richmond and his Quintet ⎭
Ivy Benson and her Ladies' Dance Orchestra/Girls' Band (35)
Carroll Gibbons and the Boyfriends/Orchestra
David Java and his Band
Jay Wilbur and his Orchestra (40)
Dance Band of the Royal Army Service Corps
Dance Band of the Manchester Regiment
Stephane Grappelly and his Quintet/Sextet
Billy Smith and his Music
Ted Heath and his Music
Frederick Hargraves and his Band

225

Dance Orchestra of the London Fire Forces
Oscar Rabin and his Band/Orchestra (36)
Dance Orchestra of the Welsh Guards
Ronnie Munro and his Dance Music/Orchestra
Frank Weir and his Orchestra (41)
Vernon Adcock and his Dance Orchestra (25)
Cherry Simmonds and his Albany Players
Maurice Winnick and his Orchestra
Howard Baker and his Band
Charles Smart and the Moonrakers
Johnny Denis and his Novelty Septet/Novelty Swing Quintet/
    Ranchmen
Stanley Black and the Dance Orchestra (42)
Walter (Wally) Chapman and his Band
Art Thompson and his Band
The Organ, The Dance Band and Me
    (Billy Thorburn and his Music with H. Robinson Cleaver – Organ)
Ralph Wilson and his Dance Orchestra (55)
Al Tabor and his Band
Howard Lucraft and his Music (40)
Dudley Beaven and his Players
Harry Gold and his Orchestra/Pieces of Eight/Band (52)
Eddie Shaw and his Band (39)
Cecil Norman and the Rhythm Players (466)
The Melodians (25)
Tommy Kinsman and his Dance Orchestra (138)
Jack Amlot and his Band
The Blue Rockets (Eric Robinson/Benny Daniels/Ronnie Rand)
Jack Coles and his Music Masters
Bill Savill and his Band/Orchestra (308)
Harold Geller and his Band/Sextet/Orchestra (51)
Roy Wallis and his Band/Quartet (27)
Billy Munn and his Music
Syd Dean and his Band (178)
Cyril Stapleton and his Orchestra
The Stardusters (George Birch/Andy Wilson)
Ian Stewart and his Orchestra/Quintet/Quartet (264)
Nat Temple and his Octet/His Clarinet and Woodwind/Orchestra (35)
Vincent Ladbroke and his Dance Orchestra
Jan Wildeman and his Orchestra

Paul Adam and his Mayfair Orchestra
Harry Gerrard and his Orchestra
Norman Griffiths and his Sextet
Bob Robinson and his Dance Orchestra
Leslie Douglas and his Orchestra
George Crow and the Blue Mariners
Al Flush and his Orchestra
Chappie D'Amato and his Band
Reggie Goff and his Sextet
Ken Beaumont's Music/Ken Beaumont and his Sextet (289)
Felix King, his Piano and his Orchestra/Orchestra/Quintet (100)
Ronnie Pleydell and his Band/Orchestra (129)
Sid Buckman and his Music
Dick Denny Orchestra
Jack Nathan and his Band (146)
Harry Farmer and the Electronomes
Leslie Baker and his Music
Jack McCormick and his Orchestra
Ivor Moreton and Dave Kaye (Two Pianos)
Lou Simmons and his Orchestra
Styx Wilkinson and his Orchestra
Hedley Ward and his Band
Charles Henesy Sextet
Tommy Smith and his Band
Sonny Rose and his Orchestra
Ken Mackintosh and his Orchestra
Frank Baron and his Quintet/Sextet (110)
The Frank Baron Sextet (directed by Harry Knight)
Percy Pease and his Band
Bill Hawkins and his Band
Eddie Francis and his Orchestra
Dennis Cracknell and his Sextet
Roland Peachey and his Mayfair Orchestra (26)
Alan Young and his Organtones
Les Garrett and his Band
Hal Graham and his Band/Orchestra (22)
Skyrockets Dance Orchestra (Stanley Andrews/Woolf Phillips) (24)
Maurice Little and his Music
Sid Phillips and his Band
Bob Bissetto and his Rumba Band

Paul Fenoulhet and his Orchestra
Ralph Sharon Sextet
Phil Tate and his Orchestra (144)
Bill Gregson and his Band
Frank Chacksfield and his Orchestra/Tunesmiths (26)
Ted Astley and his Band
Tito Burns and his Sextet
Len Goodwin Quartet
George Smith and his Band
Norton Colville and his Ballroom Music
Danny Levan and his Sextet/Quintet (27)
Johnny Gray and his Orchestra
Jerry Allen and his Trio
Andy Currie and his Dance Orchestra
Dave Shand and his Orchestra
Denny Boyce and his Orchestra (46)
The Jack Emblow Sextet (54)
Claude Cavalotti and his Orchestra (154)
Ronnie Keene and his Orchestra/Octet (20)
Lew Stone and his Band/Sextet (41)
The Gough-Adams Music/Geoff Gough and his Music (35)
Eddie Strevens Sextet/Eddie Strevens and his Quartet (85)
The Don Harper Sextet
Laurie Gold and his Orchestra
Eric Galloway and his Orchestra (26)
Stan Reynolds Octet (20)
Chris Allen and his Sextet (22)
The George Birch Six (34)
Freddie Ballerini Sextet
Johnny Howard and his Orchestra
Jack Dorsey and his Orchestra (37)
Alan Hurst and his Orchestra
Garry Brown and his Orchestra
Graham Dalley and his Music
The Dennis Mann Orchestra
The Kenny Salmon Quintet
The Dennis Wilson Quartet
Bob Potter and his Orchestra
The Phil Cleary Sextet
Iain Kerr and his Keyboards

The Roy Herbert Quintet
Johnny Kildare and his Orchestra
The Alex Sutherland Orchestra
The Johnny Cooper Band
Grisha Farfel and his Music
The Sandy Blair Quintet
The Freddie Stafford Orchestra
Colin Hulme and his Orchestra
The Jack Jordan Eight
Johnny Wollaston and his Music
The Cyril Harling Sextette
The Bill Jackman Group
The Derek Cox Quartet

Cinema Organists

Dudley Beavan	Robin Richmond	Nelson Elms
Sandy Macpherson	Thomas Dando	Reginald Foort
John Bee	Leslie Simpson	Edward O'Henry
Henry Croudson	Sidney Torch	Lloyd Thomas
Phil Park	Fredric Bayco	Donald Thorne
Joseph Seal	Frederic Curzon	Clarence Barber
Reginald Dixon	Ronald Brickell	Jack Dowle
Richard Telfer	Gordon Banner	James Bell
Bobby Pagan	Terence Casey	Ena Baga
Harold Smart	Stanley Miller	H. Robinson Cleaver
Harold Coombs	Florence de Jong	Andrew Fenner
Reginald Porter Brown	Al Bollington	Eric Lord
Charles Smart	Stanley Tudor	Horace Finch
John Madin	Lewis Gerard	Eric Spruce
Tom Jenkins	Norman Briggs	Reginald New
Stuart Barrie	Roy Page	Henry M. Millen
Rudy Lewis	Don Larusso	

Brass & Military Bands

BBC Military Band
Harton Colliery Band
Blackhall Colliery Band
County Borough of Swansea Band
Fairey Aviation Works Band
Clydebank Burgh Band
Darvel Burgh Band
Manchester L.N.E.R. Band
Scottish C.W.S. Band
Royal Marines (Chatham)
Coldstream Guards
Fodens Motor Works Band
Brighouse and Rastrick Band
Bickershaw Colliery Band
City of Sheffield Police Band
Scots Guards
Irish Guards
Sheffield Transport Dept Works Band
Royal Horse Guards (The Blues)
Black Dyke Mills Band
Grimethorpe Colliery Band
Creswell Colliery Band
Duke of Cornwall's Light Infantry
Royal Artillery Mounted Band
The Loyal Regiment
Ransome and Marles Works Band
Royal Berkshire Regiment
Barry, Ostlere and Shepherd Works Band
Metropolitan Police Band
Carlton Main Frickley Colliery Band
Royal Dragoons
Royal Army Ordinance Corps
Oxfordshire and Buckinghamshire Light Infantry
Border Regiment
Royal Artillery (Portsmouth)
Welsh Guards
Cory Workmen's Band
Royal Artillery (Woolwich)

C.W.S. Manchester Band
Coltness Works Silver Band
Manchester Regiment
Royal Marines (Plymouth)
Park and Dare Workmen's Band
South Lancashire Regiment
Wellesley Colliery Band
East Yorkshire Regiment
Sankey's Castle Works Band
Band 'A' RAF Technical Training Command
East Surrey Regiment
The Life Guards
South Wales Borderers
RAF Bomber Command
Coventry Colliery Band
Royal Canadian Airforce Overseas Band
Bedfordshire and Hertfordshire Regiment
Crookhall Colliery Band
Central Band of the Royal Air Force
Chopwell Colliery Band
East Lancashire Regiment
Royal Artillery (Salisbury Plain)
Gwaecurgurwan Silver Prize Band
Worcestershire Regiment
King's Own Scottish Borderers
Queen's Royal Regiment
13th/18th Royal Hussars
Dorsetshire Regiment
Bristol Aeroplane Company Works Band
City of Coventry Band
Royal Army Service Corps (later Royal Corps of Transport)
Band No.1 Pre-Officer Cadet Training Unit (R.A.C.)
Band 'B' RAF Technical Training Command
Royal Corps of Signals
Queen's Own Royal West Kent Regiment
Command Band of the Air Defence of Great Britain
RAF Coastal Command
5th Inniskilling Dragoon Guards
Royal Canadian Artillery
Green Howards

Central Band of the London Fire Forces (later London Fire Brigade)
RAF Fighter Command
2nd Btn Northamptonshire Regiment
Barrow Shipyard Band
1st Btn Welch Regiment
Royal Marines (Portsmouth)
Royal Canadian Naval Band of HMCS Niobe
King's Royal Rifle Corps (later 2nd Royal Greenjackets)
King's Own Yorkshire Light Infantry
Grenadier Guards
Band 'B' RAF Flying Training Command
2nd Btn Gloucestershire Regiment
RAF Regiment
Royal Irish Fusiliers
Queen's Own Highlanders (Seaforth and Camerons)
Reconnaisance Corps R.A.C.
London Military Band
No.1 Regional Band RAF
Fisher and Ludlow Works Band
National Military Band
Royal Inniskilling Fusiliers
10th Royal Hussars
Morris Motors Band
St Hilda's Band
17th/21st Lancers
Royal Lincolnshire Regiment
Corps of Royal Engineers (Chatham)
Melingriffith Works Band
British Legion (Standard Motors Branch)
Rifle Brigade
Durham Light Infantry
Royal Sussex Regiment
Middlesex Regiment
Callenders' Band
Royal Tank Regiment
RAF College, Cranwell
Royal Electrical and Mechanical Engineers
Enfield Central Band
Royal Army Medical Corps
No.4 Regional Band, Royal Air Force

Hanwell Silver Band
12th Royal Lancers
Royal Military Academy (Sandhurst)
2nd Parachute Regiment
3rd Btn Caribiniers
Royal Fusiliers (City of London Regiment)
Royal Artillery (Plymouth)
Pressed Steel Company Works Band
Munn and Feltons (Footwear) Band (later G.U.S. (Footwear) Band)
Alamein Band, Royal Tank Regiment
Royal Marines School of Music
Corps of Royal Engineers (Aldershot)
R.A. Lister Military Band
Ford Motor Works Military Band
Ferodo Works Band
Rhine Band, Royal Tank Regiment
John White (Footwear) Band
Rushden Temperance Band
Queen's Own Irish Hussars
Royal Ulster Rifles
Yorkshire Imperial Metals Band

Contributors to the Revival Series
1982–1983–1990–1991–1995

Nat Temple and his Orchestra
The Banjoliers (directed by Jack Mandel)
Lou Whiteson and his Southern Serenade Orchestra
Jack Dorsey and his Orchestra
Phil Tate and his Orchestra
Neville Hughes and his Orchestra
Tony Evans and his Band/Tony Evans Latin
The Gordon Langford Sextet
Iain Sutherland and his Orchestra
Dave Hancock and his Orchestra
Chris Allen and his Band
The Alan Downey Big Band
Geoffrey Brand and his Orchestra
Pete Winslow's Tijuana Sound/Band

Ray Davies and the Button Down Brass/Orchestra
The Don Lusher Big Band
The Francis-Langford Duo, Their Pianos and Orchestra
Sound Of Strings (directed by David Francis)
David Francis, his Piano and Strings
Ronnie Hazlehurst and his Band
Terry Walsh and the Golden Guitars
Alec Gould and his Band
The George French Orchestra
Roland Shaw and his Orchestra
The Bill McGuffie Sextet
Neil Richardson's Satin Brass
The Bill Geldard Tentette
Jack Coles and his Orchestra
Stanley Black, his Piano and Orchestra
The Pete Smith Seminar
John Huckridge and his Band
The Brian Dee Quartet
Central Band of the Royal Air Force
The Pete Allen Jazz Band
Andy Ross and his Band
Bones and Fifes
The Henry Mackenzie Quintet
The Burt Rhodes Band
John Clark and his Band
Sidney Sax Strings Unlimited
Acker Bilk and his Paramount Jazz Band
Johnny Howard and his Orchestra
The Zack Laurence Trio
The Bernard Ebbinghouse Orchestra
Ronnie Smith and his Band
Fairey Engineering Works Band
John Fox and his Orchestra
The Pete Hughes Quintet
Syd Lawrence and his Orchestra
The Sound of Horns (directed by John Pigneguy)
Barrie Forgie's Thames Eight
Jack Peberdy's Flutes and Things
Geoff Love's Banjo Sound
Band of the Coldstream Guards

John Brown's Bodies
Ronnie Aldrich and his Orchestra
The Vic Ash Quartet
Ray McVay and his Band
The Christine and Sandy Blair Two-Piano Rhythm
Reginald Leopold and his Orchestra
John Gregory and his Orchestra
The Geoff Eales Sextet
Bryan Smith and his Orchestra
Joe Loss and his Orchestra
The Robert Docker Sextet
Grant Hossack and his Orchestra
George Chisholm and the Keith Smith Hefty Jazz
Gordon Rose and his Orchestra
Pearl Fawcett (Accordion) with Orchestra (conducted by Harold Rich)
Frank Chacksfield and his Orchestra
Brian Sharpe, his Organ and Things
The Cory Band
The Frank Stafford Quintet
The David Snell Quintet
Johnny Edwards Slightly Latin
The Dave Shepherd Quintet
Cyril Ornadel and the London Theatre Orchestra
Carlos Romanos and his Orchestra
Band of the Welsh Guards
Harry Leader and his Band
The Harry Stoneham Six
The Allan Ganley Sextet
Alan Tew and his Orchestra
The Bill Jackman Group
The G.U.S. Band
Pianorama (directed by Harold Rich)
The Harry Roche Constellation
The Mick Urry Showband
Pete Moore and his Orchestra
Band of the Royal Military School of Music (Kneller Hall)
The Victor Silvester Orchestra (directed by Victor Silvester Jr)
Ken Mackintosh and his Band
Band of the Irish Guards

Picture Acknowledgements

The author and publishers gratefully acknowledge the permission given for the use of the following photographs:

Front jacket (main image) from the Library of the Vintage Light Music Society, courtesy of Mrs June Upton; front jacket (background image) and page 3 Music by Eric Coates, © 1940 Chappell & Co Ltd/ Marlowlynn Ltd/Chappell Recorded Music Library Ltd, All Rights Reserved; frontispiece by permission of the BBC; page 2 *Southport Visitor*; page 4 by kind permission of the estate of the late Eric Fraser; page 7 (all) *Radio Times*; page 9 *Radio Times*; page 8 by permission of the BBC Written Archives; page 15 *Radio Times*; page 16 *Light Music Society Journal* (1957); page 18 *Radio Times*; page 23 middle left by kind permission of Pearl Adriano, middle right *Radio Times*, right Andre Garde; page 25 courtesy of Jack Dorsey; page 27 (top) courtesy of the late Jack Mandel, (bottom) courtesy of Chris Hayes; page 29 by permission of the BBC Written Archives; page 30 *Radio Pictorial*; page 31 Gerald Crossman; page 32 *Radio Times*; page 36 courtesy of the late Hugh James; page 38 Gerald Crossman; page 39 Gerald Crossman; page 42 courtesy of Sheila Tracey; page 44 *Radio Times*; page 46, 71, 73 Brian Reynolds; page 75 Christine Blair; page 77 (top row, left) courtesy of Sheila Tracey, (top row, middle) *Radio Times*, (top row, right) courtesy of Sheila Tracey, (bottom row, both) courtesy of Sheila Tracey; page 80 Brian Reynolds; page 91 courtesy of Fred Alexander; page 94 *Radio Times*; page 101 *The Accordion News*; page 104 *The Accordion Times*; page 106 *Radio Times*; page 108 *Radio Times*; page 11 courtesy of the late Chris Hayes; page 114 courtesy of Jack Dorsey; page 115 courtesy of Jack Dorsey; page 117 *Radio Times*; page 120 *Radio Pictorial*; page 122 *Radio Times*; page 127 courtesy of the late Hans Geiger; page 131 courtesy of the late Hugh James; page 135 Houston Rogers; page 137 Polydor Records; page 143 courtesy of the late Harry Leader; page 146 courtesy of Sheila Tracey; page 149 Pye Records; page 152 Memory Lane; page 157 *Radio Times*; page 160 *Radio Times*; page 163 President Records; page 170 *Radio Times*; page 173 Decca Records; page 176 President Records; page 178 *Radio Times*; page 182 Fontana Records; page 185 VJM Records; page 187

Oriole Records; page 190 *Radio Times*; page 193 *Radio Times*; page 195 *Radio Times*; page 199 *Radio Times*; page 202 *Radio Times*; page 207 from the Library of the Vintage Light Music Society; page 208 *Radio Times*; page 211 *Best of British*; page 212 from the Library of the Vintage Light Music Society, courtesy of Mrs June Upton; page 213 Rediffusion Records; page 214 (top) Maestro Records, (bottom) courtesy of Gerald Crossman; page 215 John Merivale; back of jacket Brian Reynolds.

Index

239

242

To be of practical use, this index is not all-inclusive. It is confined to the names of musicians and others associated with *Music While You Work* as well as incorporating references to other programmes in which they participated. Where a musician has also had an involvement with other broadcasting ensembles, these have been included in many instances. I have not included references to artists appearing as composers in the programme schedules. I have also excluded references to the comprehensive lists of bands and orchestras (many of which are not referred to elsewhere in the book) as each of these listings is an index in itself.